Studies on Traditional Freemasonry

Studies on Traditional Freemasonry

By
Fabio Venzi

For my wife Emilia

This edition first published 2013

ISBN 978 0 85318 4461

Original Title, *Introduzione alla Massoneria*, Atanòr, Rome, 2012
Translation by Cinzia Mamberti and Anne Farmer

Published by Lewis Masonic
an imprint of Ian Allan Publishing Ltd, Hersham, Surrey, KT12 4RG

Printed and bound by CPI Group (UK) Ltd, Croydon, CR0 4YY

Visit the Lewis Masonic website at *www.lewismasonic.co.uk*

COVER IMAGE 'The Doom Fulfilled', Burne-Jones, Edward: Die Erfüllung des Schicksals, 1888, Staatsgalerie Stuttgart, © Foto: Staatsgalerie Stuttgart

Contents

Therefore, intelligence can never be reconciled, and can never be denied, with the compactness of the sole massive oppressive reality: of unlimited "facts" or "data" or "notions" "surrounding" the same; of the "driving force", the "reason of State", the "reason of party", "societal reason", and "mass reasoning", all "reasons" lacking in intelligence as going too far, reaching beyond the limit.

Intelligence is unfailingly critical, rebellious, 'heretical' towards anything that, by going too far, will tend to overpower it, to obscure it. It reacts by detonating repeatedly, endlessly: a book or other sort of intelligent work is a never-ending explosion, despite it being obliged at times to sleep for centuries.

Michele Federico Sciacca
L'oscuramento dell'intelligenza

Chapter One

The Origins

Other people fall into time; I have fallen out of it. The eternity that set itself above time gives way to that other eternity that lies beneath, a sterile zone where I can desire only one thing: to reinstate time, to get back into it at any price, to appropriate a piece of it, to give myself the illusion of a place of my own. But time is sealed off, time is out of reach: and it is the impossibility of penetrating it which constitutes this negative eternity, wicked eternity.

Emile Cioran
The Fall into Time

1. Theory of the Origins

The origins of Freemasonry undoubtedly constitute one of the most widely discussed and difficult arguments. The numerous theories that have been put forward over the years have embraced a series of interpretations, ranging from historic to sociological, economic, and religious aspects.

The largest debates have been conducted between historians who view the modern-day "speculative" Freemasonry as having descended "directly" from the Medieval Guilds, and those who, on the contrary, see it as a purpose-created endeavour developed towards the mid-seventeenth century. This excursus into the origins of Freemasonry will use these two theories as a starting point.

The main advocate of the "direct" descent of modern Freemasonry, although devoid of any degree of continuity, from the builders of Medieval cathedrals, was without doubt Harry Carr, one of the most widely renowned English historians in the field of Masonic studies. The theory known as *The Transition Theory* was deemed by Carr to be demonstrable on the basis of a series of facts and documents (the oldest of which dates back to 1356) which, over a period of 600 years provided proof of the descent of modern-day Freemasonry from the Medieval Guilds.

The first of these documents was related to a dispute that took place in London in 1356 between the *stonemason builders* who hewed the raw stone and the *bricklayers* and *labourers* who erected the walls of a building. The specific details of the dispute are not known, but asa result, 12 expert master builders, some of whom were of high renown, went before the Lord Mayor of London and his Councillors in the *Guildhall* and were officially authorised to draw up a simple *Code of Regulations*.

The organisation thus established evolved over the next twenty years into the *London Masons' Company*, the first Masons' Guild and, according to Carr, one of the direct progenitors of modern-day Freemasonry. The document dated 1356, together with subsequent documents (the first testimony of an "Admissions" ceremony is purported to date back to 1390), confirms, in the opinion of Carr, how the "speculative" form of Freemasonry was achieved through a "transition" that evolved without any form of continuity from the "operative" Freemasonry of the time, with everything starting from this Guild, the *London Masons' Company*:

"The transition from operative to speculative masonry was not the take-over of an old business under new management. It was the original business, which gradually changed its character according to the needs of its time, but with perfect continuity throughout."[1]

Carr moreover opined how Freemasonry developed mainly in Scotland rather than in England, purporting that the oldest documents were indeed Scottish, which were subsequently added to by the English papers.

To support his theory, Carr referred to the oldest existing testimony of a two-Degree ritual, the handwritten *Edinburgh Register House Manuscript* dating back to 1696 that had been discovered in the General Register Office in Edinburgh. The portion of the document of particular concern is entitled *The form of giving the Mason word.* The chapter starts with the ceremony conveying the Degree of "Entered Apprentice" to an Apprentice (usually 3 years after the start of his contract), followed by the ceremony for admission to the Second Degree of "Master Mason or ordinary member of the Art", a ceremony that comprised only a few questions.

The two Degrees are mentioned not only in this document, but also in another two similar texts, the *Chetwode Crawley Manuscript* dated *circa* 1700 and the *Kevan Manuscript*, discovered more recently, and dated *circa* 1714. Carr underlines how all three documents hail from Southern Scotland and all illustrate the same dynamics.

Carr's *Transition Theory* has met with considerable criticism from historians who reject the idea of a 'direct' descent of modern-day Freemasonry from the Medieval Guilds.

One of the most strenuous opposers of this theory was the historian Eric Ward, who underlined how, in his opinion, the group established within the confines of the *London Company of Masons*, the so-called "Accepted" Masons, was a completely *new* movement

1 Harry Carr, *600 Years of Craft Ritual*, AQC Vol.81, 1968.

that emerged in the seventeenth century in England, being free from and unassociated with commerce, and which bore no connection to Medieval Masonry. Ward referred to how learned gentlemen from the *Royal Society* with an interest in scientific medicine, and the study and publication of antique books and manuscripts, used the tools of the "Operative" Masons as symbolic objects, and adopted the precepts of the Regius Poem of 1390".[2]

John Hamill, an internationally renowned British historian, previously Librarian and Curator of the United Grand Lodge of England, was of a similar opinion, and, in the same way as Ward, totally excluded the possibility that there could have been a "transition" without any form of continuity, from the "Operative" Masons of Medieval times to the "Speculative" Freemasons of the seventeenth century.

Hamill moreover opines how numerous historians, in an attempt to prove the direct descent of the "speculative" form of Freemasonry from the "operative" form by means of a phase of transition, frequently in a blatantly arbitrary fashion, put together fragments of information gathered from the four corners of the British Isles, although he goes on to say how the information provided contained little more than vague pretexts. For this reason, Hamill suggests that studies on Freemasonry should be *differentiated* into those he defines as being of the *Authentic* or *Scientific School*, based on irreproachable documents and consequential conclusions, and the *Non-Authentic School.* Hamill furthermore underlines how the *Authentic School,* in examining and assessing the English documents pertaining to the origins of Freemasonry, found no evidence of the existence of "operative" Lodges.

Hamill similarly opposes other aspects put forward in Carr's *Transition Theory*, including the purported connection between the English and Scottish operative contexts of the period; Hamill forcefully denies any such connection, categorically excluding equal working conditions in England, Scotland and Ireland for the cathedral builders, particularly in view of the vast social, cultural and religious differences present in each of these countries. Indeed, confirmation was provided by the fact that up until the date of the Act of Union in 1707, although linked by the Crown since 1603, England and Scotland were separate countries.

Hamill goes on to recall how in the Middle Ages the "operative" Lodges were no more than sites on which to store materials and seek rest; in addition to the fact that as early as 1600 the Guild system, with the exception of the London Livery Companies, was dying a fast death. Moreover, Hamill finds no evidence of an *English Mason Word* or of a particular sign of recognition among the English "Operative" Masons. Indeed, evidence of "non-Operative" or "Accepted" Masons was relegated to contexts unrelated

2 Eric Ward, *The Birth of Free-Masonry*, AQC Vol.91, 1978.

to the trade – the names listed in the documents available have no connection to the building or architectural trades.

As reported by Hamill, therefore, the "Accepted" Masons (there is some doubt as to whether they can be termed "Speculative" in the seventeenth century), seem to have been first encountered in England as a *new* organisation which had no previous association with an "operative" "Craft." Furthermore, this new "Free and Accepted" or "speculative" Freemasonry first originated in England, not in Scotland.

Hamill goes on to state that, although the presence throughout the territory of "operative" Lodges with their own *Statutes* was first observed in Scotland, with documents providing evidence of the admission of "non-Operative" individuals into the Lodges in the early seventeenth century, there is however no proof that the admission of the above "non-Operatives" in any way *altered* the work carried out by the "operative" Lodges until the end of the seventeenth century, by which time "Accepted" Freemasonry had become well established in England. Hamill is of the opinion therefore that all the evidence would appear to demonstrate that the "Accepted" Freemasonry was first established in England and only *subsequently* spread to Scotland.

To conclude, what does Hamill maintain were the dynamics that led to the birth of the modern form of Freemasonry? He states that, although it is true that the *London Masons' Company* originated from the operative Guilds of Masons governed by the London Trade, carrying out a purely operative role devoid of any speculative features, in the seventeenth century the *London Masons' Company* introduced a fundamental new phenomenon known as "Acceptance". All the documents held by the *London Masons' Company* dating back to before 1620 have been lost, although a document dated 1619 demonstrates the presence of paying members who were associated with the trade, and of others, on the contrary, who paid "for making" and who were in no way linked to the trade. Thus, the latter gathered together to form an "inner circle" within the Company, and were known under the term of "Acceptance" from which modern-day Freemasonry subsequently originated.[3]

In the debate over the origins of Freemasonry, in the same way as Hamill, the historian Colin Dyer likewise denies that this may be attributed to Scotland. Dyer maintains that there are sufficient reasons to cast doubt on the purported influence of the Guilds of Scottish Masons on "Speculative" Freemasonry, as listed here: 1) Up until the time of the Act of Union in 1707, Scotland and England were "enemy" nations 2) The building methods applied in Scotland and in England were totally different; 3) It is unlikely that the "Operative" Scots could have influenced the "Speculative" Englishmen 4) English "Speculative" Freemasonry should have already been well established by

3 John Hamill, *The Craft*, Crucible, London, 1986, page 32.

1660 (if Ashmole had been appointed a Freemason in 1646, it stands to reason that others had been appointed as well).

Dyer proposes moreover a theory to explain the origins of Freemasonry, defined by the author himself as *The Religious Base Theory*, which is briefly summarised here. In his theory, Dyer essentially asserted that "Speculative" Freemasonry was first introduced during the reign of Elizabeth I (1558-1603) on a *religious base*, in secrecy, and with no association with the Guilds of Masons. In support of his theory, he highlights how the *Grand Lodge Manuscript* (1583) begins with a beseechment to the Trinity, thus confirming the undeniably Christian origins of the document; moreover, following the Restoration in 1660, when the English Episcopal Church was re-established, Dyer states how writings by Milton and Bunyan came to be observed in the Masonic rituals, demonstrating how Freemasonry clearly reflected the religious panorama of the period, featuring a peculiarity (*Trinity*) common to all three religions (Anglicans-Protestants-Catholics) on which the movement was based.[4]

Similar to Hamill, Dyer also maintains that in the late seventeenth century the *London Company of Masons* hosted an *inner conclave* featuring characteristics that differed substantially from those of a normal Company (or Guild). It constituted a sort of *spiritual movement* that aimed towards a better life, and Dyer believes that this organisation may possibly have acted as a progenitor to the stronger philosophical movement that was to be manifested in its multiple forms throughout the following century, known as the Age of Reason, during which Freemasonry developed into the form that is still present today.

The main characteristic underlying admission into this *inner conclave* was not being an apprentice of "operative" Freemasonry, but rather being a responsible citizen who behaved in an honest fashion. With the endorsement of the other members of the *inner group* these citizens were "Accepted", and accordingly the practice was subsequently known as "Acceptance".

Admission into the society (Initiation) transformed the candidate into a *Freemason*, although only on subsequently becoming an "Accepted Mason" would he be able to take part in other ceremonies. In line with this theory, Dyer stated that the expression "Free and Accepted" could at the time have been given to those who had indeed obtained the Grades of both "Free" and "Accepted" Masons. This aspect of the ceremony was subsequently modified and an Apprentice was no longer known as "Free", but only as "Accepted". The latter can be observed during the opening and closure of the ceremony for the First Degree approved by Grand Lodge in 1815. The word "Mason" is used extensively, whilst the term "Freemason" is applied only during the Opening and Closure of the 2nd Degree.[5]

4 Colin Dyer, *Some Thoughts on the Origins of Speculative Masonry*, AQC Vol.95, 1982.

5 Colin Dyer, *Symbolism in Craft Freemasonry*, Lewis Masonic, Shepperton, 1991, page 16.

Immediately subsequent to the creation of the first Grand Lodge in 1717, continues Dyer, Freemasonry started to gain in popularity with London society of the period and to become fashionable. Unfortunately, this gave rise to the scourge of the revealing of the "secrets" of the new society; one of the most meticulous and harmful documents was undoubtedly the pamphlet *Masonry Dissected* published by Samuel Prichard in 1730.

Despite the differences observed, the theories examined previously seemed basically to agree that the origins of the "movement" can be traced to the *London Masons' Company*. To this regard, an additional feature which should be underlined is how documents that can be traced to the 'Operative' Masons, although relating to a 'non-operative' context, were first published by the *London Masons Company*, as mentioned by Yasha Beresiner, an antiquarian and renowned historian of Freemasonry:

"Without any documentary evidence, we can surmise that, at the time when Western European architecture was at its infancy, London Bridge, initiated in 1176 by Peter Colechurch and built entirely from stone, would have brought English masonry and specially the London Masons' trade into some prominence. Then in 1355, the Fabric Rolls of York Minister provide condition of employment and guidance to Masons. A year later, in 1356, similar regulations by the City court of Aldermen are issued as guidance for members of the London Company of Masons (Worshipful Company of Masons of the City of London also known as the Company of Freemasons). This is swiftly followed by the earliest of the ancient charges and regulations, also referred to as Manuscript Constitution – the Halliwell MS or Regius Poem. Accepted as penned on or before 1390, and certain not later than 1425, it was the first of some 113 such English documents to be discovered over the next few centuries. The significance of these early documents, though operative in their intent and content, is that they are nonetheless found to be used in a non-operative context." [6]

To return to the theory of the origins, Douglas Knoop and G.P. Jones, viewed as keynote experts in the field of Masonic studies, largely agree with Carr in indicating Scotland as the place of origin of Freemasonry. Accordingly, these authors maintain that one of the fundamental elements in establishing the birth of Freemasonry in Scotland is constituted by the term "Masonic word", which, in the view of the authors, was first used to denote *practical* connotations in the sixteenth century in Scotland. Subsequently, the "Masonic word" was used increasingly throughout the Scottish Lodges during the ceremonies for the "Accepted" Masons, with the "Masonic word" starting to give rise to strange legends maintaining how it was a *magic* word which could even make one invisible.

6 Yasha Beresiner, 'Origins of Freemasonry: The Anglo-Scottish Zig Zag', *Heredom*, The Transactions of the Scottish Rite Research Society, Edited by Robert G. Davies, Vol.17, 2009, page 9.

The date of June 24th 1717, commonly taken as the date of foundation of modern Freemasonry, would therefore, in the view of the authors, represent the acknowledgement (originally confined to the City of London) of a new situation in which the Masonic Lodges were made up almost exclusively of "Accepted", prevalently overt "Speculative" members.

The "speculative" modern form of Freemasonry was thus established in London, although the first "Accepted" Masons had been admitted to the Corporation in Scotland. Knoop and Jones explain this by stating how in Scotland at the beginning of the eighteenth century the "Operatives" and "Accepteds" cohabited in the same Lodges, whilst in England Lodges were frequently totally separate and made up exclusively of "non-Operative" members (it indeed occurred that a builder with an interest in esotericism could belong to two distinct Lodges: an "operative" Lodge where he could discuss problems relating to his profession, and an "accepted" Lodge in which he cultivated philosophical and esoteric interests). The last remaining pure "Operatives" were gradually pushed to the edges of the "accepted" Lodges in London, who thus chose to adopt new Constitutions following the substantial changes implemented: the transformation of the Trade Guilds into *philosophical-esoteric* societies had completely deprived them of all corporative functions.[7]

An interesting figure among the theorists supporting the Scottish origins of Freemasonry is Prof. David Stevenson. Stevenson maintains that the handwritten document of the *Dundee Lodge* allows us to observe, year after year, the transformation from a Trade Guild into a society governed constitutionally by gentlemen. The author highlights the extreme rarity of this document, particularly in view of its detailed nature. Indeed, although numerous Scottish Lodges still possess archives of documents attesting this type of transformation, none provide such a detailed organic representation as that of the *Dundee Lodge*. The sheer extent of information persuaded Stevenson, the historian who has examined the document more than any other, to hypothesise that eighteenth-century Freemasonry was a heritage of Scottish origin. Stevenson was convinced that the *transformation* of a stonemasons' Guild into a gentleman's society, lacking the presence of any labourers amongst its members, first took place in Scotland, gradually spreading subsequently to England.[8]

Furthermore, Stevenson maintains that the mysteries and secrets associated with Freemasonry, and particularly the mystic-style language that refers to God as the *Great Architect*, to Solomon's Temple as a Masonic building, to the search for knowledge and enlightenment, can largely be ascribed to the influence of cultural traditions dating back

7 D. Knoop & G.P. Jones, *Masons in the Middle Ages*, AQC Vol.98, 1985.

8 David Stevenson, *The First Freemasons*, Geo. Stewart & Co. Ltd, Edinburgh, 1988.

to at least a century prior to the Age of Enlightenment in Europe. Stevenson continues by stating that that this propensity of Freemasonry for the mystical and the search for perfection first developed in the context of cultural traditions implemented at the start of the seventeenth century by the Scottish Masonic reformers. During this development and transformation of the old "operative" Freemasonry, Stevenson maintains that a key role was played by William Schaw, *King's Master of Works*, a man, in the words of the Scottish historian, steeped in ideas of mystic Hermeticism and a reformer during the late Renaissance period who contributed towards spreading these ideas throughout the Lodges towards the end of the 1590s.

Several decades later, according to Stevenson's theory, the Freemasons had developed a certain affinity with the Rosicrucians, i.e. with a form of mystic idealism of German origin that preached universal perfection and reform along similar lines to those adopted during the late Renaissance period in the hermetic search for human perfection. In support of his theory, Stevenson argues that the hermetic school of thought was first introduced into Scotland by various means, including the work of one of Giordano Bruno's disciples, Alexander Dickson, who introduced it to the Court of the Stuarts in 1590; William Schaw was closely linked to these circles.

Stevenson is persuaded that Schaw would have had the opportunity to substantially alter the nature of the Scottish "operative" Lodges in the early years of the seventeenth century, creating an association between the existing crafts and trades, the use of secret passwords, and the knowledge of principles of mathematics and architecture with the search for mystical knowledge and mnemonic techniques as a key to the secrets of the universe (the ultimate aim of a specific line of hermetic research).

Similarly, the North American historian Margaret Jacob, a fervent supporter of Stevenson's theories, firmly believes that these were the type of activities undertaken by Schaw in the realms of Scottish Freemasonry, maintaining how his followers contributed decisively towards raising awareness of their history among the bricklayers of the ancient Lodges, and rousing a certain interest in esotericism.[9] I shall attempt to disprove Stevenson's theory in a subsequent chapter.

To continue in my analysis into the theory of the origins of Freemasonry, Frederick W. Seal-Coon puts forward the interesting *Theory of Conspiracy to Fellowship*, in which he affirms how, during Cromwell's era, Royalist Lodges were present in England (the antiquarian Elias Ashmole was an obvious example), constituted of conspirators who used secret signs to conceal their political activities. Following the Restoration of the Monarchy, these clandestine Lodges were revealed and transformed into places for meetings and pastimes; subsequently,

9 Margaret C. Jacob, *Massoneria illuminata*, Einaudi, Turin, 1995, pages 57-58.

the discussion of religious and political matters was abolished, adopting the Masonic symbols to indicate a natural propensity for archaeology and architecture.[10] The theory thus advanced by the historian Seal-Coon, a member, as many of the authors mentioned previously, of the *Quatuor Coronati* Lodge in London, underlines how Freemasonry can be identified as an Initiatic Society, featuring, consequently, an esoteric pathway leading to a change, a spiritual "transformation" of man which, the author maintains, is of little importance. Indeed, in describing the period of their formation, the author views the Masonic Lodges essentially as political "sects" which were subsequently transformed into pleasant "places for meetings and pastimes". There is no need to emphasise how I am in complete disagreement with such a disparaging and ridiculous theory.

Michael Spurr, in *The Age of Enlightenment Theory*, underlines important analogies between the principles of Freemasonry and the ideals of the Enlightenment. In his opinion, these common principles include the concept of Fellowship, Equality, compliance with the laws of the land, loyalty to the king and belief in a supreme being.[11] This theory, which detects in the origins of Masonic thought an influence of the principles of the philosophy of the Enlightenment, is also supported by another English author, Trevor Stewart, who writes:

"Freemasonry was the product of English Enlightenment thinking, and the teachings which those 17th century initiates espoused in their gatherings would not be recognised by most speculative freemasons today as being 'Freemasonry'. Their doctrines, such as we can determine from the paucity of documentary evidence, were relatively primitive, whereas what most member of the English Craft consider now to be 'Freemasonry' is embodied in much more elaborate schemes – such as William Preston's Lectures – where the symbolism and the quasi-historical matters are thoroughly worked out in a fully-integrated and highly structured scheme. It is only in the early 18th century that the various components that make up what is now called 'Freemasonry' came to coalesce together. It was only in that era and in London that a suitable format was devised which gave those elements the means of wide expression. There are key features of 'Freemasonry' that could only have been married together in the early 18th century. They may have existed separately before the first Grand Lodge was formed but it was only with that institutional framework in place and with the sort of men who were active within it that opportunities and means existed to bring that eclectic process into effect. There were, broadly speaking, two stages:

1) *A preliminary 'Stage I' when the 'Freemasonry' was relative primitive, so far as can be ascertained from the lamentably small amount of actual hard evidence that is available, and*

10 Frederick W. Seal-Coon, *The Birth of Freemasonry (Another Theory)*, AQC Vol. 92, 1979

11 Michael Spurr, *Freemasonry – Child of the Enlightenment? Or Vice Versa?*, AQC Vol.109, 1996.

2) *A second, Enlightenment 'Stage II', for which there is a variety of evidence and which is still regarded throughout the English constitution at least as proper 'Freemasonry".*

Stewart, after listing the elements in common with the Enlightenment, concludes:

"As has been stated already: these themes had emerged separately and at earlier times but it was only in the first half of the 18th century that they all eventually coalesced to provide that range of material upon which Preston could draw." [12]

I will expound and discuss my total disagreement with this theory in the following chapters.

Michael Baigent, renowned author of esoteric books on Freemasonry, and currently editor of the journal *Freemasonry Today*, has put forward *The Royal Society Theory*. The author from New Zealand links the birth of "speculative" Freemasonry with *hermetic* thought and with the establishment of the *Royal Society* in London. This theory, presented, in the same way as many of the theories discussed herein, at the *Quatuor Coronati* Lodge in London, was rejected during the discussions that followed by other members of the same Lodge; the latter were indeed of the opinion that, with the exception of the All-seeing Eye and the Pentalpha, there are no other similarities or points of contact with other Masonic symbols or with notions of hermetic thought. Furthermore, the members of the *Royal Society* who were also Freemasons were relatively few, with the obvious exception of those mentioned by Baigent, including Ashmole, Moray and Kincardine. However, none of these individuals played a decisive role in the origins of Freemasonry.[13]

Among the many theories put forward, the hypothesis whereby the origins of Freemasonry were deemed of a *charitable* rather than a *philosophical* nature should not be overlooked. Andrew Durr, one of the proponents of this theory, saw Freemasonry as a development of the growing *self-help* movement of the seventeenth century. In the absence of a Welfare State, people of the time who became ill or fell on hard times could only rely on local charity; consequently, various groups of craftsmen took on the task of solving this problem independently. During convivial meetings, money to be used in times of need was collected in a box, for this reason the associations came to be known as Box Clubs. The author states that, in the same way as occurred on "operative" Scottish Lodges, the Box Clubs started to admit members who were in no way linked to the trade, thus reaching the conclusion that Freemasonry in its modern

12 Trevor Stewart, *English Speculative Freemasonry: Some Possible Origins, Themes and Developments* AQC Vol.117, 2004.

13 Michael Baigent, *Freemasonry, Hermetic Thought and the Royal Society of London*, AQC Vol.109, 1996.

form initially developed as a Box Club for "Operative" Masons, subsequently opening up membership to those who were not associated with the Craft.[14]

Cyril N. Batham puts forward a theory entitled *Monastic Origins*. In his theory Batham initially refers to, and subsequently rejects, Carr's theory, according to which when the Craftsmen's Guilds started to decline, the "Accepted" Masons grew in number and were able to gain control of the Lodges; they changed both the ceremonials and the very structure of the Lodges, resulting, in Carr's opinion, in the creation of the modern-day "non-operative" or "speculative" Freemasonry. Batham, in the same way as Hamill before him, disagrees with this theory arguing that, with the exception of a border Lodge which was more Scottish than English, there was no evidence that "non-operative" Masons had been admitted to "operative" English Lodges. Moreover, Batham is of the opinion that no documents are available that demonstrate the transformation of an "operative" English Lodge into a "non-operative" Lodge.

In his theory, Batham maintains that when, during the Middle Ages in England a new society started to emerge, *Inner Sancta* Monasteries were established with elderly members acting as teachers for the younger brethren. Following the dissolution of the Monasteries in 1538 (by Henry VIII), and the subsequent abolition of Fellowships in 1547, several of these *Sancta* survived as secret cells up until the late sixteenth century. Once more favourable conditions were established following the Restoration, these cells re-emerged and expanded, evolving into the form of Freemasonry we know today.[15]

The studies conducted by the French historian Paul Naudon, who identified in the Fellowships and subsequently the Templars the origins and development of early Freemasonry, are partly correlated to Batham's theory.

In particular, Naudon reports how the dynamics resulting in the origin of Freemasonry had been implemented by a series of institutions, as listed below:

1) The Roman Collegia, the remains of which continued to be present in the West after the invasions, and survived as institutions throughout the Oriental Empire, where they were found by the Crusaders at the end of the eleventh century;
2) The Ecclesiastical Associations of Builders, which had been set up by the Bishops, particularly by Benedictines, Cistercians and Templars in the Middle Ages;
3) Under the aegis of the above and in the form of both lay Fellowships and Guilds, the birth and the organisation of the Freemasonry of Craftsmen.

14 Andrew Durr, *The Origin of the Craft*, AQC Vol.96, 1983.

15 Cyril N. Batham, *The Grand Lodge of England (1717) and its Founding Lodges*, AQC Vol.103, 1990.

In his theory, Naudon highlights a progressive transformation of Freemasonry from the art of building into the art, *stricto sensu*, of thinking and living. Particularly, Naudon states how this transformation took place under the aegis of the Temple and in the context of the sovereign jurisdiction of the latter, with the first Parisian groups of masons and carpenters.[16]

In his study, Naudon delineates an evolutionary line which, starting from the Roman Collegia and following their subsequent exportation and marked development and transformation of the original model, reaches as far as Gaul and Great Britain, where Freemasonry ultimately originated.

The conservation and transmission of secrets by the Collegia, devastated by the Barbarian invasions and dissolved in the advent of the feudal societies, is purported to have been undertaken subsequently by ecclesiastic bodies, mainly monasteries, and in particular the Benedictine Order. The Templars, pupils of the Benedictines, prolonged the work of the monasteries for a considerable period and, from the twelfth century onwards gave rise to lay groups of builders, communities that were entitled to specific exemptions, and were thus know as "free crafts". Therefore, in the mid-twelfth century the first lay Fellowships were established which, created from a vast religious and social movement of the time, initially gathered people from all crafts under a common global aim. Subsequently, the aims were refined and focused on a professional level in order to bring together people working in the same craft: first the merchants, followed by the craftsmen. Masons and church builders subsequently founded Fellowships featuring mystical and corporative elements.

The Fellowships, stemming directly from the monastic bodies, lived under the dominion of the abbeys and were subjected to feudal jurisdiction, whilst frequently continuing to benefit from extensive exemptions and privileges deriving from the Church. Naudon comments on how these Fellowships would ultimately give rise to the development of free crafts and Freemasonry.

The French historian goes on to recount how the true creators of the Fellowships of builders were indeed the Templars, the first builders of churches and fortresses acting on orders from the Crusaders, particularly due to their knowledge of architecture and secrets of the craft that, as mentioned previously, they gained from the Benedictines and the Cistercians. How then did we get from the Templars to modern-day Freemasonry? Naudon illustrates the following design:

1) The Templars formed monastic associations of builders trained in the use of Greek and Roman building traditions by the Benedictines and the Cistercians.

16 Paul Naudon, *Le Origini della Massoneria*, Atanòr, Rome, 2008, pages 9-10.

2) They were in close contact with the associations of Christian and Oriental Muslim architects, being affected by their operative and initiatic influences.
3) In Europe, the Templars were at the heart of the creation and development of the community of builders entitled to enjoy specific privileges, later giving rise to the free crafts and Freemasonry.
4) Following the dissolution of the Order, a number of Templars opted to join the community of builders.[17]

Naudon states that, from the fifteenth or sixteenth century, neither the Crafts communities nor the Fellowships could be considered the holder of the traditions of the ancient Collegia. The communities were strictly governed in minute detail and their role was limited solely to dealing with professional issues, whilst the Fellowships lost sight of their religious, spiritual and charitable aims. They all too frequently focused on profane issues, justifying the bans that were repeatedly issued against them by the Royal authorities or the Church. Among other things, Naudon mentions how the communities and the Fellowships had become particularists and operated on an increasingly local level, no longer occupying the universal position of the Roman Collegia and the Fellowships of the Middle Ages. Moreover, their diffusion had been largely hampered by the bans issued, and their activities had been limited merely to defending the interests of their Brethren.

The role that the Fellowships were not able to undertake in transmitting initiatic ideals and values was subsequently covered by English and Scottish corporative Freemasonry; the latter would prove capable not only of conserving the ancient heritage, but also of invigorating and enriching it with the addition of new initiatic rites, thus freeing it from the "operative" contingencies and transforming it progressively into the modern "speculative" form of Freemasonry.[18]

These dynamics took place within the Guilds. Naudon explained how the Guilds were the last to be established following the Roman Collegia, the Culdees, the Benedictine monks, the monastic bodies and the Fellowships, and were first seen in Northern countries, Normandy and England, conveying an immediate juridical contribution to the organisation of the Crafts. The first advantage provided by the Guilds was their being characterised by the professionalism of the community of French craftsmen with the pious nature of the Fellowships. Moreover, the English Guilds were not affected by the strict control that the King of France attempted to exert over the Crafts, nor by the restrictions

17 Paul Naudon, op. cit., page 94.
18 Paul Naudon, op. cit., page 155.

and interdictions forced upon the Fellowships. Indeed, they were even encouraged by the Crown and by the English Church, thus enabling them to safeguard their traditions.

Subsequently, throughout the centuries the Guilds gained a wealth of initiatic content thanks to provisions made by the Hermeticists and the Rosicrucians, particularly when they terminated their operative dealings and admitted a large number of speculative members.[19]

To conclude, whilst traditions were being lost on the Continent, thanks to English Freemasonry the ancient heritage has been handed down to the present day.

The various theories put forward with regard to the origins of Freemasonry could not fail to include that relating to the Brotherhood of the Rose Cross; the following historians have also sought to prove the origins of Freemasonry in the Rosicrucian Order: J.S.M. Ward in his *Freemasonry and the Ancient Gods* (1926) and A. E. Waite with *The Secret Tradition in Freemasonry* (1911).

More recently, the theory of the Rosicrucian origins was once again put forward by A. Cosby F. Jackson, a historian expert in Freemasonry and member of the *Quatuor Coronati* Lodge in London. He maintains that the two Brotherhoods – the "speculative" Freemasonry and the Rosicrucians – were first established round about the same time by men having similar cultural interests. They both had essentially the same aims – self-perfection and religious mysticism and both first came to light in the seventeenth century. Rosicrucianism, explains Jackson, also sustained ideas and concepts borrowed from Alchemy and developed in a rapid fashion, whilst Freemasonry featured a much slower growth. Critics of this theory have underlined how the plausible points of contact between Freemasonry and the Rosicrucians were rather few, the importance of Christian pity and self-perfection, together with the fact that members of both may have also belonged to the newly formed *Royal Society*.[20]

Richard Sandbach proposes a theory that he himself defines as a "*Darwinian Concept*". In his theory, he examines how, where and when Freemasonry first originated and highlights several fundamental points:

a) The "operative" form of Freemasonry provided a safe haven against betrayal by the enemy. This help may have been extended to those who wished to be "made" Masons (*Passport Theory*).
b) The Masonic movement in the late 17th century may have been influenced by religious factors, which would explain "why" and "in what form" the Masonic Lodges survived during the 17th century.

19 Paul Naudon, op. cit., page 167.
20 A. Cosby F. Jackson, *Rosicrucianism and its Effect on Craft Masonry*, AQC Vol.97, 1984.

c) In the world of social evolution (as in Darwinian evolution), events were frequently modelled on social and environmental circumstances rather than on politics. The only comment to be made here is that in the *Origin of the Species* Darwin explains how the individual species evolved from their forerunners, and not how the new species originated.[21]

Sandbach moreover states his conviction that "speculative" Freemasonry first originated in England. Referring to the theories of the previously mentioned Prof. Stevenson, he emphasises how, although the Scottish historian cites a number of cases in which "non-Operative" members were admitted to Scottish Lodges at the end of the sixteenth century, there is no firm proof that "speculative" Freemasonry did not first develop in Scotland before spreading to England. We have seen (the Ashmole case is paradigmatic) how in England "non-Operatives" members had been admitted since the mid-seventeenth century, and maybe even earlier; however, according to Sandbach it is important to ascertain when men "Accepted" in this way first started to meet in Lodges and to develop this 'system of morals' that led to current modern-day Freemasonry. What was the evolution of the first "makings"? It should be pointed out that there was a marked spirit of social curiosity at the time in scientific and philosophical issues; when two or more people realised that they had a common Masonic knowledge it was natural for them to arrange private meetings to talk about Freemasonry, during which, after the 'agape' (or Festive Board), they would discuss the significance of the things they had been taught when they had been "made", and, most likely, the use of the Signs of Recognition.

In the light of these premises, therefore, concluded Sandbach, we are able to confirm that the onset of "speculative" Freemasonry was clearly evident during the last decade of the seventeenth century and at the start of the eighteenth century in the context of clubs and coffee-houses between men who, for practical reasons or reasons of self-preservation had been "made" Masons in the early, chaotic times. In England during the seventeenth century the Lodges of "Operative" Masons, in an era in which political and religious issues could lead to one's death, were to afford a safe place to stay and protection against betrayal by the enemy thanks to the secret signs of recognition; it may be for this reason that the "Operative" Masons started to accept the "non-Operative" members. Later, following the defeat of James II at the Battle of Boyne in 1690, and with the onset of the 'Age of Reason', as the social situation started to quieten, particularly in London, discussions of a varying nature started to be held between the "non-Operatives"; this led to a desire to possess their "own" Lodge together with their "own" friends, possibly even

21 Richard Sandbach, *The Origin of Species – The Freemason*, AQC Vol.108, 1995.

boasting their own "secret" acquaintances. In this climate, the birth of "speculative" Freemasonry would have represented a necessary outcome.[22]

In another document, Sandbach illustrates his theory schematically, and in my opinion very clearly. This theory however continues to be one of the most widely debated among scholars of Freemasonry:

"In medieval times when a great building project was begun the work was entrusted to professional Masons (often called Freemasons from working in freestone). A Masons' Lodge for the project would be formed and only duly qualified men admitted; it is almost certain that there were passwords and a grip required to gain admission. The ceremony of initiation was formal and apparently involved communicating two things, a mythical history of the Craft and a password or words, by a minimum of a Master and two Wardens.

1) *It seems certain that in Scotland (where feudal hierarchy persisted long after it had died out in England) some of the clan chiefs and local lairds only allowed these meetings if they could attend and they consequently became technically Masons though they would have no intention of becoming practising operatives. While I do not agree with Dr. Stevenson that this was in any sense the beginning of Speculative (as distinct from Operative) Masonry, it clearly provided a precedent for the transmission of the recognition signs (including the grip and 'masons word') to non-operatives and under the pressure and dangers of the Civil War these could hopefully act as some guarantee of safety in travel which was a dangerous enterprise in war-torn England. At all events, the custom seems to have spread from the north.*
2) *The first evidence of the admission of a non-operative in England is that of Elias Ashmole in 1646 at Warrington. He was a royalist and on parole in north Cheshire. Another military man was admitted at the same meeting. Ashmole's immediate land was in Parliamentarian hands. It is tempting to assume that Ashmole deliberately postponed his departure until he had the security of the Masonic signs and words.*
3) *After the Restoration Ashmole – who became prominent in society and a member of the Royal Society – attended a meeting of the 'Acception' of the London Company of Masons, a trade guild who seem to have formed this unit to cater for those who were or wished to be Freemasons but had no intention of training as operatives. He was able to attend by virtue of his Initiation at Warrington.*
4) *So far this has been factual. We now come into the role of speculation.*
5) *In the 'coffee house' and scientific curiosity atmosphere that followed the Restoration (including the foundation of the Royal Society) it would be natural for men who had been Initiated as*

22 Richard Sandbach, *Talks for Lodge & Chapter*, Ian Allan, Addlestone, 1996, pages 13-15.

Freemasons to gravitate together; inevitably that would lead to a discussion of experiences and of the 'ancient history' communicated as part of the Initiation Ceremony. There may well have been a feeling of resentment at the attempt of the London Company to control this new phenomenon. At all events, in 1717 a Grand Lodge was formed independent of the London company. It grew and prospered though from 1751 to 1813 there were two conflicting Grand Lodges, the new one (confusingly calling itself 'Ancients') protesting against what they saw as innovations – primarily the establishing of a third degree. The original Grand Lodge was thus stigmatised as the 'Moderns' – my own 'red apron' London Lodge (Lodge of Antiquity, now No.2 because it lost in the renumbering ballot at the reunion in 1813) and of which I am a Past Master, is the oldest extant Freemasons' lodge in the world.

6) *In the liberated world of the Restoration the enquiries into science which the arid rule of the Commonwealth had suppressed were eagerly resumed and it was in that 'coffee house' atmosphere that speculative Freemasonry began to form its standard ceremonies and customs. So here we see the beginnings of modern rituals. Procedural matters seems to have been loosely regulated but there was considerable latitude in philosophising until the Union of the two Grand Lodges in 1813 when, almost by accident, rituals became much more standardised – but that is another story.*

7) *To sum up: I suggest that the earliest initiation of non-masons into operative lodges first occurred in the feudal society of Scotland, that the practice spread to England as providing safety in the turbulent times of the Civil War, that it was institutionalised under the aegis of the London Acception and finally took the form of independent 'speculative' — as distinct from 'operative' lodges —under the control of an independent sovereign Grand Lodge in 1717."* [23]

I would like to close this section by mentioning one of the most interesting studies, in my opinion, on the origins of Freemasonry, particularly as it does not overlook examining the *initiatic* aspect. I refer to the essay by Eric Ward, entitled *The Birth of Free-Masonry*, published in 1978.

Ward is one of those people who believe that Freemasonry was born *ex novo* towards the mid-seventeenth century, borrowing legendary material from the medieval stone masons and, subsequently, the rituals from the Scottish body of masons. The author opines that there is still today no reliable proof that modern-day Freemasonry originated from the Medieval corporations of cathedral builders; consequently, the "Accepted" Freemasonry is a movement established in England, free and independent of the corporations, no earlier than the seventeenth century. This movement, affirms

23 Richard Sandbach, AQC Vol.120, 2007.

Ward, encompassed the old English "operative" duties, which at the time had become almost obsolete, and during the first stage of its growth borrowed some of the coeval traditions of the Scottish Craft Masons.

There is no doubt whatsoever that other influences also contributed towards nourishing the fledgling organism; this does not however mean that these circumstances may have generated the same. Indeed, Ward is persuaded that, although Scotland and Ireland contributed towards the development of Freemasonry, was undoubtedly formed in England.

Ward, as previous authors, criticises Carr with regard to his conviction of the direct descent of Freemasonry from the Scottish Guilds, demonstrated, according to Carr, throughout 600 years of ritual development without any degree of continuity. Ward categorically rejects this theory and, in referring to the ritual, underlines how, although of fundamental importance, the latter does not represent the beginning and the end of Freemasonry, but rather a *means*, a *tool*, with which to achieve the aim. Moreover, Ward continues, even if it were true that Freemasons existed in the fourteenth century, we would still be far from establishing that the men who bore this name had anything in common with the "Free Masons" who belonged to the "speculative" order, and identifying them as one and the same. To summarise, concludes Ward, if we hope to demonstrate an organic degree of continuity we should necessarily compare like things with their counterparts.[24]

It is however mainly on the term "Freemason" that Ward focuses, particularly to highlight the lack of links or continuity with the Medieval Masons. He states that during the seventeenth century in England groups of men belonging to a range of trades organised themselves in small independent groups or Lodges bearing a merely symbolic connection to the corporations of builders. Although in some cases several members may have been stonemasons belonging to these corporations, this had absolutely no influence on the activity of the Lodges concerned that had marked *philosophical* and *social* characteristics; these institutions represent, in his opinion, the first *prototypes* of the current "speculative" Masonic Lodges.

Ward maintains that the first of these Lodges was probably situated inside the *London Masons' Company*, the records of which provide proof of its existence under the name of *The Acception* as early as 1630; the members of this Lodge were known as "Accepted" Masons, possibly giving rise to the name of the institution itself.

The first known use of the term "Accepted" Mason is found on a printed parody going by the title of *Poor Robin's Intelligencer* dated October 10th 1676. Elias Ashmole use the term "New-Accepted" Masons in his diary in 1682, but also "Free Mason" in both the latter and in a previous diary dated 1646. Charles Burman, his biographer, modernised the term

24 Eric Ward, *The Birth of Free-Masonry*, AQC Vol.91, 1978.

in *Free-Masons* in 1717. In 1686, Dr. Robert Plot wrote of the Society of *Free-Masons* and, in 1688, Randle Holme III used the same term in *An Academie of Armory.* John Aubrey is said to have used both "Free-Masons" and "Accepted Masons" in his notes on Wiltshire in 1691, whilst an anti-Masonic pamphlet dated 1698 used the term "Freed Masons". Richard Rawlinson, in 1719, referred to the "Fellowship of Adopted Masons, Accepted Masons or Free Masons", Thomas Vaughn in *Long Livers* in 1722 referred to these as *Free Masons* and the Roberts *Constitutions* (likewise dated 1722) used the term "Free-Masons".[25]

In conclusion, Ward maintains that a debate into the various terms used to refer to the "non-Operative" Masons, irrespective of their institution, highlighted three important findings:

a) There *had* to be a difference in terminology as there were still many true "Operative" Masons, i.e. Masons of the Craft who worked approximately during the 18th century. Their names and institutions are recorded on several town registers and other rolls, in circumstances which clearly denote that they were stone masons.

b) This difference was acknowledged at the time. Randle Holme III in 1688 stated: *"I cannot but honour the Fellowship of the Masons because of its antiquity; and more so, being a member of the society known as Free-Masons."* Thus, for Randle Holme, the Fraternity of Masons and the society known as "Free-Masons" were two distinct entities. In the first report of an initiation in England Elias Ashmole mentioned how he had been made a "Free Mason" in Warrington in 1646. Not a "Mason", and not even a "Freemason", but a member of the society that, literally, was quite separate from both.

c) The term *free* in "Free and Accepted" had acquired a different significance to *free* as used in *freemason*, which was a contraction of the term *freestone mason*. As the Company of Free and Accepted Masons was quite separate from the builders' corporations, *free* had clearly assumed the meaning of not being bound to these corporations. The word had assumed exactly the same meaning as used in Free House, an inn or public place which was not associated with a particular brewery. In the 17th century the status of Master Mason as the supervisor of an important construction project had changed, as his role had been taken by the skilled amateur, the predecessor of the modern-day consultant architect. Likewise, the organization and building methods employed were changing, and the result was a downgrading of operative bricklayers to a subordinate position. A few succeeded in changing their *status*, for example Robert Smythson, founder of a well-known class of architects who, according to a wall plaque in Wollaton Church, started his working life as a "Freemason" and ended it in 1614 as an "architector".

25 Ibid.

Thus, during the period in which our form of "non-operative" Freemasonry started to take shape, the distinction between a Craft "Freemason" and any other form of stonemason started to become somewhat blurred. The growth of the movement that was to become the "speculative" Freemasonry, together with the changes to the Builders' corporations smoothed the way for further changes to the word. Having adopted the term "Free and Accepted Mason", the less cumbersome "Free-Mason" was a natural contraction for the printed word; however, by the end of the eighteenth century, the unpronounceable hyphen had become so bothersome that the term "Freemason" was adopted, subsequently receiving the seal of approval when Freemasons' Halls came into everyday use.

To summarise, proof has been provided that the word "Freemason" in its Medieval context was derived from French Latin/Norman elements which had been anglicised, compounded, and likely simplified. The identical, although semantically diverse term of "Freemason" intended as commonly used today to indicate a member of our society is a relatively modern adaptation that has been handed down by means of a progressive contraction of more specific terms and borrowed words. As use of the word in its modern sense was enabled solely following the obsolescence of the description of the corporation, the tendency to assimilate the new with the old is etymologically unsound.[26]

With regard to the aspect of "Acceptance", Ward maintains that the fact that the corporations habitually elected as members important persons who had no concern for commercial activities or trade is indeed a stereotype. He opines that there is no proof that corporations of English stonemasons have ever proceeded in this manner. Undoubtedly, there are Scottish Masonic Lodges registered as having members of this type from 1634, although it should be underlined that, despite the presence of these "non-Operative" members, the Scottish Lodges continued without exception to be of an "operative" nature right up until the eighteenth century. The same is true also for the Haughfoot Lodge, originally made up entirely of "non-operative" members and later integrated by men belonging to the corporation. The traditions employed in this Lodge do not appear to have been any different from those used in other Craft Lodges in the area. The 'non-Operatives' in Scotland evidently did not possess any authority to change the corporative traditions, and indeed I know of no case where such changes took place. Conversely, in England in the seventeenth century a completely different and unprecedented situation developed when Lodges which were totally independent of the Masonic corporations from the outset started to be established. In view of this autonomy, members were not banned from making changes to the rites and traditions used in the Lodges, which can thus be considered as prototypes preceding the establishment of modern-day Freemasonry.

26 Ibid.

Therefore, Ward is of the opinion that the difference between these English Lodges of "Accepted" or "Adopted" Masons that were independent of the builders' corporations, and the Scottish Lodges, substantially of an "operative" nature and which employed standardised ceremonials that the "non-Operative" members were not in a position to change, is historically significant. Moreover, this provides a key to the explanation as to why the first English Lodges borrowed, assimilated and developed such a large amount of ritual material which was so blatantly of Scottish origin.[27]

Therefore, Ward views "Accepted" Freemasonry established in England at the start of the seventeenth century initially as an extremely small company that gradually grew and was extensively diffused throughout the following decades. The members of this movement seem to have been gentlemen of culture or successful employers for the majority, thus, ward maintains, largely resembling the stereotype of a "better type" of person reported by Anderson in the eighteenth century. There is no documented evidence that induces us to maintain that any efforts were made to recruit the more humble workers, the salaried stonemasons, and thus the term *Free-Mason* was used to indicate "free from the corporation of masons".

In the light of the theories examined, I wish to conclude this section by emphasising once again the key role played in the search for the "origins" of Freemasonry by the *London Masons' Company,* indicated by the majority of historians mentioned here as the place in which, with all probability, the first "speculative" Freemasonry was incubated. Yasha Beresiner succinctly confirmed the concept as follows:

"In England, meanwhile, the wide void between the emergence of the gothic charges in 1400 and the founding of Grand Lodge in 1717 is a yawning gap. During these three hundred years the London Company of Masons stands alone as the backbone to any Masonic activity that is to be encountered in the Kingdom. The company itself, clearly, is not a Lodge (in the Scottish sense) and no such body as a 'Lodge' is to be found associated with the Company. Instead, from about 1619/20, the earliest date of which records of the London Company of Masons survive, a ceremony known as the 'Accepcion' or 'acception' takes place at unspecified intervals and totally independent of the Company itself. The ceremony admits into an apparent inner circle within the Company, candidates already members of the company and, from 1642, strangers, bestowing on them a standing beyond the freedom of the Company. They are easily identified in the existing Treasurer's records because they are charged double the dues." [28]

27 Ibid.

28 Yasha Beresiner, op. cit., pages 13-14.

2. The Great Deceit of an Enlightened Freemasonry

As highlighted in the previous section, one of the most commonly acknowledged theories maintains that Masonic symbolism and school derive from the philosophy of the Enlightenment.

I will therefore attempt to explain why the theory purporting that the principles of Freemasonry express the philosophy underlying the Enlightenment movement is devoid of any truth, being, in my opinion, rather the daughter of the tradition associated with the Neoplatonic ideals of the Renaissance, therefore far removed from the empiricism and rationalism of the eighteenth century that are clearly *incompatible* with the esoteric and metaphysical principles of Freemasonry.

Indeed, the Masonic "Method" makes use of a symbolic language to express the integration, denied from the time of René Descartes onwards, between *spirit* and *matter*, an esoteric language differing from philosophic and scientific languages in its way of communicating by means of images intended to arouse knowledge through *intuition* rather than by rational means.

Indeed, this *intellectual intuition* constitutes the instrument, the "Method" on which the Masonic process is based, a method facilitating the implementation of an *active process* of inner transformation leading to the development of an actual change in status. The fundamental issue is represented by the fact that any transformation will occur in a *personal* rather than a *social* context, as the aim of Freemasons is to be reunited with the Supreme Being, and in doing so free themselves of material bonds ("metals"), thus undertaking a true *spiritual development.*

However, the theory whereby Freemasonry is the offspring of the eighteenth-century movement of enlightenment and progressivism is hard to eradicate, and the damage produced by this forcing of history has been considerable. Undeniably, during the eighteenth century several Masonic societies introduced principles pertaining to the school of thought of the Enlightenment into the realms of Freemasonry, thereby distorting the esoteric and initiatic origins. These were however only sporadic occurrences.The most outstanding case was that of the *Grand Orient of France*, the oldest French Masonic Obedience, which increasingly absorbed the ideals of the Enlightenment movement, so much so as to ultimately remove, in 1877, all reference to the *Great Architect of the Universe* from its rituals. Indeed, rituals performed by the *Grand Orient of France* display clear features reminiscent of enlightenment and progressivism. Merely as an example, the ceremony performed on occasion of the Inauguration of a Temple, essentially the Consecration of a Masonic Temple, contains the wording the *"flame is the symbol of Reason" (capital letters)"* and *"let the Flaming Star lead us towards progress"* (reason and progress being the singular features of the Enlightenment).

This ritual moreover is articulated by the triptych *Liberté, Egualité, Fraternité,* and contains no prayers, invocations, Bible readings, circumanbulations and esoteric formulas, all of which are features unfailingly present in traditional Masonic ceremonies. Furthermore, the ceremony concerned is no longer even known as Consecration, with all that the term implies from an esoteric-initiatic point of view, but is now called Inauguration, a term of undeniably "profane" connotations. It can thus be asserted that during the eighteenth century several Masonic bodies in Europe and overseas (for example a few Obediences in South America) included the enlightenment principles in their rituals, thus distorting their esoteric and initiatic origins. In these cases the ritual, an indispensable element in an initiatic organisation, has been gradually deprived of its true symbolic significance and replaced by commentaries and exegeses characterised by a desolating banality and a dull moralism reminiscent of the "century of the Enlightened". Naturally, this cannot be arbitrarily applied to all forms of Freemasonry, either in the eighteenth century or indeed today.

The Enlightenment was a vast philosophic movement first developed in England during the seventeenth century and which subsequently extended to France and the rest of the European continent. The movement was denoted by its unerring faith in reason and the capacity of the latter to emancipate mankind from religious fanaticism and, particularly, to free it from ignorance and superstition. The Enlightenment focused on the study of daily, mundane issues, reducing knowledge to the mere data gained from experience. The assumptions underlying its establishment were to be found in the rapid development of science in the eighteenth century, evolving from the Renaissance naturalism to the new science of Galileo. Subsequently, Newton demonstrated how the universe was a mechanism the movements of which were regulated by the force of attraction that holds the parts together. Thus, in the eighteenth century the positive method of science was applied to all life domains and a mechanical explanation provided for all types of phenomena.

Its general characteristics included an absolute *worshipping* of science and an empiricism based on experience, abandoning and fighting against the *innate ideas* and concepts produced by pure reason, applying an inductive research method (study of the phenomena will *necessarily* lead to the laws underlying the same). One of the consequences of this philosophical approach, probably the one that resulted in Illuminist thought being deemed incompatible with the principles and essence of Freemasonry as an initiatic society, was an *anti-metaphysical agnosticism* that saw experience as being limited by fact, and therefore incapable of solving problems linked to the supersensitive world and the *transcendent*.

It is clear therefore that a school of thought that tends towards a process of perfection based on symbol and allegories such as that adopted by Freemasonry and inserted in an "esoteric" and "metaphysical" spatial and temporal dimension has little in common with the experimental nature of the empiricism of the Enlightenment.

In support of this notion, I shall now take into consideration some of the main characteristics of enlightenment principles and analyse the lack of common issues with the principles and singularities on which an "Initiatic Order" is based.

First of all "Empiricism", a new philosophy which, in the same way as science, was based on experience, and consequently maintained that all ideas and principles were unequivocally derived from experience. Intellect is conceived as a blank slate on which the marks made by experience are gradually etched, thereby refuting the existence of innate ideas. This denial of the presence in mankind of "innate" ideas *irrespective* of experience is clearly contrary to Masonic principles, according to which the concept of *religio perennis* (a "transcendental unity", primordial wisdom in which the various forms of religion that contemplate manifestation of a divine entity are not mutually exclusive and do not propose different truths, the Truth being *one* alone) referred to by Freemasons in justifying tolerance towards all creeds divergent from their own, is indeed based on an *innate* predisposition of mankind to the sacred.

As mentioned previously, another characteristic of the Enlightenment school of thought is the "Anti-metaphysical agnosticism" according to which experience is an action strictly limited to actual facts, consequently *incapable* of reaching the very essence of things, and totally unable to comprehend anything pertaining to the "supersensitive". Conversely, the Masonic "Method", tending towards knowledge based on intuition, refers to knowledge gained as the fruit of a transcendent and supra-rational *Tradition*.

On the contrary, the characteristics of modern thought and of the essentially atheist Freemasonry that sought inspiration from the latter, represent the negation of all forms of knowledge diverse from scientific and empirical dogma. Accordingly, one of the major concepts underlying Initiatic organisations, the *secret*, becomes totally incomprehensible, being unable to grasp the essentially symbolic value of the latter, referred rather to an inner *initiatic secret* that is "revealed" solely through *spiritual development* and which, due to its inexpressible nature, *cannot be communicated* to others. Metaphysical truths can never be wholly expressed in words, concepts or formulas, thus hindering the clear defining of metaphysics in view of its boundless essence. The inexpressible may be effectively grasped and conceived by means of intellectual intuition within the limits of one's personal intellectual capacities, but it cannot be conveyed to others. In conclusion, it is the existence of a hidden *Truth* and its unique and personal process of *revelation*, that constitute the true essence of the *initiatic secret*.

Let us now examine Rationalism and Anti-historicism as further aspects of the Enlightenment ideals. The thinkers of the Age of Enlightenment, based on the premise that truth can only be secured from experience, maintained that *Tradition*, the voice of the past, the authority exerted by the ancient thinkers, could only cause harm as it constituted a *prejudice* hindering a clear unimpeded vision. Furthermore, as a consequence of their anti-historic attitude, the enlightened concluded that prior to the eighteenth century there had only been errors, barbarisms, obscurantism. But on the contrary, Freemasonry is the most recent form of *Tradition,* and similar to all traditional forms gathers and conveys in an *uninterrupted chain* all aspects present from the beginning, unchanged by the ravages of time, beyond the realms of history and time. In the context of *Tradition* the transmitting of primary principles occurs in a vertical fashion, from super humans to humans, implying perfection from its very outset. The means best suited to instilling knowledge of the truth of a higher order associated with this *Tradition* is represented by symbolism, a tool that has been rejected or ignored by the modern world, which views truths as belonging to the order of *pure intellectuality*. If modern language is an analytical and discursive form of language, in the same way as human reasoning of which it is the tool, conversely, "symbolism" is essentially synthetic, and for this reason is *intuitive*, thereby more suitable than the spoken language in lending support to "intellectual intuition". Being of a synthetic nature, symbolism affords the possibility of a truly unlimited wealth of conceptions, proving superior to spoken language characterised by more specifically defined meanings imposing considerable limitations on one's intellect.

Lastly, Relativism, one of the major characteristics of the Enlightenment school of thought. Relativism maintains that all our ideas are closely linked to *external impressions* and to associations formed by the latter; they are undeniably moulded on experience. These ideas therefore could vary from their current status if our experience and the external phenomena were to change. In this case, ideas would not be based on a universal, eternally constant, firm foundation, but would merely convey the *experience* of the moment. No reference could be made to the True, the Beautiful or the Good in *absolute* terms. Indeed, the latter is one of the accusations levelled by the Catholic Church against Freemasonry, although it is, as I have already had occasion to underline in a conference focusing on this topic, totally groundless. [29] Indeed, the entire Masonic ritual is a journey undertaken with the sole aim of seeking a metaphysical Truth, eternal and unchangeable, of which the human soul bears the original mark.

Incredibly, it was two scholars of Freemasonry, Eugen Lennhoff and Oskar Posner, who first applied the term "relativist" to the Masonic school of thought, thereby providing the Catholic Church with the opportunity, punctually exploited several decades later, to use this inanity against Freemasonry. Indeed, the book written by Lennhoff and Posner, the *International Lexicon of Freemasonry* was awkwardly included among the texts presented by the *United Grand Lodge of Germany* to the *German Episcopal Conference* to evaluate the presence of elements of incompatibility between the Catholic Church and Freemasonry. The book by Lennhoff and Posner states that:

29 Fabio Venzi, in *Chiesa Cattolica e Massoneria*, conference organised by Pontificia Facoltà Teologica Seraphicum, Rome, 2008.

"Freemasonry may therefore be conceived as a movement aimed at attracting men of relativistic tendencies," a statement which led the *German Episcopal Conference* in 1980, following six years of discussions with representatives of the *United Grand Lodge of Germany*, to include among the six items of incompatibility between the Church and Freemasonry the issue of Relativism, verbatim *"essentia massoneriae est relativismus et subiectivismus, ersiae negatur obiectiva veritatis cognitio"*, as reported in *Quaesitum est*, the Declaration on Masonic Associations dated November 26th 1983 by the *Prefect for the Doctrine of the Faith* at that period, Cardinal Joseph Ratzinger.

Yet others have defined the Masonic school of thought as "deist", which is even more ridiculous. It is an established fact that in the deist doctrine there is no place for a relationship between God and man; God exists but is in no way involved in the historic events of man. Then how can the constant reference to the "assistance" of the *Great Architect of the Universe* in our rituals be explained? Not forgetting moreover the Royal Arch in which we address the *"True and Living God Most High"*, therefore to a *personal* theistic God. The damage caused by books such as the one written by Lennhof and Posner is incalculable. Supporters of the relativist theory maintain that Masonic rituals are in no way associated with knowledge "concerning the ultimate questions of being", underlining that if Masonry has any *esoteric secret* it is surely of an *ethical* nature, focusing on a spiritual agreement between Masons throughout the entire world, all pertaining to humanity and tolerance.

However, among the theories that have most affected the correct interpretation of Freemasonry, those put forward by the writer Margaret Jacob, considered one of the leading experts of the history of Freemasonry, should not be overlooked. I shall commence with statements such as:

"It would seem that the constitutional and legislative environment was what attracted men on the Continent to the first lodges. Within their confines brothers adjudicated new forms of personal power and they could imagine themselves as involved in governance as well as in opposition;[30] *Those historians who have emphasised only the democratic elements in Masonic government miss the obvious: The lodges mirrored the old order just as they were creating a form of civil society that would ultimately replace it.*[31]*, Masonic discourse, in whatever western European language, although permitting the expression of local interests and circumstances, did so within the framework of a rhetoric that was British in origin as well as invariably civic, hence political, and most frequently progressive and reformist.*[32] *Certainly the historical*

30 Margaret C. Jacob, *Massoneria illuminata*, Einaudi, Turin, 1995, Page 5.Original title: *Living the Enlightenment: Freemasonry and Politics in Eighteenth-Century Europe*, Oxford University Press, 1991.

31 Ibid. page 13.

32 Ibid. page 14.

phenomenon of freemasonry has significance in the interesting similarity of its rhetoric with that of the first modern democratic and radical movements.[33] *But we shall approach it for what it can tell us about the eighteenth-century Enlightenment; For all of its strengths it misses the distinctively civic quality of Masonic sociability – its building of the polity within sociability, the political content of its moral vision and its discourse; its imitation and initiation of form of governance, not lest its quasi-religious quality.*[34] *The point about the Masonic impulse wherever we find it is that it strove to be political.*[35] *It is the contention of this book that the Masonic experience in every western European context, from Edinburg to Berlin, from the 1730s to the 1780s, was resolutely civil and hence political"*[36] *and we could continue further.*

It is clear therefore how these are theories based wholly on the idea that the origins of Freemasonry are founded on essentially "political" motivations, and on the possibility that Freemasonry may also have been represented as an "Initiatic Order" does not even cross the mind of Jacob:

"These small private societies came to be seen as organised around a constitution in the post-1688, or parliamentary, sense of that term. The goal of government by consent within the context of subordination to 'legitimate' authority was vigorously pursued by the Grand Lodge of London and was demanded of all lodges affiliated with it … the lodges practiced a civil administration, derived from British political practice and tradition. Predictably in a British context lodges were, on the whole, remarkably supportive of established institutions, of Church and State."[37]

As is clear, throughout the entire text there is no explicit reference to rituals, to their esoteric and initiatic content, absolutely nothing. Freemasonry is reduced to a mere association on a par with numerous others, with Jacob underlining that:

"Certain characteristics of Masonic association differ not at all from the many other private societies that sprang up throughout Europe in the course of the eighteenth century. Members, proposed and chosen by other members, paid dues, attended meetings, voted and discussed, gave loyalty, and sought conviviality, if not self-improvement, from their association."[38] *The same pathway of self-perfection is viewed as an incidental component and, where pursued, in the opinion of Jacob, was merely: "They taught men to speak in public, to keep records, to pay 'taxes', to be tolerant, to debate freely, to vote, to moderate their*

33 Ibid. page 20.
34 Ibid. page 22.
35 Ibid. page 26.
36 Ibid. page 27.
37 Ibid. pages 75-82.
38 Ibid. page 32.

feasting."[39] *What need was there therefore to consecrate Temples and Lodges, to create rituals and symbols with such deep esoteric and philosophic connotations, to wear vestments, merely to achieve aims that could have been accomplished in any club?*

However, I would like to mention the most incredible theory which is undoubtedly constituted by Jacob's account of the reasons underlying the exclusion of women from initiation into the Masonic Obediences. In her words: "And throughout the century they [Freemasons] will be harassed by charges of libertinism and sodomy. Partly in response, freemasons would alternatively encourage women's participation and seek to exclude them. In the eyes of their frequently clerical opponents the reason for this exclusion was simple: Why would women wish to be involved in the practices of government -"[40] There is no need for further comment.

What fruits has the Illuminist school of thought left us? An *unconditioned trust* in the value and powers of science has undoubtedly led to progress on a technical level, although frequently not reciprocated by progress in one's spiritual life. The idea advanced by the Illuminist school of thought, of an *indefinite* progress has been manifested solely with regard to *material* progress, which is devoid of a parallel *moral* progress. History has taught us that ethico-moral progress and technical progress do not necessarily go hand in hand, and all too frequently technical progress has not heralded a reciprocal progress in ethics and morality, thereby completely overlooking the *transcendent* face of mankind.

Several thinkers were of the opinion that Illuminism should be seen as an arch-enemy, among which are Giambattista Vico, Johann Gottfried Herder, Edmund Burke, Joseph-Marie de Maistre and subsequently Thomas Carlyle and Hippolyte Taine.

Herder and Burke, progenitors of so-called anti-illuminism, a reaction to modernity, denied that reason could represent the sole *criterion of legitimacy* for any human institution, thus shedding constant doubt on the existing order and identifying in rationalism the cause of social disintegration. For Herder, doubt, scepticism, philosophy, abstractions, and enlightened thought would kill the vital forces present in humans. Burke was among the pioneers of this idea, destined to play an important role in the changes of the twentieth century, in which the prevailing quality of mankind would be primitivism rather than reason. He was the first to oppose John Locke, one of the fathers of Illuminist thought, and his theory of *tabula rasa*, according to which man is born with innate ideals and *Traditions* deriving from his predecessors, and which complicated the possibility of "progress" of civilisation itself.

39 Ibid. page 35.
40 Ibid. page 9.

In the view of these authors, during the supporters of the French Enlightenment presented all the symptoms of decline and transmitted their disease to the whole of Europe.[41]

As we have seen, the prevailing error in the theories advanced by Jacob is to be found in her representation of Freemasonry as a tool to be used in the achieving of an ethic, but rather a *democratic*, *political* ethic, an ethic that can be achieved by means of a parliamentary democracy; neither Herder nor Burke, on the contrary, gave any "moral" importance to legislation, specifically with the intent of avoiding the creation of *lay morals* stemming from rationalism and universal regulations.

Carlyle also views rationalism, reason, as an enemy to be fought against, writing in this regard:

"Logic is good but is not the best thing we have…a healthy intellect is not the logic, the argumentative, but rather the intuitive,"[42] *and in the renowned work Sartor Resartus he writes: "Man is driven and governed by Symbols, that may render him pleased or displeased…we are not upheld by a power of Logic and Measurement, but rather by our power of Imagination."*[43]

Illuminist thought may be viewed as the last expression of a phenomenon that from the time of Ancient Greece to the Oriental civilisations has invariably been manifested during periods of decadence, historic moments in which reason attempts to annihilate *Tradition*. For this reason thoughts similar to those expressed by the Illuminists remain a constant threat for *Traditional* societies.

It is evident that something has been lost over time, and we have an impelling need to recover it. The flattening of Masonic thought over the Illuminist philosophy is the result of this; scientific progress, law, justice and freedom have all resulted, in several cases, in the *transformation* of Freemasonry from an "Initiatic Society" into a "Lay Religion", accompanied by demands, at times, of substituting for the true religion.

Traditional Freemasonry should thus be interpreted, in my opinion, as an overt Initiatic organisation that has no ambition to "act" on a social or historic plane, but which was established on the basis of an ancient knowledge. Accordingly, it may likewise be defined as a "summation" of Western Initiatic traditions.

The movement does, however, "operate" on both an individual and universal level. Indeed, in pursuing the design of a Divine Being who has transcended the pure, raw material to become an accomplishment of his own expression, through the actions undertaken by an individual, the Brotherhood changes and uplifts the whole of mankind to a level of awareness of its history and purpose situated markedly beyond the limits of mere human events.

41 Zeev Sternhell, *Contro l'Illuminismo*, Baldini Castoldi Dalai, Milan, 2007, page 210.

42 Thomas Carlyle, *Essais choisis de Critique et de Morale*, Mercure, Paris, 1907, pages 50-51.

43 Thomas Carlyle, *Sartor Resartus*, Liberilibri, Macerata, 2008, pages 265-267.

3. The Schaw Statutes and the "Art of Memory" of Ramon Llull

As mentioned in the previous section, two main schools of thought are manifested with regard to the "context" in which modern-day Freemasonry originated; the first supports the English origins of the movement, whilst the second opts for a Scottish source.

With regard to the second, one of the versions which has gained an appreciable number of supporters recently relates to the *Schaw Statutes* dated 1598/99, a document that, according to the historians concerned, would appear to attest to the unequivocal proof of the birth of Freemasonry from the Scottish Lodges of the time. I have opted to examine this theory in a separate chapter in order to provide for an exhaustive analysis of the content.

I will therefore illustrate, and at the same time attempt to reject, the theory put forward by a previously Scottish historian Prof. David Stevenson, Lecturer of Scottish History at the University of Aberdeen. Stevenson's theory is based on the influence of the *Schaw Statutes* on the birth of seventeenth century Scottish Freemasonry; I will moreover analyse references made to the "Art of Memory".

In the *Statutes* promulgated at the end of the sixteenth century by William Schaw, Stevenson is persuaded that he has found conclusive documentary confirmation of another widely debated theory put forward by a renowned historian of the Warburg Institute, Frances A. Yates, famed for her studies on the history of the Renaissance and in particular her research on the Italian philosopher Giordano Bruno. The phenomenon known as the "Yates paradigm" maintains that in the work of Giordano Bruno various components (comprising Lullism) perform a specific function, thus contributing towards the success of the mission of the Supreme Magus responsible throughout the whole of Europe for spreading the Hermetic tradition.

On reviewing and further developing the suggestions made by Yates, the theories put forward by Bruno were, in Stevenson's opinion, those that provided William Schaw with the cue with which to *modify* the Scottish Freemasonry of the time, transforming it into something entirely different to the previous model, and using, among other things, the Hermetic principles of the Brunian "Art of Memory".

As mentioned previously, Stevenson takes over where Yates left off, with the latter commenting on the cultural climate in which the famous essay *Giordano Bruno and the Hermetic tradition* was collocated:

"Where is such combination as this of religious toleration, emotional link with the medieval past, emphasis on good works for others, and imaginative attachment to the religion and the symbolism of the Egyptians? The only answer to this question that I can think of

is – in Freemasonry, with its mythical link with the medieval masons, its toleration, its philanthropy, and its Egyptian symbolism." [44]

Stevenson embraces this theory fully and, developing it further, affirms that the Scottish Lodges at the end of the sixteenth century, thanks to the contribution provided by William Schaw, influenced by the Hermetic movement and the Brunian theories, combined this philosophy with the "operative" tradition and with other features of the Renaissance school of thought, resulting in the creation of modern-day Freemasonry.

I will attempt here to demonstrate the lack of sustainability of this theory, based on several assumptions, on the Hermeticism of the sixteenth-century Scottish Lodges and the influence produced by the philosophical theories of Giordano Bruno which, in my opinion, are not only indemonstrable but are moreover incompatible with the context concerned.

The Two Statutes *of William Schaw, 1598/1599*

William Schaw was born in Scotland in 1550, a member of an important Scottish family from Sauchie, a small village in the county of Clackmannanshire. Little is known of his life, with the exception that he received a liberal education and was interested in architectural studies. Close to the Royal Family of Scotland from an early age, on December 21st 1583 James VI appointed him King's Master of Works in Scotland with responsibility for all royal palaces and castles, and Chamberlain to the Queen.

In particular, William Schaw is remembered for having devised a system for the organisation of Scottish Lodges culminating in the enactment of the *Statutes* published in 1598 and 1599. He was an authoritative man and one of the most powerful members of the period of his standing in Scotland. He died in 1602 at the age of 52. He is buried in Dunfermline Abbey and his tomb, built at the expense of his friend Alexander Seton, bears a Latin inscription recalling his moral and intellectual qualities:

INTEGERRIMO, AMICO, GVGLIELMO SCHAW.
VIVE. INTER. SUPEROS. AETERNVMQUE. OPTIME. VIVE.
HAEC. TIBI. VITA. LABOR. MORS. FUIT. ALTA. QUIES.
ALEXANDER SETONIVS. D.F.
D.O.M.
HVMILIS HAEC. LAPIDVM. STRVCTVRA. TEGIT. VITVM.
EXCELLENTI. PERITIA. PROBITATE. EXIMIA. SINGVLARI.

44 Frances A. Yates, *Giordano Bruno and the Hermetic Tradition*, Routledge & Kegan Paul, 1964 pages 300-301.

VITAE. INTEGRITATE. SVMMIS. VIRTVTIBVS. ORNATVM.
GUGLIELMUM SCHAW. REGIIS. OPERIBVS. PRAEFECTVM. SACRIS.
CEREMONIIS. PRAEPOSITVM. RAGINAE. QUAESTOREM.
EXTREMVM. IS. DIEM. OBIIT. 18. APRILIS . 1602.
MORTALES. INTER. VIXIT. ANNOS. QVINQVAGINTA. DVOS.
GALLIAS. MVLTAQUE. ALIA. REGNA. EXOLENDI ANIMI. STVDIO.
PEREGRAVIT. NVLLA. LIBERALI. DISCIPLINA. NON. IMBVTVS.
ARCHITECTVRAE. PERITISSIMVS. PRINCIPIBVS. IMPRIMIS. VIRIS.
EGREGIIS. ANIMI. DOTIBVS. COMMENDATVS. LABORIBVS. ET
NEGOTIIS.
NON INDEFESSVS. MODO. ET. INSVPERABILIS. SED. ASSIDVE.
STRENVVS, ET, INTEGER. NVLLI. BONO. NON CARISSIMVS. CVI.
NOTVS. AD. OFFICIA. ET. DEMERENDOS. HOMINVM. ANIMOS.
NATVS.
NVNC. INTER. SVPEROS. AETERNVM. VIVIT.
ANNA. REGINA. NE. VIRTVS. AETERNA. COMMENDATIONE.
DIGNA. MEMORVM. MORTALITATE. LABESCERET. OPTIMI.
INTEGERRIMIQVE. VIRI. MEMORIAE. MONVMENTVM. PONT.
MANDAVIT.

As mentioned, William Schaw was appointed by James VI *King's Master of Works and Warden-general* or *Chief Master of Masons*, positions that, as emphasised by George Draften: *"were entirely administrative being those, so it is said, of a Guild Officer for the Craft of masons in Scotland regarded as a body of lodges and quite separate from the control exercised in the cities and burghs by the Trade Incorporation"*.[45]

It was indeed within the framework of his position of *King's Master of Works* and *Chief Master of Masons* that in 1598 and 1599 Schaw promulgated two series of decrees regulating the profession of mason in Scotland. An original copy of the *Statutes* bearing the signature of William Schaw is conserved in the Minute-Book of the Edinburgh Lodge (Mary's Chapel) No.1.

The *Statutes* promulgated by William Schaw represent the first existing form of organisation of the Scottish Lodge system; an organisation presided over by a *General Warden*. The first *Statutes*, introduced on December 28th 1598, are divided into 22 items. They open with an undertaking of the *Master Mason* to observe the ordnances established by his predecessors.

45 George Draffen of Newington, *The Schaw Statutes*, AQC, Vol. 94, 1981, page 138.

In spite of its importance, this document has been frequently underestimated by historians of Freemasonry, and irrespective of one's belief or lack of belief in his theory, Stevenson should undoubtedly be given due acknowledgement for having once again drawn the attention of historians of Freemasonry to the *Statutes*.

Stevenson maintains that, although known by the same name, the Lodges belonging to the organisation governed by Schaw differed radically from those of the ancient medieval builders, likewise performing markedly different rituals. Stevenson writes: "*It is also no doubt the case that the earlier lodges had rituals and ceremonies – it is difficult to conceive of a medieval craft organisation not having rituals of some sort. But there is nothing to indicate that these rituals were identical to those of the new Schaw lodges, the rituals of the latter were based on the Mason Word, and there is no pre-seventeenth-century evidence for the existence of the Word ... Just as there is no evidence of continuity of ritual, so there is none of organisations. Doubtless some of the new-type lodges which appeared around 1600 claimed from the first links with these shadowy earlier lodges (as many certainly did later) but there is not a single scrap of evidence to give plausibility to the idea of the direct and continuous descent of any of the Schaw lodges from earlier organization. Of the two types of medieval lodge, the semi-permanent lodges sometimes attached to great churches probably disappeared before the 1590s, a process which would have been hastened by the coming of reformation to Scotland in 1560. As to temporary building-site lodges, they continued to exist alongside the new lodges ... Service's office of warden over a site lodge was nothing to do with the lodge of the Schaw Statutes and their wardens, and the fact that the Medieval-style site lodge could exist alongside the new Schaw Lodges but entirely separate from them emphasises that they were very different even if they had the same name. In both ritual and organisation William Schaw may have built on fragmentary tradition of the craft, but the central theme appears to be innovation rather than continuity.*"[46]

Therefore, according to Stevenson, there was no degree of continuity between the previous medieval "operative" Lodges and the *new* Lodges as conceived by Schaw, which differed from the former in both structure and aims, in spite of having maintained the same name.

The possibility that William Schaw in reorganising the entire administrative system of Scottish Lodges may have "modified" other previously existing features is also supported by another renowned Scottish scholar, Robert Cooper, Librarian of the *Grand Lodge of Scotland*, who writes:

"Schaw did not 'invent' lodges nor did he invent the oath that stonemasons took to look after each other. All of this was already in existence by the time he became Master

46 David Stevenson, *The Origins of Freemasonry*, Cambridge University Press, 1988, pages 36-37.

of Works. Taking this into consideration together with all the other rules in Schaw's First Statutes, it would appear that he was intent on formalising an existing but loose and informal association of Scotland stonemasons and their lodges...Schaw's lasting impact was to formalise a pre-existing, probably very casual, system of stonemasons' lodges that were already in possession of a number of traditions, lore, ceremonies and a system of esoteric knowledge. In doing so he began a process that would ultimately lead to modern Freemasonry. His statutes meant that lodges had for the first time to keep records, which is why the oldest lodge records in the worlds exist in Scotland. Aitcheson's Haven's records commence on 9 January 1599, followed by those of the lodge of Edinburgh on 31 July 1599... It seems obvious that by putting his statutes in place, Schaw was attempting to create a National organization with himself at his head... It is clear that the stonemasons' lodges have long been associated with systems of esoteric knowledge or a secret 'code' such as that which William Schaw seems to have formalised with his statutes. Medieval crafts had 'Mysteries', systems of esoteric knowledge appropriated to each trade, and they used their working tools – the items with which each member was intimately acquainted — as visual aids to teach the trade's particular moral lesson. Obviously such knowledge was restricted to members." [47]

Therefore, Cooper likewise opines that Schaw should be seen as the *inspirer* of modern-day "speculative" Freemasonry created through a reorganisation of a concern existing previously in Scotland at the end of the sixteenth century, using traditions, ceremonies (including the taking of an oath by members) and, above all, a system of "esoteric knowledge". Esoteric knowledge of which, in my opinion, there is no demonstrable proof or presence in the documents currently available.

The "Art of Memory"

The numerous historians who have studied the Statutes, particularly the 1599 items, have frequently overlooked the aspect which, in my opinion, represents the true singularity comprised therein: their reference to the "Art of Memory". Indeed, the 1599 Statutes first referred to the term "Art of Memory", a frequently misinterpreted expression, often construed as a mere "memory test", a mnemonic technique applied in memorising the Statutes or, presumably, the scant rituals existing at that period.

I am in agreement on this with Stevenson that Schaw was referring to something quite different, to the "Art of Memory" that from Ramon Llull up until the Renaissance and to Giordano Bruno, represented something considerably more complex than a mere mnemonic procedure.

47 Robert L.D. Cooper, *Cracking the Freemason's Code*, Rider, London, 2006, pages 20-25.

I wish to concentrate specifically on the second *Schaw Statutes* promulgated at Holyroodhouse on December 28th 1599. These *Statutes* comprise 14 items, some of which are specifically addressed to the *Kilwinning Lodge*, whilst yet others pertain to all Scottish Lodges. Item 13 contains the sentence at the centre of the present debate; in this statement: *"The warden of Kilwinning Lodge was ordered to test every entered apprentice and fellow craft in 'the art of memorie and science thairof."*

As mentioned above, numerous historians have failed to give due consideration to the implicit reference made to the "Art of Memory". A first example of this underestimation is constituted by the important keynote *Freemasons' Guide and Compendium* by Bernard Jones, which whilst providing an irrefutable explanation of the *Statutes*, makes no reference to, or rather deals with in an extremely superficial manner, the fundamental item 13 of the 1599 *Statutes*, in which reference to the "Art of Memory" is contained.

Bernard Jones provides a clear description of the *Statutes*:

"The first set of the Schaw Statutes order the Brethren to observe the ordinances and to be true to one another, to be obedient to the Wardens, Deacons, and masters, and to be honest, diligent, and upright. No one may undertake work unless able to complete it satisfactorily, and no Master may supplant another or take an uncompleted work unless the previous Master is duly satisfied. There is to be an annual election of one Warden. No Master may have more than three Apprentices during his lifetime, and an apprentice is not to be bound for less than seven years, and is not to be made a Fellow Craft until he has served an additional seven years. Masters are forbidden to sell their Apprentices without informing the lodge Warden, so that his name and date of reception may be duly booked. No Master or fellow of Craft may be received or admitted except in the presence of six Masters and two Entered Apprentices, the Warden of that lodge being one of the six, the date thereof being orderly booked, and 'his name and mark insert' in the said book, together with the names of the six Masters, the apprentices, and Intender. No one to be admitted without an assay and trial of skill. A Master is not allowed to engage in work under charge of any other craftsman, or to receive cowans to work in his society, or company, or to send any of his servants to work with them. Entered Apprentices are forbidden to undertake work beyond the value of ten pounds. Any strife among Masters, servants, or Apprentices is to be notified to the lodge within twenty-four hours, and the award accepted. Masters and others are ordered to take all needful precautions as to the erection of scaffolding, and if accidents occur through their negligence they shall not act as Masters but be subject to others. Masters may not receive runaway Apprentices. All members must attend meetings when lawfully warned, and all masters present at any assembly or meeting are to be sworn 'by their great oath' not to hide or conceal any wrong done to each other or to the owners of the work. Finally, the various penalties attaching to the foregoing were ordered to be collected and distributed by the officers

of the lodge. The second set of Statutes confirm the Edinburgh Lodge as being the first and principal lodge in Scotland, that of Kilwinning as the second, and the lodge of Stirling as the third. They make the wardens of any lodge answerable to the presbyters (civic elders) within their sheriffdoms for the masons subject to their lodges, and regulate the election of Wardens. They also empower the Wardens of Kilwinning to test the qualifications of the Fellow Crafts within their district 'of their art, craft, scyance, and ancient memorie,' to the intent that the said Warden shall be duly responsible for such persons as are under them. Fellow Crafts at entry and prior to admission must pay to the lodge ten pounds with ten shillings' worth of gloves, this including the expense of the banquet and none are to be admitted without 'ane sufficient essay' and 'pruife of memorie and art of craft'.[48]

Subsequently, on describing item 13 of the 1599 *Statutes*, Jones confuses mnemonic techniques with the quite different "Art of Memory", and writes: *"There does not appear to be anything of esoteric interest in these statutes, but writers from time to time have tended to direct special attention or to give slight 'colour' to a phrase here and there in what may be a 'wishful' attempt to detect veiled references. The quiet, unbiased reading of the Statutes fails, however, to discover (with one possible exception) anything other than provisions for regulating the mason trade and for investing the lodge at Kilwinning with certain powers. That possible exception is the inclusion of the phrases 'of ancient memorie' and 'pruife of memorie and art of craft'. These words could bear the interpretation that the craftsmen were expected to have learnt by heart something of a traditional or secret nature not expedient to name; but, since the Wardens have to answer to the civic presbyters for the masons under their charge, it reasonably follows that no such interpretation can be regarded as very likely."*[49]

Thus, Jones underlines how item 13 of the *Statutes* contains nothing beyond an incentive to memorise things that it is deemed preferable not to convey in a written form.

This confusion between mnemonic techniques and the "Art of Memory" is also encountered in the work of other scholars, with a further example being provided by the work of Tobias Churton who, on referring to Stevenson's theories writes:

"The 'Art of Memorie', advocated as a form of metaphysical psychology by the Dominican friar, Giordano Bruno, was linked to his belief that the magus could stand foursquare upon earth with his higher mind illuminated by celestial and solar influences. Bruno took the old, medieval 'Lullian Art' of integrating knowledge in complex mind-pictures away from its basis as an aid to memory function, through visual links and association placed in an imagine 'Theatre' construction, and on towards an illuminist parapsychology. This occult system was

48 Bernard E. Jones, *Freemasons' Guide and Compendium*, George G. Harrap & Co. Ltd, London, 1950, pages 128-129.
49 Ibid. page 130.

surely well beyond the capacities of most masters, wardens and prentices of stonemasons' lodges. Even had it been a private interest of the most daring and gifted masters, it was an unlikely candidate for a national Masonic curriculum! The later phrase 'the art of memorie and science thairof' – it would seem that the most likely meaning of the test was a simple test of memory." [50] *It is clear that Churton, as Jones previously, is not aware of the fact that to refer to a mere mnemonic technique would have been a redundant repetition for Schaw who, in the previous paragraphs, had twice made explicit reference to a memory test.*

Indeed, items 6 and 10 unequivocally refer to a request for an actual memory test; item 6 requires the wardens of the Lodge of Kilwinning to elect.

"sex of the maist perfyte and worthiest of memorie within (thair boundis), to tak triall of the qualificatioun of the hail masonis within the boundis foirsaid, of thair art, craft, scyance and antient memorie," whilst item 10 underlines how no fellow craftsman will be eligible:

"without ane sufficient essay and pruife of memorie and art of craft to the warden, deacon and quartermasters". It is clear therefore that the memory tests are *explicitly* requested by Schaw and are clearly identified as such, thus providing an undeniable distinction from the "Art of Memory" of the subsequent item 13.

The Unsustainable Stevenson-Yates Theory

I would now like to address the issue of the distortions made by Stevenson. He affirms that the *mystical* and *occult* currents of the Renaissance school of thought were deliberately introduced into the Scottish Lodges by Schaw in his *Statutes*:

"The reference to the art of memory in the Second Schaw Statutes provides the only direct evidence, as opposed to strong circumstantial evidence, that in remodelling the mason craft William Schaw was deliberately introducing Renaissance influence into the craft, and for that reason it is immensely important," and continues, *"As regards the Second Statutes, the three simple words 'art of memory' may be taken as proof that from the first the Schaw lodges were at least dabbling in occult and mystical strands of late Renaissance thought."* [51] With regard to these considerations, I am in full agreement with the likelihood that the contents and symbology of *several* currents of the Renaissance school of thought, namely Neoplatonism, may have exerted a successive influence on Masonic rituals, but this undoubtedly occurred *much later* than the period examined herein.[52]

Stevenson subsequently reiterates his theory of a Hermetic influence on Scottish operative Freemasonry:

50 Tobias Churton, *Freemasonry: The Reality*, Lewis Masonic, Hersham, 2007, pages 224-225.

51 David Stevenson, op.cit., pages 49-50.

52 Fabio Venzi, *The Influence of Neoplatonic Thought on Freemasonry*, Book Guild, Brighton, 2007.

"The Hermetic movement was soon to be discredited on historical grounds, but its influence on the Scottish Masonic lodges was permanent, for they combined elements with their own traditional lore and other aspects of Renaissance and Reformation thought to create freemasonry." [53] Thus, in his view, the Hermetic 'movement' of the Renaissance exerted a permanent and marked influence on the Scottish Lodges at the end of the sixteenth century. This is solely an opinion for which no objective support has been provided; indeed, documents in our possession, the *Old Charges*, reveal a complete lack of Hermetic components, with the exception of an insignificant reference to Hermes in the legend narrated.

The oldest reference to Hermes was first made in the *Cooke Manuscript* (1450), the second oldest of the *Old Charges*, subsequently being reiterated in many of the approximately 130 *Old Charges* (in some being replaced by Euclid) in a more or less similar context. Indeed the legend narrated in the *Old Charges* recounts how following the biblical "Great Flood" the two columns on which all knowledge was inscribed were found by Pythagoras and Hermes who in turn handed down their knowledge to their successors.

I am in complete agreement with Michael Baigent as to the hypothesis whereby the introduction of Hermetic thought into Freemasonry took place only much later. In an article published in *AQC* in 1996, *Freemasonry, Hermetic Thought and the Royal Society of London* in referring to Elias Ashmole, Baigent mentions an encounter in 1651 with the alchemist William Backhouse, during which Ashmole apparently underwent a sort of Hermetic initiation. We do however know that Ashmole had been initiated five years previously, on October 16th 1646, in Warrington. On analysing these two events Baigent comments:

"What can we deduce from this? Surely, given his comments, it is that whatever he received in his hermetic initiation was something other than that which he had received in his Masonic initiation. Such was his desire for hermetic knowledge that, after the latter, he had continued searching for another five years. It is, the, reasonable to conclude that speculative Freemasonry of the type joined by Ashmole in 1646 did not contain anything of Hermetic importance. As I have argued with my examination of Elias Ashmole's Hermetic initiation, 1651 would appear to provide the earliest possible date for the inclusion of the Hermetic strand into Freemasonry." [54]

However, Stevenson's theory becomes even more daring when he goes on to identify the Nolan philosopher Giordano Bruno as the source of inspiration for the "project" of William Schaw. Stevenson writes: *"Giordano Bruno visited Paris in 1581-3, and his first*

53 David Stevenson, op. cit., pages.86-87.

54 Michael Baigent, *Freemasonry, Hermetic Thought and the Royal Society of London,* AQC, Vol. 109, 1996.

two works on memory were published there in 1582. He then moved to England, where his third work was printed in 1583, and almost immediately a controversy erupted over his ideas. In the course of this his cause was championed in print by a Scot living in London. Alexander Dickson had been born in Perthshire in 1558 and studied at the University of St Andrews. Early in 1584 he published a treatise based on Bruno's first work, outlining the classical art of memory but setting it in a hermetic Egyptian context much more openly than Bruno had done. It is likely that Bruno and his disciple Alexander Dickson met while the former was in England in 1583-5; but whether they did or not, the episode reveals the foremost supporter of Bruno in Britain was a Scotsman. Dickson was, moreover, not alone at the Scottish court in taking an interest in the art. William Fowler, poet, man of letters and secretary to the queen, Anne of Denmark, includes in a list of 'My Works' a treatise on 'art of memorye'."[55] However, although Dickson was a supporter of Bruno's theories, it should once again be emphasised that although Dickson, Fowler and Schaw may have met and have had contact of a philosophical nature, there is no existing proof to demonstrate this occurrence.

Stevenson was undoubtedly aware of the existence of other forms of "Art of Memory" in that period, but, influenced by Yates, was in no doubt as to the fact that this specific "Art of Memory" was the very one mentioned to Giordano Bruno:

"Of the many variants of the art of memory, ancient, Medieval and Renaissance, which was it that William Schaw wished Scottish masons to be skilled in? The likely connection with Dickson, and the fact that other elements of the Hermetic tradition are present in the emergence of freemasonry at this time must surely indicate that it was at least influenced by the occult, Hermetic art of Giordano Bruno...If it was in part Bruno's art that Schaw introduced to the masons, then he was attempting to implant elements of a secret Hermetic cult into the mason craft, with the art of memory intended to lead to spiritual advancement and knowledge of the divine."[56] Stevenson is indeed persuaded that he has found in the *Schaw Statutes* documentary confirmation of the theories put forward by Yates:

"Frances Yates, though not aware of the reference in the Second Schaw Statutes to the art of memory, suggested a connection between the art, which used an architectural framework in the search for wisdom, and freemasonry. She suggested that in England 'the Hermetic form of the art of memory perhaps goes more (than in Italy) underground, becoming associated with secret Catholic sympathisers, or with existing secret religious groups, or with incipient Rosicrucianism or Freemasonry'.[57] *To continue with a lengthy citation by Yates herself: "Masonic historians have to leave as an unsolved question the problem of the origin*

55 David Stevenson, op. cit., page 91.

56 David Stevenson op. cit., page 95.

57 David Stevenson op. cit., page 96.

of 'speculative masonry', with its symbolic use of columns, arches, and other architectural features, and of geometrical symbolism, as the framework within which it presents a moral teaching and a mystical outlook, directed towards the divine architect of the universe. I would think that the answer to this problem may be suggested by the history of the art of memory, that the Renaissance occult memory may be the real source of a Hermetic and mystical movement which used, not the real architecture of 'operative' masonry, but the imaginary or 'speculative' architecture of the art of memory as a vehicle of its teachings." [58]

In Stevenson's view, therefore, for what reason did William Schaw include the "Art of Memory" in his *Statutes*? Stevenson seems to be in no doubt:

"What did Schaw and the masons use the art of memory for? The general striving for mystical enlightenment is doubtless present, but, as has already been suggested, it was probably also employed for more mundane purposes such as memorising the Old Charges. The two are not entirely separable, however: the search for knowledge of the divine was based on Hermetic theories of ancient Egyptian knowledge, and Hermes and Egypt have an important place in the Old Charges." [59] *Accordingly, Stevenson maintained that the use of the "Art of Memory" would have enabled the Scottish bricklayers of the time to achieve a "mystical illumination", although, at the same time, this achievement would also have produced the "practical" effect of allowing them to commit the Old Charges to memory. Both these aims would appear to be highly unlikely, and I will now explain why.*

Although we have already discussed the inconsistency of the Hermetic and Egyptian elements present throughout the *Old Charges*, Stevenson adds that the art of memory served a second purpose, aimed at aiding the memorisation of the *Old Charges* themselves. He is once again wrong in stating this. In practical terms, the Brunian system known as the "Art of Memory" was completely ineffectual for use in committing things to memory.

In a work entitled *La chiave delle ombre (The key to the shadows)* published in 1997, the Italian scholar Francesco Torchia clearly demonstrated how the five-wheel system devised by Giordano Bruno was completely *devoid of utility* for mnemonic purposes.[60] Furthermore, as emphasised by Paolo Rossi, one of the most eminent historians of the Renaissance period.

"The Brunian art of memory is a memorisation technique that is considerably more complicated and less easy to manage than 'Ciceronian' techniques, with Bruno displaying a marked abandonment of the art of memory conceived as a transferable technique, no

58 Frances Yates, *The Art of Memory*, Pimlico, London SW1V, 1992, pages 286-304.

59 David Stevenson, op. cit., page 96.

60 Francesco Torchia, *La chiave delle ombre*, Il Mulino, Bologna, 1997, page 131.

formulae regulate this connection and, as underlined by Bruno, one is obliged to 'rely on the pure architect of imagination." [61]

It was however Yates who in referring to the Brunian system and to the possibility of practical use of the "Art of Memory" asserts that:"We shall never succeed in understanding this business in detail," moreover referring elsewhere to the Brunian machine as "an extraordinary jumble."[62]

What then were Bruno's true intentions? Once again Yates provides the following explanation:

"In Shadows he does not hesitate to use the (supposedly) very powerful images of the Decans of the zodiac; in Circe he introduces the art of memory with fiercely magical incantations uttered by the sorceress. Bruno aimed at much greater powers than the mild lion-taming or the planetary oratory of Camillo. The reader of Shadows immediately notices the repeatedly formed figure of a circle marked with thirty letters. Some of these figures display a concentric circle marked with thirty letters. Paris in the sixteenth century was the foremost European centre of Lullism, and no Parisian could have failed to recognise these circles as the famous combinatory wheels of the Lullian Art As expected therefore, the Llull depicted by Bruno was undeniably more the Renaissance Llull rather than the medieval Llull. His Lullian circle includes more letters than in any genuine Lullian art, as well as a few Greek and Hebrew letters, which are never used in genuine Lullism." [63] *This article by Yates underlines how Bruno's aims were largely of a "magical" nature, and how he dismissed a Christian and Trinitarian use (on the contrary, Llull had made these elements a pivot for his art), an aspect which, as we shall see subsequently, was of considerable importance. Thus, the brilliant success achieved by Bruno in identifying a means of combining the classic art of memory with Lullism was based on an 'occultisation' pushed to the limits of both classic art and Lullism. He placed the image of classic art on the combinatory wheels of Llull, but the images are magical images and the wheels are wheels of beseechment.*[64] *A system therefore that had nothing to do with the memorising of the Old Charges, and which was striving towards far more challenging results.*

According to Bruno, by adapting, manipulating or using astral images one manipulates "forms" situated at a level closer to reality than those located in the lower world, which are all dependent on the influence of the stars. Bruno was persuaded he could operate on the lower world, changing the sidereal influences produced, as long as a means of adapting and manipulating the astral images were available.

61 Paolo Rossi, *Il tempo dei maghi*, Raffaello Cortina Editore, Milan, 2006, page 82.

62 Frances A.Yates, op. cit., pages 195-201.

63 Frances A.Yates, op. cit., pages 205-206.

64 Frances A.Yates, op. cit., page 208.

In truth, astral images are actually "shadows of ideas", shadows of reality, and closer to the reality of the physical shadows of the lower world. Impressing on one's mind the image of "higher agents", it should have proved possible from on high to know of things situated lower down; the inferior items would have been arranged in one's memory once the images of superior things comprising the reality of inferior things in a higher form had been organised according to a design more closely resembling the most recent reality. The latter memory would represent the memory of a divine man, a magus in possession of divine powers stemming from an imagination bridled to the action of cosmic forces.[65]

Therefore, the system devised by Bruno is addressed unmistakably towards an "*occult*" aim and to a Magus capable of making use of the same, of controlling it for the purpose of acquiring *divine powers*. I am firmly convinced that William Schaw did not expect this much of the sixteenth-century builders.

It is however undeniable that the theories put forward by Ramon Llull had a profound impact on Bruno, and it has already been mentioned how Paris, the city where Bruno stayed and wrote several of his major works, was the most important centre of Lullism in the sixteenth century. In the *Shadows of Ideas*, written in Paris, a circle bearing thirty letters, a form inspired beyond all doubt by the combinatory art of Ramon Llull, is used repeatedly. However, the letters used are greater in number than those contemplated by Llull, and are mainly Greek and Hebrew letters. Consequently, it may be concluded that the Llull depicted by Bruno is a Llull *affected* by the Renaissance, differing markedly to the authentic Llull, comprising the introduction of *pseudolullian* theories and texts such as *De auditu kabbalistico*, thus featuring alchemical and kabbalistic influences which were not present in the genuine medieval Llull. Indeed, the "Art" of Ramon Llull was in a certain sense "occultised" by Bruno.

The Antitrinitarianism of Bruno and the Christian Component in the Origins of Freemasonry

A further objection to Stevenson's theory is based on the fact that it would seem scarcely plausible to maintain that the ideas of a heretic who only several months later would be burnt at the stake in Piazza Campo dé Fiori in Rome for the theories he believed in could be professed in the court of James VI, a Catholic king. Furthermore, he who was reported as having included those theories into Freemasonry of the period, William Schaw, was himself a Catholic, accused in 1593 by the English of being a "suspect Jesuit" in the court of James VI.

65 Frances A.Yates, op. cit., page 213.

The true weakness of Stevenson's theory however is the *impossibility* of reconciling the Masonic rituals, if they may be so termed, of the period, and the Antitrinitarianism of Giordano Bruno. Antitrinitarianism features constantly throughout the works of Bruno, not only when applied to foment the anti-Christian controversy (in his *Lo Spaccio della bestia trionfante* when he ridicules the dogma of the Incarnation, likening Christ to the centaur Chiron, half man and half beast), but also because Antitrinitarianism is deep-rooted in a philosophical theme underlying Bruno's entire school of thought, from *De umbris* to *De la causa* to *Heroic Frenzies*.

In the *Lo Spaccio della bestia trionfante*, three dialogues focusing on a moral theme, Bruno likens the triumphant beasts to the signs of the celestial constellations represented by animals. These must be expelled from the sky, or "banished" as termed by Bruno, as they represent ancient vices which need to be replaced with modern virtues, a new series of values to be used as a reference point by mankind. According to Bruno, Christianity is the main culprit responsible for this breakdown in values and thus a change, a reversal of values, is needed. In the context of this new hierarchy proposed by Bruno, the first place is occupied by Truth, followed by Prudence, Wisdom, Law, Fortitude, Philanthropy and Magnanimity. In the *Expulsion of the Triumphant Beast* Bruno does away explicitly and once and for all with the Christian model of the creation, in the context of a wholly naturalist perspective. As stated previously, the contemptuous and mocking judgements uttered by Bruno about Christ, initially likened to Orion "*who made the sky urinate in fear*", and subsequently to the centaur Chiron, leave the reader in no doubt as to his views on Christianity.

Thus, in the view of Stevenson, into which Masonic context would Bruno's theories, with, as we have just witnessed, the rejection of Christianity as the leitmotiv, have been introduced by William Schaw? In this regard, we should take into account several characteristics of the Freemasonry of the period in England and Scotland through examination of the sole reliable documents capable of providing documentable elements of certainty; naturally, I refer to the *Old Charges*. In *The Genesis of Freemasonry*, D. Knoop and G. P. Jones, two renowned historians of Freemasonry, provide an excellent definition and a conclusion that delves deep into the heart of the issue at hand:

"The MS. Constitution of Masonry, or more familiarly the Old Charges, of which the Regius and Cooke MSS. of circa 1400 are the oldest known versions, consist of a Body of regulation relating to masters, craftsmen, and apprentices, and to wages and other matters affecting masons. These regulations, describe in the documents either as Articles and Points, or as Charges general and singular, are prefaced by a legendary narrative of how the building craft and the regulations came into being. About 115 versions of the Old Charges have been traced In an endeavour to trace changes in the form of the MS. Constitution, we

propose to leave aside the Regius MS., which is in a class by itself...Instead, we treat the Cooke MS. as the oldest version. This consists of five elements: 1) a statement of man's debt to God; 2) the New Long History; 3) the Old Short History; 4) the Articles and Points; 5) a brief Closing Prayer. The first element is replaced in most of the later versions by an invocation to the Trinity." [66] *In point number 5 the two authors highlight the undeniable presence of a "Christian" element, an invoking of the Trinity. Indeed, further confirmation and support is given by J.R. Clarke in his article The Change from Christianity to Deism in Freemasonry when he writes:*

"There is no doubt that the old operative masons were expected to be Christians. In nearly all the documents known as the Old Charges, the first and principal charge, from the Cooke MS. (circa 1400) to the Grand Lodge No1 MS. (1583), is that a mason shall love God, Holy Church, and all Saints. The saints were omitted after 1583 but the others remained, as in the William Watson MS. (1637): 'Ye shall be true man or true men to God and ye Holy Church and that ye shall use neither error nor heresy". With regard to Scotland, the catechism known as Dumfries No4 MS. (1710) commences: "with a prayer of admittance: 'The Almighty Father of Holiness, the Wisdom of the Glorious Jesus give us grace so to govern ourselves...". Thus, Clarke concludes that "the Scottish masons also were assumed to be Christians". [67]

Alex Horne, referring to the presence of Christian elements in *The Saints John in the Masonic Tradition* writes: *"The use of the Bible opened at the Gospel of St. John is a Masonic custom going back to the early beginnings of speculative Masonry,"* [68] a concept confirmed by Neville Barker Cryer in *The De-Christianizing of the Craft*: *"It was on the Gospels that medieval masons would often take their obligation or oath."* [69]

It is a given fact that the *Old Charges*, although originating in England, had also been acknowledged in Scotland by the year 1600 (*Grand Lodge MS. No1*, dated December 25th 1583; this document therefore bears a date which is four days subsequent to the appointment of William Schaw as *King's Master of Works* in Scotland) and is likewise supported by Stevenson. The question arises therefore as to how Stevenson could even have imagined, in the context of an undeniably Christian, and thus Trinitarian, Freemasonry, that William Schaw, likewise a Christian at the service of a Christian sovereign, could have been so incautious as to advance theories mocking Christianity. I confess that of all the issues discussed, it is this that perplexes me most.

66 Douglas Knoop & G.P. Jones, *The Genesis of Freemasonry*, Manchester University Press, 1948, pages 62-81.

67 J.R. Clarke, *The Change from Christianity to Deism in Freemasonry*, AQC Vol.78, 1965.

68 Alex Horne, *The Saints John in the Masonic Tradition*, AQC Vol. 75, 1962.

69 N. Barker Cryer, *The De-Christianizing of the Craft*, AQC Vol.97, 1984.

The "Art" of Ramon Llull

In spite of the above, Stevenson's theory seems to attract numerous supporters. Accordingly, in Italy Giuseppe Giarrizzo, recalling the theory advanced by the Scottish scholar, writes: *"The Art of Memory by Giordano Bruno was in no way similar to the work of Giulio Camillo, displaying rather a marked discrepancy. The traditional components were deemed less important than the occult and mystical features. In his opinion, art was a highly important Hermetic secret from the remote past, a revelation of Egyptian doctrines, the true aim of which was to assist the human mind in its ascension towards an understanding of God, towards a unity with God. Affirmations of this kind, contained in Ars reminiscendi, were bound to give rise to an immediate controversy: this was indeed the case and the art of memory would subsequently be introduced by Alexander Dickson, a Scottish follower of Bruno, into the Masonic lodges in its newest hermetic-kabbalistic version."* [70] The dynamics through which Alexander Dickson seemingly introduced the "Art of Memory" into the Masonic Lodges, and the reasons behind this choice, are not explained by Giarrizzo, and indeed he would not have been able to do so, being unable to rely on a single document to support this hypothesis.

Another advocate of Stevenson's theory is the US historian Margaret Jacob who in referring to this matter writes: *"To tell the truth this association between Freemasonry and Renaissance Hermeticism is no novelty; indeed, its existence had been hypothesised since the 1960s by Frances Yates, a renowned scholar of Hermeticism and author of a monograph on Giordano Bruno. The original feature is that this hypothesis has now been definitively documented and confirmed. Stevenson notifies us of the possibility that Schaw may have visited the Scottish lodges in the early years of the XVIIth century, emphasizing the relationship existing between their artisan craftsmanship traditions, the use of secret passwords, knowledge of the principles of mathematics and architecture, coupled with research into the mystical knowledge of nature using mnemonic techniques as a key to gain access to the secrets of the universe (supreme aim of a specific vein of Hermetic research). This association would have seemed quite feasible to the craftsmen who, on the basis of verbal traditions, had been initiated to undeniably imaginative myths such as that maintaining that Euclid was an Egyptian builder. The philosophical Hermetic currents emerged once more in Scottish articles written in the XVIIth century, underlining the association between 'Masonic word', the secret password of members of the lodge, with practices carried out by the Rosicrucian Knights. Moreover, several Masonic documents mention the sun using mystic Hermetic terms."* [71] As on previous occasions, Jacob naturally does not state which Scottish documents

70 Giuseppe Giarrizzo, *Massoneria e Illuminismo*, Marsilio, Venice, 1994, pages 17-19.

71 Margaret C. Jacob, *Massoneria illuminata*, Einaudi, Turin, 1995, page 57.

link the "Masonic word" with the Rosicrucians, and likewise fails to explain which "philosophical Hermetic currents" were apparently derived from the same.

Therefore, as frequently happens, Stevenson's theory attracted fervent followers, but having already deemed this theory unreliable, I would now look at the alternative theory I aim to adhere to in *interpreting* the meaning of the expression "Art of Memory" as used in the Schaw *Statutes*. Naturally, in view of the evident lack of supporting documents available to date, I shall be confined to the area of sheer hypothesis, although making every effort to demonstrate the validity of the former through the use of logic and common sense.

It should first be stated that William Schaw undoubtedly intended to transform Freemasonry into a more "exclusive", *elite* system, a project blatantly stemming from the prohibition for Masons to work together with "Cowans", the less skilled labourers.

As mentioned previously, in conceiving his "Art of Memory" Bruno was inspired by the theories advanced by Ramon Llull. This was supported by Yates in her important article entitled *The Art of Memory*:

"For there was another kind of art of memory which began in the Middle Ages, which continued into the Renaissance and beyond, and which it was the aim of many in the Renaissance to combine with the classical art in some new synthesis whereby memory should reach still further heights of insight and of power. This other art of memory was the Art of Ramon Llull." [72]

Thus, the protagonist of our theory is introduced, the Catalonian theologist and philosopher Ramon Llull (Palma de Majorca, 1235-1315). Referring to the Augustinian tradition, at convergence with Averroism, Llull maintained that philosophy was subordinate to theology. In Llull's opinion the mistakes made by philosophy are closely linked to ignorance of the truth of faith, in the light of which all worldly knowledge should be interpreted and organised. Llull is convinced that if knowledge were presented in a Unitarian manner, whilst however maintaining an association with the essence of faith, even the unfaithful would be prevailed upon. It is indeed mainly, although not solely, for this purpose that he elaborated "General Art", based on principles capable of embracing the foundations of all sciences, of which the "Art of Memory" is an important component. Yates continues:

"In one of its aspects, the Lullian Art is an art of memory. The divine attributes which are its foundation form themselves into a Trinitarian structure through which it became, in Llull's eyes, a reflection of the Trinity, and he intended that it should be used by the three powers of the soul defined by Augustine as the reflection of the Trinity in man. As intellectus,

72 Frances A. Yates, op. cit., page 175.

it was an art of knowing or finding out the truth; as voluntas, it was an art of training the will towards loving truth; as memoria, it was an art of memory for remembering truth. One is reminded of the scholastic formulations concerning the three parts of Prudence, memoria, intelligentia, providentia, the artificial memory belonging to one of the parts." [73]

However, Lullism intended as an art of memory did not stem from the classic rhetoric tradition in the same way as the other art of memory, but derived rather from the philosophical tradition of Augustinian Platonism combined with other increasingly Neoplatonist features. It claims it is aware of the first causes: to use the terminology of Llull, the *dignity* of God. All Lullian arts are based on this *Dignitates Dei*, all divine or attributed names deemed to be first causes in a similar fashion to the Neoplatonic system devised by Scotus Eriugena, which markedly influenced Llull. Secondly, in Lullism, at least as it was initially taught by Llull, there is no mention of anything resembling the images of traditional mnemonics, no efforts at improving one's memory through use of emotional or dramatic corporeal symbols heralding the fruitful interaction between the "Art of Memory" and figurative arts observed in the works of Giordano Bruno. Indeed, Llull designed the concepts he used in his art using a letter of the alphabet, thus conveying an almost algebraic feature to Lullism.

Yates however points out how the most significant aspect of Lullism in the history of knowledge is the introduction of the *movement of memory*. The figures used in his art, in which concepts are portrayed by means of letters of the alphabet, are rotating rather than static. One of the figures is made up of *concentric circles* marked with the letters depicting each single concept, and as the wheels start to turn a varied combination of concepts is obtained. In yet other mobile figures, *triangles* inscribed inside a circle illustrate the associated concepts. These are of course modest artifices, but are concomitantly revolutionary in their attempt to represent the world of the psyche.[74]

If, as observed, Stevenson's idea was based on a belief in the *occult* connotations of the "Art of Memory", as proposed by Schaw, it is my opinion that Schaw's intentions were quite different. Accordingly, based on the Brunian rather than Llullian principles of the "Art of Memory", implying therefore more a *universal language* than an *occult method,* Schaw could have proposed the introduction into the Lodges of the concept of *universal brotherhood* by means of a *common language*.

In this regard, Llull elaborated a "General Art" based on principles capable of embracing the foundations of all sciences. He maintained that there were eighteen such principles; nine were the divine attributes (dignity) achieved by attributing to God

73 Frances A. Yates, op. cit., page 176.

74 Frances A. Yates, op. cit., page 177.

on a superlative level the perfection encountered in finite beings, namely goodness, greatness, eternity, power, wisdom, will, virtue, truth and glory; nine terms indicate the relationships existing between contingent beings: difference, concordance, adversity, beginning, halfway, end, majority, equality and minority. Llull indicated these elements using *letters of the alphabet* and other symbols, achieving combinations through use of *concentric circles* or other *mobile figures*. The numerous combinations subsequently reveal the typical reasoning representing the solution to all problems.

The four abovementioned *mobile figures* are merely the syntactic rules of the Lullian *language* representing the geometric shapes dear to Llull; they include a *straight line*, *triangle*, *pentagon* and *circle*. Contrary to Bruno's aims, their function here serves no magical purpose, but solely as a practical example of how the elements of "Art" should be grouped.

The ultimate aim of the "Art" is to lead intellect towards the full awareness of reality. Once the principles and rules of the "Art" have been imparted, the first step is to establish questions to aid the progression of the discursive process. Accordingly, the numerous pages that Llull filled with questions are not an attempt at reproducing the questions potentially asked of the "Art", but rather an overt display of the fecundity of the "Art" itself.[75]

In commenting on Llull, Elémire Zolla writes:

"Memory, which constitutes part of prudence together with intelligence and providence (Cicerone, de invenzione, II, 53, 160, quoted by Alberto Magno, De bono, IV, 2) has a mystical and primary function, being a mention of God. Llull secures to establish an art of memory through which any means of remembering shall be addressed to God. He therefore observes how memory obtained through the use of drugs displeases God and provides only rarely any degree of science."[76]

At first sight, therefore, the "Art" was invented for theological purposes, as Llull wished to make it accessible to all people, many of whom were lacking the university education required to comprehend the Latin terms. In his search for a doctrinal basis capable of providing a common starting point for discussion or debate, Llull achieved a nucleus with two central themes focusing on the definition of God through his dignity and the ability of human knowledge to reflect on the truth of faith, whilst his desire to identify means allowing him to facilitate an ongoing discussion based on these premises, devoid of linguistic and scholastic constraints, led him to use universal *symbols and geometric figures*. "Art" therefore is intended as an actual *system to be used in interpreting*

75 Jordi Gayà Estelrich, *Raimondo Lullo una teologia per la missione*, Jaca Book, Milan, 1999, page 102.

76 Elémire Zolla, *I mistici dell'Occidente*, Adelphi, Milan, 1997, page 789.

reality with the essential characteristics of stability and permanence, and above all a *universal* nature.

The main aim of Lullian "Art" therefore was to represent *knowledge* in a unitarian fashion, revealing features of rigorous evidence, unfailingly closely associated with faith, in an attempt to identify a *common language* capable of simplifying the relationship between mankind, a *universal language*. Thus, it represents the first attempt at establishing a *universal language* possessing the requisites of clarity and universality, the formalising of which would result in a clarity of expression and reference to terms based on reality, known and participated, to guarantee the *universal* nature of communication.

The formal aspect of the Lullian "Art" is the intention to simplify human speech and return to the original concept of the various realms of knowledge. Llull put forward his theory on the basis of *principles common to all three religious traditions*, a theory aimed at maintaining the unity of these traditions according to a common basis of philosophy, science and mysticism.

As mentioned previously, Llull applied a *symbolic geometry*: the *triangle* stood for the divine; the *circle* represented the skies (by which Llull unfailingly implied the seven planets and the twelve signs of the zodiac); the *square* symbolised the four elements. The dominant philosophy was a form of Platonism, with Llull adhering to the tradition of medieval Christian Platonism based largely on Augustine. The Lullian dignities are nearly all listed as divine attributes in Augustine's works, and a following chapter will examine the association with Renaissance Neoplatonism.

Symbolic geometry is a constant presence throughout Masonic rituals. It a well-known fact that in Freemasonry the use of *geometric symbols* represents a common basis for all Brothers who have undergone their Initiation; through the use of symbols Freemasons are capable of interpreting and assimilating the principles of the "Art" irrespective of the differences and obstacles posed by specific languages and cultures. Should a Freemason enter into a Masonic Temple in any country whatsoever, through use of symbols he will be able to take part in the functions of the Lodge as the symbolic language used in Freemasonry is indeed a *universal* language.

The language devised by Llull may therefore be rightly defined as a sort of *Clavis Universalis*, a *universal language* capable of uniting men of all creeds and origins. As emphasised by Paolo Rossi:

"The term Clavis Universalis was used between the sixteenth and seventeenth centuries to indicate the general science or procedure that enables man to grasp, beyond the semblances of phenomena or 'shadows of ideas', the ideal structure or theme constituting the sheer essence of reality. To decipher the alphabet of the world; to succeed in reading the great book of nature, the marks left by the divine mind; to discover the full correspondence between the

original forms and the chain of human reasoning; to construct a perfect language capable of removing all misunderstandings and revealing the essence, putting mankind in touch with things rather than signs; to compile entire encyclopaedias of orderly classified material that faithfully reproduce the harmony present throughout the cosmos." [77]

The interest shown in the Kabbalah, in artificial and universal scriptures, in the discovery of the first principles underlying all forms of knowledge, the "Art of Memory" and the continual call towards a logic seen as a *key* that opens the secrets of reality: these themes are all associated with the rebirth of Lullism during the Renaissance; indeed, it may have been this that attracted William Schaw and persuaded him to include the Lullian "Art of Memory" in his 1599 *Statutes.*

A *universal symbolism* forms the root of this "Art" that assumes a capacity to speak, at the same time and concomitantly, of logics and metaphysics, to enunciate the rules underlying the discussions and rules on which reality is based. Llull sees God and the divine dignities as *archetypes* of reality and the entire universe arranged as a giant group of symbols recalling, beyond mere appearances, the structure of the divine being: *"The similes of Divine Nature are impressed in all creatures, according to the more and the less."*

To conclude, as stated previously, no documented proof is available to affirm that in adopting the expression "Art of Memory", William Schaw was referring to the "Art" of Ramon Llull rather than, as upheld by Stevenson, to the work of Giordano Bruno. An attempt has however been made to provide a logical explanation to our alternative theory, deeming it more appropriate to the Masonic context to which it is referred.

Moreover, in this paper I have focused on setting to rights a series of distortions that have contributed towards creating further confusion in the field of studies on Freemasonry. Stevenson's theory actually features numerous incongruities of both a philosophical and ritualistic nature. Furthermore, the theory is based on yet another theory formulated by Yates portraying Bruno as a preponderant expression of Renaissance hermeticism, which at the time was vigourously challenged. Recent studies have criticised the above approach, and demonstrated how Bruno was indeed interested in Hermetic doctrines, but in a lot more besides. In her *Giordano Bruno and Renaissance Science* Hilary Gatti writes:

"Yates saw the Brunian vitalism, with the consequent divinisation of the mechanisms of nature, as a mystical, hermetical conception, according to an interpretation that would have had a considerable influence. The epithet of 'Hermetic Magus' assigned to him by Yates did not correspond to views pronounced by the philosopher himself. It is quite true that in the fourth Italian dialogue, the Expulsion of the Triumphant Beast on which Yates bases

77 Paolo Rossi, *Clavis universalis*, Il Mulino, Bologna, 1983, page 17.

the majority of her thesis, at the end of a lengthy quotation of the Hermetic Asclepius, the Brunian Isis refers to the people whose religious cult is yearned after by Trismegistus, calling them 'my Egyptians'. However, although this step is subsequently construed by Yates as proof of the predilection of Bruno for a type of religion in which the divine communicates directly and eloquently with mankind by means of natural objects, even the most humble and commonplace, the remarks made by Yates suggesting that Bruno was largely and persistently influenced by Hermetic doctrines rather than by the older schools of thought he frequently refers to, are simply not feasible.[78]

Furthermore, as noted by Gatti, it is not indeed Hermes Trismegistus who represents for Bruno the source and main model for his ideas, but rather Pythagoras, thus shedding a totally new light on Brunian cosmology.[79] The hypothesis put forward by Gatti is that Bruno should be re-evaluated first and foremost as a "philosopher of science" rather than as a Renaissance "magus", commenting:

"The Ash Wednesday Supper depicts the ongoing revolution of the time in the European culture affected by a moment of marked religious and intellectual crisis linking this culture to its ancient philosophical roots and attempting to re-establish a sense of continuity between the ancient Pythagorism and the emerging sciences, particularly with regard to the new form of cosmology based on Copernicus… Thus, situated at the two opposite ends of the cultural history of the Occident, Pythagoras and Copernicus are celebrated by Bruno in the first dialogue of the Ash Wednesday Supper as the two sources of a truth in the light of which he was to construct a radically revisited and extended, homogeneous and unified cosmological structure, thereby creating optimal conditions in the search for scientific and theological truths. In this sense Bruno is rightly considered a precursor of Newton who likewise identifies Pythagoras as a key figure of ancient times, not only for the role played as the founder of Greek science but also as warden of the true religion."[80]

78 Hilary Gatti, *Giordano Bruno e la scienza del rinascimento*, Raffaello Cortina Editore, Milan, 2001, page 15. Original title: *Giordano Bruno and Renaissance Science*, Cornell University, 1999.

79 Hilary Gatti, op. cit., page 17.

80 Hilary Gatti, op. cit., pages 31-33.

Chapter Two

The Principles and the Inspiring Traditions

"But first thou must tear off from thee the cloak which thou dost wear [the physical body] – the web of ignorance, the ground of bad, corruption's chain, the carapace of darkness, the living death, sensation's corpse, the tomb thou carriest with thee, the robber in thy house, who through the things he loveth, hateth thee, and through the things he hateth, bears thee malice. Such is the hateful cloak thou wearest – that throttles thee [and holds thee] down to it, in order that thou mayst not gaze above, and having seen the Beauty of the Truth, and Good that dwells therein, detest the bad of it; having found out the plot that it hath schemed against thee..."

Corpus Hermeticum VII, 2, 3

1. Association or Initiatic Society?

In 1984, the Board of General Purposes of the Grand United Lodge of England issued a document entitled *What is Freemasonry?* which provides, for the use of neophytes, a first, generic, definition of Freemasonry. The document briefly defines Freemasonry as *"One of the world's oldest secular fraternal societies... a society of men concerned with spiritual values. Its member are taught its precepts by a series of ritual dramas, which follow ancient forms and use stonemasons' customs and tools as allegorical guides. The essential qualification for admission and continuing membership is a belief in a Supreme Being. Membership is open to men of any race or religion who can fulfil this essential qualification and are of good repute..."*

On examination, it becomes rapidly evident that, in spite of the formal correctness of the definition, its *initiatic* and *esoteric* aspects present in the ritual and in the principles and aims of Freemasonry are not sufficiently emphasised. These aspects represent the true "peculiarity" of every Initiatic Order and consequently, the aforesaid definition, for the aims established is somewhat reductive.

From this premise it is clearly evident that, to enable a correct understanding of the phenomenon of Freemasonry, the issue of its definition undoubtedly constitutes the more complex and thorny problem to resolve, a problem that has created dissent and divided factions within the realms of Freemasonry itself.

Before embarking on a search of the origins of the movements therefore, a consensus would have to be reached as to the main focus of the search: what is Freemasonry; an "association of solidarity", based on ethico-moral principles, a "parapolitical" association, an "Initiatic Society", or better still an "Initiatic Order", founded on ancient esoteric rituals, with aims that reach beyond, although comprising, the mere *moralistic* representation that is often construed?

The problem, as mentioned previously, is not easy to solve, in view of the frequently contrasting multiple forms that Freemasonry, following its birth in English speaking lands, has assumed in the countries to which it has been introduced, and successively developed. A potential solution aimed at enhancing a friendly co-existence between the various "beings" involved in Freemasonry, at times in open contrast, if not outright hostility, would be to lay the foundations for a co-existence of the numerous representations, whilst, naturally, maintaining the essence of the Masonic *Landmarks*. This issue will be addressed in the last section of this chapter.

Freemasons and the "Sacred"

The first question to be asked by those who encounter Freemasonry for the first time is frequently, "Is Freemasonry a religion?" Obviously the answer is no, but in order to better comprehend the significance of this denial, we should examine the details of the relationship between Freemasonry and the "sacred". To clarify the issue, particularly from a strictly terminological point of view, I would therefore like to start by analysing the significance of the two words, "religion" and "sacred".

According to the field of expertise occupied, a series of options are available. From an anthropological point of view, the renowned scholar James George Frazer defines religion as: *"a propitiation or conciliation of powers superior to man which are believed to direct and control the course of nature and of human life. Thus defined, religion consists of two elements, a theoretical and a practical, namely, a belief in powers higher than man and an attempt to propitiate or please them"*;[81] on passing from anthropology to sociology, according to the French sociologist Émile Durkheim, the paradigmatic model of religion is to be intended as an *autonomous system* with a set of sacred objects interlinked by a network of co-ordination and subordination, a *cohesive system* around which a homogenous series of beliefs and rites gravitates.

With regard to the aims of the present study, an interesting definition is provided by the historian of religions Marcello Massenzio, who states: *"Religious thought is*

81 J.G. Frazer, *Il Ramo d'oro*, Bollati Boringhieri, Turin 1990, page 67.

characterised by a singular prerogative that allows it to be distinguished from other forms of thought: it implies that the world is divided into two distinct spheres, the first comprising all that is sacred, and the second all that is profane. The Sacred/Profane antithesis, the pillar that upholds the fundamental classification of the real, is the element that enhances recognition of the specific domain of the religious … The heterogeneity between these two dominions of all that is real does not automatically exclude all types of communication between the two, but rather dictates a need to comply with clear cultural regulations capable of governing the contact. As an example, a profane individual on approaching the sacred is required to some extent to absorb the characteristics of the sacred, being subjected, albeit temporarily to a mutation of state focused, in the same way as the rites of passage, on the dynamics of death-rebirth." [82]. Starting out from this definition based on the Sacred/Profane dichotomy it may be affirmed that, although Freemasonry is not a religion, its underlying principle could indeed be defined as "religious", or better still "sacred". In order to facilitate an initial collocation, it may be of assistance to establish a different point of terminological reference to substitute the word religion with the word "sacred" for the specific purpose of avoiding elementary misunderstandings. Use of the terminology and concept of "sacred" will in this way provide an appropriate instrument with which to approach, unequivocally, the substance of the principles and thought underlying Freemasonry.

During a Masonic Initiation it is indeed the idea of the "sacred" and awareness of the same to be powerfully perceived, a fundamental idea that is found inevitably in all forms of *Tradition*; the "sacred", the opposite *par excellence* of "profane", is necessarily located in a different dimension, removed, metaphysical, accessible only under particular conditions. The great scholar of the history of religions Mircea Eliade provides the following majestic definition:

"The sacred is radically opposed to the profane thanks to the presence of rites, sacraments, the imparting of myths. It is not available to all, in view of a secret capable of imparting to the select few that which is transmitted. On the other hand, it should be underlined how, before an initiation, the profane should in some way be purified, with this purification being comprised as a sacred thing. The dividing line between the sacred and the profane is more subtle than is generally maintained." [83]

The "sacred" defers to a dimension of diversity, and does not constitute a "separate" reality precluded to the human race but, on the contrary, is intersected, interacts with the latter. Undoubtedly, the "sacred" is, by sheer definition, *notionally* inconceivable

82 M. Massenzio, *Storia delle religioni e antropologia*, in *Manuale di Storia delle Religioni*, Laterza, Bari, 1998, page 491.

83 Mircea Eliade, *Initiation et Monde Moderne*, in *Travaux de Villard de Honnecourt, No1*, 1980, page 27.

and can be comprehended mainly on an emotional level; consequently, with regard to Freemasonry, it has proven necessary to accompany the "sacred" with *ethico-moral* contents, which however over time have almost entirely concealed the presence of the same, portraying Freemasonry more as a mere charitable institution.

In the light of these premises it is clear that Freemasonry may not be considered a religion or a surrogate, and is intended rather as an *initiatic philosophy* featuring an undeniable relationship with the "sacred" that provides the appropriate cognitive and methodological instruments for use in embarking on a pathway to individual and spiritual perfection.

The "Method"

The "Method" of achieving moral and spiritual perfection used by Freemasons is one that enables an active process of inner transformation to be undertaken, an overt "change of status" to be enacted. The intention is to perceive the essence of things, the *metaphysical* or *noumenic* reality that progresses beyond the visible through the implication of a faculty which, in traditional doctrines, is defined as *intellectual intuition*, although I personally would prefer to use the term *intuitive awareness.* By *intuitive awareness* or *intellectual intuition* there is no implication of reason of discursive thought, but rather, as highlighted by the poet and expert of esotericism Fernando Pessoa, *"the organ of immediate knowledge, that is the 'pure intelligence' that reaches beyond mere reason, a 'metaphysical' awareness, super-individual and super-rational, a veritable operation of the mind through which the outcome of intelligence is achieved without resorting to intelligence".*[84] Through use of *intuitive awareness* inevitably and necessarily the *sacrificium intellectus* is produced, as the protagonist of the famous novel by Thomas Mann, *Doctor Faustus* underlines *"the other-worldly intuitive awareness necessarily brings with it".*[85]

By *intuitive awareness* therefore, we mean a type of gnoseological experience which, despite being immediate in the same way as the act of intuition, is not vague and confused in the same way as the latter, being indeed a type of awareness based on a super-sensitive and super-rational perception of the "pure" state of the Being, or rather of the actual state of reality before the senses and individual reasoning divide the same into a series of "things" and manifestations characterised by (but only for men) by a particular significance.[86]

84 Fernando Pessoa, *Pagine Esoteriche*, Adelphi, Milan, 1997, page 53.

85 Thomas Mann, *Doctor Faustus*, Mondadori, Milan, 1997, page 110.

86 Massimo Scaligero, *Dioniso*, in *Testimonianze su Evola*, Mediterranee, Rome, 1973.

If the Masonic pathway is seen as inner awareness, the *reunion* of the finite Self with the Divine Principle, or likewise the *reintegration* of the individual Self with the Divine Self, thus the Masonic "Method" acts as the instrument for this pathway. This "Method" therefore, and here I refer in particular to the *ritual* that represents the expression of the same, is invariably an *external* factor transmitted through use of "forms", it will therefore only represent a 'preparation' of the Freemason prior to receiving the *true* initiatic teachings that can only be achieved only through the outcome of one's *personal* strivings.

As a consequence, the "Method" indicates the route to be adhered to, but does not constitute the actual pathway, the design to be achieved, the aim of which is merely to aid the initiate in acquiring the mental and intellectual aptitude required to comprehend the *initiatic concepts*. In my opinion, those who believe that the *memorisation* of a ritual is synonymous with *understanding* the same, with *completing* the initiatic pathway are quite mistaken. The Masonic "Method" should indeed teach the initiate to free himself of *foregone conclusions*, as it is an established fact that if our mind is conditioned in the search for Truth and God, we will only be able to increase our knowledge, gain more information as permitted by this conditioning, by undertaking an exquisitely *acquisitive* process. Wherever society conditions the individual, and this conditioning assumes the semblance of self-improvement, in reality, as emphasised by the great Indian thinker Jiddu Krishnamurti, it is the perpetuation of a perpetuation of "me", of the ego in various forms. However, this type of self-improvement may become crude or ambiguous on becoming the "practice of virtue", of "goodness", the so-called neighbourly love, that is frequently no more than a mere continuation of "me", a product of the conditioning influences of society. All our efforts are directed at becoming something, someone, in this world or another. But, according to Krishnamurti, this dynamic is subjected to the same pressure, the same urges towards preserving and cultivating Self. If we wish to discover the truth we need to be completely free from all conditioning, all dogma, all beliefs and all authority that obliges us to conform; substantially this means that we are completely alone, and this, in his opinion, is extremely difficult. Only a free mind will be capable of investigating; certainly not a mind fettered by a foregone conclusion, belief or dogma, a mind that knows no certainties, that analyses and discovers in continuation, that loses all it has learnt on undergoing any sort of experience, and is therefore in a state on non-awareness: only this mind shall be free from the routine. According to Krishnamurti, this is the highest form of thought.[87]

87 J. Krishnamurti, *Riflessioni sull'Io*, Ubaldini Editore, Rome, 2009, page 46.

The "Purpose"

The purpose of the Masonic "Method", as mentioned previously, is to achieve the union between our Self and the Divine Principle that is within us. The supreme purpose of man is indeed to be reunited with his Divine principle, freeing himself from all material bonds (leaving the "metals" behind); in order to achieve this spiritual objective Freemasonry affords a *metaphysical pathway of fulfilment* within the context of its frequently heterogeneous rituals. This *metaphysical* fulfilment will consequently lead to the gaining of a Truth, a Truth that, in so far as it is of a metaphysical nature, shall be expressible and inexpressible at the same time, although, as underlined by Frithjof Schuon, inexpressible does not imply "unknowable": *"Indeed, intellect attains the divine order and as a consequence includes everything that is; it is expressible, and crystallises in formulations that are as they should be, as they convey all that is necessary or of use to the spirit. The forms represent doors opening onto the essences of thought and language, in the same way as with other forms of symbolism."* [88]

I should like once again to emphasise how the dimension in which we are "operating" is not a *physical* domain, but is rather a *metaphysical* or *transcendent* domain that possesses dynamics, rules and even a diverse terminology, with Schuon describing metaphysics thus as: *"its transcendent character makes it independent of any human mode of thought. In order to define clearly the difference between the two modes of thought, it may be said that philosophy proceeds from reason (which is a purely individual faculty), whereas metaphysics proceeds exclusively from the intellect; the latter faculty has been defined by Meister Eckhart, who fully understood the import of his words: 'There is something in the soul that is uncreated and uncreatable; if the entire soul were thus, it would be uncreated and uncreatable, and this something is the intellect... in the case of intellectual intuition, knowledge is not possessed by the individual insofar as he is an individual, but insofar as in his innermost essence he is not distinct from his Divine Principle. Thus metaphysical certitude is absolute because of the identity between the knower and the known in the Intellect."* [89]

It follows therefore that the task of a Freemason is not to *act* on the universal society, but only to *comprehend* his personal Self; however, it is an arduous task to understand both the conscious and the unconscious Self in view of the fact that an individual is continuously at war with himself. This *realisation* that has been defined as *metaphysical* as it represents the supreme awareness, will be the highest level to be sought after and achieved, and to reach this level the initiate will be requested to resort to use of a sort of "conscious synthesis" in open contrast with the mere rational speech of an empirical and analytical mind that is relegated to the confines of the manifested and the *relative*.

88 Frithjof Schuon, *Sulle tracce della Religione Perenne*, Mediterranee, Rome, 1988, page 18.

89 Frithjof Schuon, *Unità trascendente delle religioni*, Mediterranee, Rome, 1980, pages 9-10.

Thus, if imperative Masonic ethics indeed confer the individual with a sense of *personal* responsibility in the uncovering of his authentic nature and essence, it should be taken into account that the initiatic process is likewise, and above all, is an active-implementer metaphysical domain, neither inert nor latent; consequently, the Masonic pathway may be defined as being of a *metaphysical* nature, being first addressed through *intuition* and subsequently *experienced.*

The aims and purposes therefore of Freemasonry are the perfecting of man, a pathway to the ascent of Self in which all beings, individual or collective, tend in either a conscious or an unconscious manner to strive to fulfil their achievements by using the instruments made available by their singular nature. It is at the very point of his evolution that an individual will be effectively capable of recognising these aims, and it is then that his true initiation begins; and, on having gained awareness of Self, he will now be required to conduct the latter along his *personal* pathway towards the complete fulfilment to be achieved with a complete, harmonious and hierarchical development of all possibilities implicated virtually in the essence of the same being.

Accordingly, between man and his Creator there is no rift, although, as stated by the great scholar of *Traditions*, Julius Evola:

"The traditional view of Sapience, both heathen and oriental, is that between man and God there is no appreciable difference, no heterogeneity in nature. 'My stock is celestial' – declares the orphic initiate; and likewise, in the Veda and Upanishad, man is himself considered a God, albeit in a state of unawareness and daze. Basically, this view acknowledges the possibility that man may ascend to God as soon as he wishes; a deification that man may achieve using his own means, without any transcendental or supernatural intervention. This, strictly speaking, is the religious attitude, i.e. the dualistic attitude which implies that man and God may be two possible states of a single conscience, hypothesizing these two potential states as two distinct things – here man, and there (in 'heaven' or elsewhere) God. The knowledge of God (gnosis, theosophy) is replaced by a belief in God; the spiritual experience by the dogma; the efforts to achieve a transcendent activity by prayer, reverence and devotion; sufficiency by insufficiency and dependence when facing the 'Lord Omnipotent'." [90]

It represents the completion of an arduous process, a challenging journey, a solitary itinerary full of unknowns and uncertainties, as underlined by Mariano Bianca:

"The initiate is said to undertake a journey, and this is the dimension which characterises the individual: to travel ascending and descending, going far and becoming closer, discovering lakes and deserts, drinking from new springs, gathering the roses encountered along the route, feeding off the fruits he manages to pick. He offers himself up unto himself, to the others and

90 Julius Evola, *Imperialismo Pagano*, Mediterranee, Rome, 2004, pages 131-132.

to the world, a continually new being: he is noble, an infant who revels in his enthusiasm for the world, capable of identifying all natures of fragrance and essences and adding to the richness of all places he encounters. He is likewise a senior, an aged person who takes pleasure in the places he visits, as it is they who spur him on still further: higher and lower. As highlighted by Hermes Trismegistus, he is not yet born and he offers himself unto the world as a corpse following his death."[91]

To recognise oneself in God, to "deify" oneself, is therefore the principal aim, the purpose and the plan common to all universal *Traditions*. Man becomes a complete being only when he progresses beyond his body and his mind, in an active intellect, in beatitude. This is what we are taught by the Christian traditions, and which are comparable to the achieving of *neshamah* in the Hebrew traditions, of *bodhi* in Hindu traditions, of *aql* in Islamic traditions, and so on in the language of all known traditions.[92]

Thus, the aim of Freemasonry as an "Initiatic Order" is revealed in the *Traditional* thoughts, in the *transcendent* and *metaphysical* dynamics that for centuries have been maintained, it is indeed by means of *Tradition* that man is able to undertake experiences springing from the spiritual source of his true essence, to undergo a metamorphosis and develop his forces, the testimony of a dimension underlying the visible dimension and which merely reflects the structure of an independent spirit. He is capable of experiencing a dimension from within and, should he permit this dimension to guide him in his quest, he will be freed from the fear of death, he will be able to bear things that are unacceptable to the mind and a mysterious force of love will come upon him in the exact place in which he fell into isolation.[93]

Obviously, *Tradition,* the "forms" by means of which it has been manifested historically, conveys its Truth through *esoteric* means, for the following reason, as explained by Schuon:

"The difference between the exoteric and the esoteric points of view appears clearly when one compares the respective moral attitudes: on the side of exoterism, the virtues readily give way to prejudices which, through excess of zeal, are opposed to reality and consequently to intelligence; on the side of pure esoterism – which is truly faithful to its nature – 'there is no right superior to that of truth', as a Hindu maxim asserts, and every good must result from the nature of things and not from our sentiments in so far as they lose track of this. From the esoteric or knowledgeable point of view, humility, for example, is not the desire to be low nor the autosuggestion of a lowness which in reality one does not have, but the awareness of

91 Mariano Bianca, *L'Oltre e l'Invisibile*, Atanòr, Rome, 2002, page 92.

92 Elémire Zolla, *Che cos'è la Tradizione*, Bompiani, Milan, 1971, page 133.

93 Karlfried G. Dürckheim, *Il Cammino Interiore*, Mediterranee, Rome, 1992, page 22.

a lowness that is firstly ontological and then personal – for every individual has limits if not defects – and this objective and disinterested awareness dissolves ambition and vanity at their roots. This means that esoterism or sapience operates not by means of a sentimental tendency responsible for inextricable complications, but through discernment, therefore far beyond any form of distorting and unconfessed individualism." [94]

The "Source"

The source of this process of "reunion" with the Divine is the so-called *religio perennis*, a primeval and universal *sophia,* a *transcendent unity* in which the various forms of religion that contemplate manifestation of a divine entity are not mutually exclusive and do not propose different truths, the truth being *one* alone.

This concept may be clarified by resorting to a simple, much used simile of colours that harmonise and never contrast, conveying a sole transparent light; the *sophia perennis* can be thus identified, as the common element in traditional civilisations, a *metaphysical* element in which the fundamental principles of *Tradition* reside.

As mentioned previously, all traditional forms are contained in principle in the primordial *Tradition* that forms the internal and central nucleus and is visible through the outer veils. To once again cite Frithjof Schuon:

"It has been reiterated repeatedly that the absolute Truth is written in an eternal scripture, in the actual substance of our spirit. The various Revelations merely 'crystallise' and 'actualise' on different levels and from case to case, a nucleus of certainties that is not conserved solely in the divine Omniscience, but slumbers as a refraction of the 'naturally supernatural' kernel of the individual, the ethnic or historic group or of the human race." [95]

Several authors of studies on Freemasonry, although remarkably few to tell the truth, have applied the concept of *sophia perennis* to represent the relationship of a Freemason with the "sacred"; one of these is Walter Leslie Wilmshurst who, in his book *The Meaning of Masonry* provides this definition:

"The religions of the world, though all aiming at teaching truth, express that truth in different ways, and we are more prone to emphasise the differences than to look for the correspondences in what they teach." [96]

We should today start to be more aware, particularly in the light of the above premises, of the fact that the narrators of Masonic rituals conceived the latter based on the fundamental assumption of an *essential unity between all traditional doctrines* and their principles, bearing in

94 Frithjof Schuon, *L'esoterismo come principio e come via*, Mediterranee, Rome, 1997, pages 43-44.

95 Frithjof Schuon, *L'uomo e la certezza,* Borla Editore, Turin, 1967, pages 121-122.

96 W.L. Wilmshurst, *The Meaning of Masonry*, Gramercy Books, New York, 1980, page 28.

mind that the fundamental unity of all traditional doctrines does not imply a fusion between different traditions and a consensus on the principles does not indicate uniformity. This would thus explain why the various expressions of Freemasonry assume a series of semblances according to the historic traditions they stem from, although achieving a consensus as to the *basic principles*, the so-called *Landmarks*. A traditional "form" such as Freemasonry, is represented by a "synthesis" of a transcendent order between the pure intellectual principle, metaphysical, unalterable and unique, and the particular conditions of a given historic cycle. It is for this reason that it would be nonsense to refer to Freemasonry "in general" terms.

Fundamental therefore to aid understanding of the essence of Masonic rituals is an acceptance of the idea of a departure from a primeval *Tradition*, according to which the various metaphysical and religious traditions are merely singular projections that convey the spiritual substance at numerous levels. The Masonic principle whereby members of all religious creeds are free to enter into its temples is a direct consequence of this working hypothesis. Therefore, based on the concept of a *metaphysical unity* of all religions, the confines between *esotericism* and *exotericism* must necessarily be removed, the confines between the various religious creeds and the primeval *Tradition* that should herald their unification in the ultimate metaphysical root.

To return to the concept of *sophia perennis*, Saint Augustine stated that *"wisdom itself is not brought into being but is as it was and always will be"*.[97] God's truth therefore can only be one, although the pathways leading to God are numerous because He is everything and all points of the circumference are equally distant from the centre. Consequently, the *sophia perennis* represents the *confluence* of all pathways that lead to God, to attest that He is indeed the end that man aims to achieve and man is the point of departure of this return to the divine circle. Ultimately, the aims and the purpose of the *religio perennis* are the removal of the *illusory* distance between God and man.

It is thus evident, in the light of the above, how the ridiculous accusation of *atheism* that is frequently levelled at Freemasonry appears increasingly absurd, as is made particularly evident in the example cited above how man cannot reach God without God, without the help of God, as highlighted further by the traditionalist and scholar of Islamic thought, Seyyed Hossein Nasr: *"Man is not capable of revealing alone the pathway to salvation, the 'righteous pathway'."* [98]

As mentioned in the Masonic rituals, God represents the *Centre*, a constant reference point, a *Centre* to be portrayed as a *sophia perennis* from which all traditional "forms" spring and originate. All things originate from the *Centre* and flow towards the *Centre*,

97 Saint Augustine, *Confessions* IX, 10.

98 Seyyed Hossein Nasr, *Ideali e realtà dell'Islam,* Rusconi, Milan, 1974, page 22.

and it is only in the *Centre* that the unification of the primeval *Tradition* is wrought and all historic manifestations which, despite being quite distinct and different, reveal the essence of an undividable, divine Truth: *"The centre is, first and foremost, the origin, the point of departure of all things; it is the main pint lacking form and lacking dimension, invisible therefore, and, consequently, the sole image that can be given of the primeval unity. It gives rise by irradiation to all things, in the same way that unity produces all numbers and its essence is left unchanged and not affected in any manner."* [99]

The Initiatic Component

The etymology of the term "Initiation", meaning beginning, is illustrated as the passage from a "profane" state of *torpor* to a state of *awareness*, from which time onwards the Initiate witnesses a *reawakening* of his consciousness that illuminates his being, a state that corresponds in a certain sense to a "new birth", a true ontological mutation. Initiation may thus be defined as a sort of reawakening of man to *awareness* of his own identity first, and subsequently of the position he occupies in the cosmos, the possibility of rediscovering the divine spark that is concealed within each of us.

In the world of *Tradition,* initiation in its highest forms is unfailingly conceived as an intensely real operation capable of altering, as stated previously, the ontological state of an individual, and of infusing him with the forces of the world of being, or, as Evola would say, of the "higher world".[100]

Numerous, and at times contrasting, definitions are provided for the term "Initiation". Mariano Bianca in his collection of essays *L'Oltre e l'Invisibile (Beyond the Invisible)* illustrates a "traditional" interpretation, referring to Initiation as follows:

"A process commences to achieve the psychic and noetic modification of the neophyte, of his perspectives towards himself and the world, and of his ways of being and behaving; the neophyte commences his journey into the initiatic continuity. In initiation the presence of a community in which those taking part in the rite operate according to specific philosophic, symbolic, ritual and ethical contents denoting an esoteric tradition is of fundamental importance; the participants undertake the task of mediation between the esoteric contents and the neophyte and are thus predisposed towards transmitting the same by means of gestures and words. In turn, the neophyte is prepared to receive the latter. During the ritual of initiation material and symbolic instruments are used, gestures, actions and words that convey a transmutational significance as they impress a change in the psychic and noetic status of the neophyte." [101]

99 René Guénon, *Simboli della scienza sacra,* Adelphi, Milan, 1990.

100 Julius Evola, *Rivolta contro il mondo moderno,* Mediterranee, Rome, 1998, page 108.

101 Mariano Bianca, *L' Oltre e l'Invisibile,* Atanòr, Rome, 2002, page 131.

Conversely, Claude Guérillot provides a markedly more *reductive* definition of Initiation from an esoteric point of view, maintaining that the ceremonies for the installation of the initiatic pathways in itself confers absolutely nothing, merely undertaking a "reawakening". They are therefore viewed as suggesting the provision of new horizons, new questions, new meditations, new duties, and are therefore to be considered no more than mere "rites of passage" from which *"many men and women, on having been subjected to the rites, have not achieved any benefit, and had not understood the work that still remained to be undertaken"*.[102]

In my opinion, Initiation represents a fundamental preliminary phase to aid comprehension of the true nature of an "Initiatic Order", it implies achieving a *state of awareness* that is no longer conditioned by the bodily encumbrance, all through the application of the rituals that Julius Evola describes in a way that is, in my view, impeccable, as representing *"allusive transcriptions of a series of states of awareness along the pathway to self-fulfilment"*.

Thus, by interpreting the esoteric influences not only as mere *intellectual* influences, but as full-blown *spiritual* influences, propitiatory of an *inner transformation*, Initiation should as a consequence correspond to an opening of the dimension of *transcendence*, of access to the divine, a pathway at the end of which, as highlighted by Arturo Reghini, the Roman Pythagorean, in referring to Pythagorism, *"the spiritual health was achieved by means of palingenesis, or rebirth, or by means of a new birth or birth to a new life. Pythagorean palingenesis should not be confused with metempsychosis or with metomsomatosis, nor with migration or with the various metamorphoses, and with reincarnation neither. It is not a process that is undergone in a passive or fatal manner, nor is it a general law or a reprieve granted by the gods; it is an operation, a task, indeed it is a 'Great Work' carried out deliberately and technically in line with a specific rite that Plato and Maximus Tyrius referred to as royal art."*[103]

Thus, in his opinion, Initiation will be achieved only through the work undertaken personally by the initiate, consisting in the realisation of *extracorporeal modalities* of the individual human state, a possibility of gaining access to the higher states of being, to Liberation, being a return to the Supreme Principle. In any case, we are dealing with inner states of an awareness which, therefore, cannot be communicated, in obtaining which the initiate may rely only on himself.

Jean Robin, scholar of the works of René Guénon, lists in a clear and schematic manner the three conditions that are, in his opinion, necessary for initiation: 1)

102 Claude Guérillot, *De la porte basse à la porte étroite: une approche de l'initiation*, Editions Dervy, Paris, 1998, pages 15-17.

103 Arturo Reghini, *Dizionario Filologico*, IGNIS, Roma, 2004.

Qualification, comprising a series of possibilities relating to the individual nature of the subject, and representing the raw material to which the initiatic process should be applied; 2) *Transmission*, through the reuniting with a traditional organisation of a spiritual influence that conveys the individual with an "illumination" that will allow him to develop the possibilities he possesses; 3) *Inner Endeavours*, by means of which, thanks to the help of coadjutants or help from the outside, this development will occur gradually, aiding the being in his progression from step to step, in climbing the steps of initiatic hierarchy until he reaches the ultimate goal of "Liberation" or the "Supreme Identity".[104]

Julius Evola, similarly to Guénon, underlined how Initiation will necessarily lead to an ontological mutation: *"The fundamental premise of Initiation is that the human condition, with the limits which define the common individuality, can be surpassed. This change of state, a passage from a way of being to another way of being, permits the Initiate to accede to an Olympian plane, contrary to the super-man who belongs to the Promethean plane. The latter remains unchanged, although attempting by means of a prevarication to acquire dignity and supreme powers."*[105]

In all *Traditions*, initiation should necessarily be conferred by a Master in possession of a reliable qualification, a sort of spiritual father known as *guru* by Hindus, *geron* by Orthodox Christians, *sheikh* by Muslims, and naturally corresponding in Freemasonry to the Most Worshipful Master. It is therefore clear that the Lodge is called upon to make an important choice when identifying the "right", and above all "qualified" Most Worshipful Master, and seeks in the candidate a "capacity to initiate". Following Initiation the process of growth, the initiatic pathway will be prevalently of an *active* and personal nature, and the initiative of achieving a full realisation as prescribed by the "Method" imparted by the Most Worshipful Master will be the sole responsibility of the individual Mason.

2. Mystery Societies

Mystery Societies may be considered, from a strictly chronological point of view, the first *Traditional* "forms" which inspired Freemasonry in terms of organisation and structure.

In his preface to Charles W. Leadbeater's *Freemasonry and its Ancient Mystic Rites*, Mariano Bianca describes with extreme clarity the main points of this "contamination":

"Sacred practices based on elements shared by all initiatic societies are found, to a greater or lesser extent, among the cultures of the old Eastern Mediterranean Basin and its relative societies: a) initiatic practices; b) initiatic journeys (symbolic or real); c) 'rules' for the development of

104 Jean Robin, *René Guénon: Testimone della Tradizione*, Il Cinabro, Catania, 1993, page 148.
105 Julius Evola, *L'arco e la clava*, Mediterranee, Rome, 1995, page 97.

one's 'path'; d) different stages or degrees of the interior development of initiates; e) the ultimate objective of the entire process aimed at one's own improvement, the understanding of the 'hidden' meaning of man and the universe (sometimes also known as truth) and man's place in the latter, the sense of life and death, the nature of everything 'divine'." [106]

Let's start by acknowledging the fact that no proof of a direct, documented line of descent between Freemasonry and Mystery Societies actually exists and speaking of "filiation" would therefore certainly be improper. The fact remains that a number of scholars, including the above-mentioned Leadbeater, have believed in the possibility that such a process could have actually taken place.

According to Leadbeater an underground *mystery-initiatic* movement led to the establishment of initiatic formations, the first ones coming into the open being the Mystery Societies. "Speculative" Freemasonry, the last initiatic expression of the above movement, later manifested itself following a number of other consecutive historical events. Leadbeater maintains that this "submerged" movement still existed in the Middle Ages, not only and to a lesser extent in Trade Guilds (Trade of Masons) but also in literary and *philosophical* forms, interwoven with Christianity, or in "magical currents" sharing some of their contents as in the *Fedeli d'Amore*, the Troubadour culture, and in many writers and philosophers such as Agrippa, Campanella, Ficino and Bruno, to name but a few.[107] It is clear we are dealing with pure guesswork.

Nevertheless, although no concrete succession from man to man can be detected, the essence of Mysteries, their heading towards the sacred and divine that is within us, through a moral and epistemological journey, through "secrets" and initiatic processes, undoubtedly survived for over two thousand years, ideally moving from one initiatic "form" to another, finally reaching Freemasonry. As emphasised by the great Pythagorean scholar Arturo Reghini:

"The central idea of Masonic Mysteries is therefore the ancient Mediterranean idea of privileged survival, resurrection from death, immortality, of palingenesis achieved through mystic death. It is the Egyptian, Orphic, Pythagorean, Hermetic idea; it is the main reason behind the Mysteries of Eleusis, Ceres and Mithra." [108]

Based on the above premises, Freemasonry can rightly be considered an "up-to-date" representation of an old *mystery-initiatic* society, that is, an Initiatic society featuring what used to be referred to as Mysteries, meaning rituals characterised by an *esoteric* component, decipherable only by Initiates.

106 Mariano Bianca, *Preface to La Massoneria e gli Antichi Misteri*, by Charles W. Leadbeater, Atanòr, Rome, 2008, pages 9-10.

107 Mariano Bianca, op. cit., page 13.

108 Arturo Reghini, *Le Parole Sacre e di Passo*, Atanòr, Rome, 2008, page 25.

Whereas Mystery societies, and their cults, could not resist the forceful strength of Christianity and slowly but inexorably disappeared, their initiatic and esoteric contents did not suffer the same fate, as proved by the fact that a number of components of their rituals are still nowadays used in modern Freemasonry.

Mysteries

Despite the fact that the "sacred" pervaded all aspects of the public and private live, Mystery Societies clearly distinguished themselves from official religions and cults. In this regard it should be emphasised how mystery cults have always thrived particularly in times of crisis and social uprisings, when individuals started to develop a certain dissatisfaction with traditional forms of life and thought, and started asking themselves new *existential* questions to which they could find an answer within the traditional institutions. These dynamics have repeatedly occurred in the course of history, even in recent times in the period preceding the First World War, with the rediscovery of Oriental religions and the birth and development of Theosophy and Anthroposophy.

In the case of Mystery societies, the official cult, the gods who made up the Olympus of Greek mythology, did not fully satisfy the religious needs of men of the time, and a new system was therefore created in which the dynamics for the approach of the "sacred" presented a different emotional and spiritual involvement, thus giving rise to the Mysteries.

The relationship of a Mystery initiate with his relative deity is of a different nature to that of a man of the ancient world with the god of an official cult. I could go so far as saying that the relationship with the Divine, in Mysteries of a *deeper* nature, is almost *metaphysical* as initiates are left the "freedom" to experiment with the "sacred", and in the official cult, is non-existent. In this regard, in her *Mystery Religions in the Ancient World,* Marion Giebel stresses that:

"At the time of initiation, mystery disciples are delivered a secret knowledge that allows them to deepen their understanding of the divine and human thus reaching a special relationship with their mystery deity, which promises them support and protection. Although showing similar characteristics, the development of mysteries cannot be attributed to a direct descent from tribal initiation or fertility rites. The Eleusinian Mysteries, for instance, present similarities and differences, but a certain aspect never varies: initiation always grants access to a more noble existence, extending beyond human life and portraying man as the link on a chain connecting divine to human life." [109]

At any rate, when dealing with Mystery societies, we should not envision realities that were completely detached from their time context; indeed, even Mysteries

109 Marion Giebel, *I culti misterici nel mondo antico*, ECIG, 1993, Genoa, pages 10-12.

performed in the Greek world designated some of the several festivities recognised by the official calendars of the most important cities and, as public societies, they could not and did not differ from the other cults followed in Greek city-states. It is therefore unwise to mark a sharp separation between one and the other in order to distinguish a precise category of mystery cults. Furthermore, the definition of Mysteries from a terminological point of view is not an easy task either, as the progressive semantic evolution undergone by the term transformed it from container, with regard to its ritual and ceremonial context, into content and thus an object of study and examination.

The use of the term Mysteries could thus risk causing confusion and misunderstanding. Károly Kerényi, the great scholar of religious studies and myths, clarifies how the term altered its meaning depending on the context and historical period in which it was used:

"There are however mysteries, sacraments, doctrines and experiences of Christianity that in Greek could only be defined using the term 'mystery'. These mysteries, in the same way as all the pathways of initiation comprised in the immense field today referred to as 'mystical', feature a common characteristic. This characteristic is observed in Plotinus, the heathen philosopher who indeed belongs to the non-classical world of mysticism. We are dealing with the 'flight of one towards the one': a 'flight', an escape from the world in which man as 'one' was 'alone' and his subsequent union with he who is 'one' by his very nature. Whether this One is intended in a monotheist sense, as the one who exists, or in the pantheist sense as the Universal Being – the orientation towards a Being who is beyond the multiplicity of one's natural experience is most characteristic. Whether the Being is conceived as a mere supernatural element such as Christianity, or as being diversely opposed to the multiple world of nature, as intimated by the other religions of salvation, mysticism tends to redeem man by freeing him from all natural bonds.

We should not be faced with these forms of great oriental and western mysticism if we wish to become familiar with the original Greek-pagan use of a group of words correlated to mysterion. The Classical Greeks' use of the adjective 'mystical' did not imply ideas that tended to remove themselves from the world and project themselves towards the mystical. On the contrary. The 'mystical aura' that, in the Frogs of Aristophanes caressed those who drew close to the beatific mysti, the initiates who danced in the other world, is the smell of the burning torches. For the Athenians of the 5th century the word 'mystic' re-evoked the atmosphere of nocturnal festivities with all their sensitive details: a 'mystical' experience for him is a specific festive experience. In the history of Greek religions the 'mystic' – from the time in which it was first subjected to philosophical interpretation – was represented in the form of a festive occurrence. Mysteria was the name given to a specific type of feast in Athens.

According to the goddesses they were devoted to, these festivities could have been called Demeter, Koreia or Perrephattia, and may even have been thus known. Ancient tradition refers to mysteria – mysteries' which, in line with its modern use, should also be written in Greek with a capital lette…How does the situation stand with regard to Mysteria? Likewise, this term refers to a festivity, a period of atmospherically distinguished sacred events rather than sacred activities, rites and celebrations, which were demonstrated by a classical Athenian orator in referring to a ritual act, the teletes of the Mysteria themselves, in viewing the teletes of the Mysteria as the festive rite. Moreover, the name Mysteria is limited exactly to the period of time passed in the practising of rites … The basic nucleus of the term Mysteria – and likewise of the terms mystes and mysticos – is constituted by a verb, the ritual significance of which 'to initiate' is the ulterior formation of 'to close one's eyes or mouth'. The monuments – two replicas of a representation of the initiation of Herakles into the mysteria – underline how we should not think of subjects becoming mute in front of the arreton, but of a ceremony of closing one's eyes. We see Herakles sitting with his head draped in veils: the Mysteria commence for the mystes in the moment that he, as a passive participant in the event, closes his eyes and sits in total darkness. On entering initia (plural), as known by the Romans in their Latin translation, is not only this initiatory act of closing one's eyes, myesis, a more accurate translation of which is initiate, but is the Mysteria themselves. A feast to celebrate the gaining of obscurity – to what exit or ascent can this then lead —: this is, in the original sense of the term, the feast of Mysteria." [110]

I can summarise by stating that, literally, Mysteries can be considered an expression of the "sacred" that allowed the achievement of a certain degree of Knowledge, whatever that may have been. And, as sacred expressions, they were in turn included in the larger context of public festivities, within which all divinities found their specific place, both as objects of cult and mythology.

Officially a part of institutionalised religious dynamics, Mysteries revealed a whole cultural complex linked to deities carrying out their duties *within* a specific competence area – thus not necessarily a deity — similar to Pantheon gods. Above all, as cults and ritual practices playing a role in the updating of mythic events, Mysteries gave shape to death, periodically rescuing it from the original chaos, as gods had already done in the era of myths, and, in some ways, taming it and making it ritually – and culturally – controllable. This way death was made *accessible* by culture, a *"mask using cyclicality to temporarily erase history as an unstoppable process"*.[111]

110 Károly Kerényi, *Miti e Misteri*, Bollati Boringhieri, Turin, 1979, pages 144-153.

111 Paolo Scarpi, *Le Religioni dei Misteri*, Fondazione Lorenzo Valla, Arnoldo Mondadori Editore, Milan, 2002, pages XIII-XIV.

Hymn to Demeter

Our knowledge of the ritual undertaken in the Eleusinian Mysteries is based mainly on a poem *Hymn to Demeter* that is one of the so-called "Homeric hymns" traditionally attributed to Homer as they were written in the same dialect used in the *Odyssey* and the *Iliad.*

The mythical tale on which the hymn is based tells of the abduction of Persephone, Demeter's daughter, who, whilst gathering flowers on the Nysa plain together with the daughter of Ocean, saw the earth open beneath her feet and was forcibly dragged into the underworld by Hades who was determined to make her his bride. After nine days of wandering desperately, Demeter was informed of the happening by the goddess Hecate and the god Helios and, furious with Zeus who had agreed to the union between Hades and Persephone, decided to no longer return to Mount Olympus.

Demeter, therefore, after having taken on the semblance of an old woman, walked to Eleusis where she sat near to the Well of Virgins and was approached by four of the daughters of Celeus, King of Eleusis who asked her where she was from. Demeter replied that her name was Doso and that she had escaped from the hands of pirates who had abducted her. She was taken to the Royal Palace and put to work as nursemaid for Demofonte, the infant son of the king and his wife Metanira. Once settled in the palace Demeter, sad and silent, was cheered by the playfulness of the servant Iambe who even managed to get her to smile. Subsequently, on invitation of Queen Metanira to join her in a cup of red wine, Demeter replied that instead of wine she preferred to drink kykeon, a drink made up of barley, water and mint leaves.

Demeter, however, instead of feeding Demofonte as a normal infant, decided to temper him in the flames in order to render him immortal; during the rite she was however discovered and interrupted by Metanira who, horrified at the sight of her baby in the fire, started to scream. At this point Demeter decided to reveal her true identity and showed herself in all her splendour, demanding, to placate her fury, that the Eleusinians build her a Temple with a great altar where she could teach humans her rites.

Once the sanctuary had been constructed, Demeter retired there and, still angry at the thought of her daughter's fate, induced a terrible drought. The lack of produce would subsequently result in a failure of men to offer sacrifices and oblations to Olympus, with Zeus repeatedly asking Demeter to return to Olympus and calm her fury, although receiving the reply that Demeter would never return until she had been reunited with her daughter Persephone.

Thus, Zeus, forced by the obstinacy of Demeter, sent Hermes to Hades requesting that he return Persephone to her mother. Hades, accepting the invitation begrudgingly, prior to releasing the girl, tricked her into eating some pomegranate grains. As pomegranates were the food of the dead, this artifice would connect Persephone forever to the reign of Hades, forcing her to return there for four months every year.

On being reunited with her daughter, Demeter once again returned to Mount Olympus and the soil once more flourished. Here Demeter, prior to returning to the gods, revealed the rites of the Mysteries to Triptolemos, Diocletian, Eumolpus and Celeus. (This is a summarised version of the myth.)

On careful reading of the *Hymn to Demeter*, one can observe the presence of two different rituals of "initiation", two rites featuring diverse dynamics both aimed at achieving the same purpose, knowledge of the Divine and identification with the same.

I shall now examine separately these two initiations: the Eleusinian ritual practised in the sanctuary, and the failed initiation of Demofonte described in the *Hymn*.

The Eleusinian Ritual

Among the Mystery societies, that referring to the Eleusinian Mysteries is undoubtedly, in view of the documentation available, the most widely acknowledged and, in my opinion, the one which has inspired several aspects of Masonic ritual.

For more than 2,000 years in Eleusis the Mysteries were celebrated; it is therefore quite plausible that over time the ritual may have undergone substantial transformations. Undeniably the vicinity and the protection afforded by Athens contributed towards making Eleusis a veritable centre of the Greek religious scene.

The literary and figurative testimonies available refer particularly to the first stages of initiation, those not containing any secrets. Initiation was indeed divided into different stages and degrees, comprising the Lesser Mysteries, the Greater Mysteries (*teletes*), and the fundamental final experience (*epòpteia*), the apex of the ceremony and of the initiatic pathway. We however have only a few pointers as to the *teletes* and the *epòpteia*.

In the Eleusinian rite two classes of Initiates were present, known as *mystai,* together with those who had already undergone initiation, the *epòptai*. The mystagogue was the person that guided the initiate to the sanctuary in Eleusis and assisted him during the ceremony, much of which saw the *mystai* blindfolded.

The Lesser Mysteries were celebrated once a year in Kheria, a suburb of Athens, during the month of Anthesterion in the spring. The ceremonies comprised a series of rituals, fastings, purifications and sacrifices, all regulated by a mystagogue. It is thought that the initiates reproposed in an updated version episodes of mythical tales of the two goddesses narrated by Homer in the *Hymn to Demeter*.

The Greater Mysteries were also celebrated once yearly, from the 7th to the 13th of the month of Boedromion (September-October); the ceremony lasted for eight days, the first seven of which were taken up by preparations for the ceremony. All citizens of

Athens, women and slaves included, were permitted to take part, as long as they spoke Greek and had "unsoiled hands". The absolute requirement was that they had to have completed the Lesser Mysteries of Kheria.

The *Eleusinion*, a sort of Athenian version of the Temple of Eleusis, was used for celebrations on the first day of the Mysteries. The day before, the sacred objects, the *hiera*, had been transported to the building from Eleusis by the *Epheboi* and enclosed in a wrapping, with the Priestess of Athens meeting them and escorting the sacred objects into the *Eleusinion*.

The following day the procession headed towards the sea where each initiate carried a piglet which was washed in the water and offered as a sacrifice on their return to Athens; this act, the sacrificing of the animal, should be interpreted as representing the disappearance of Persephone into the underworld with Hades. Subsequently, the initiate, or *mystai*, fasted for two days inside the *Eleusinion*. On the fourth day, the *Archon Basileus* (chief magistrate) and his wife, before the representatives of the city of Athens, carried out the great sacrifice. On the 19th of Boedromion everyone returned to Eleusis; the procession left at dawn and comprised the initiates, their tutors, and numerous citizens of Athens, and acted as an escort to the priestesses on the return journey to Eleusis where the *hiera* were returned to their rightful place. The procession was preceded by a wooden stature of Iacchus, the incarnation of the ritual scream, which was followed by the *hiera* wrapped in their cloths on a cart, during the journey, on crossing the bridge over the River Kephisos, masked men challenged the noblemen present in the procession. In the evening, the procession entered the outer yard of the sanctuary where, during the night, dances and singing took place in honour of Demeter and Persephone, and the next day the initiates, after fasting, offered their sacrifices.

Behind the entrance to the Temple there was a grotto that symbolised the entrance to the underworld, obviously devoted to Hades. The ritual took place in the *Telestérion*, a vast area built to accommodate a large number of people who watched the hierophant in the act of "demonstrating the sacred".

Once the initiates had entered into the sanctuary, the fundamental phase of the initiatic ceremony commenced; little or nothing is known of this, however. As highlighted by Mircea Eliade:

"With regard to the two secret rites (teletes) we can only put forward hypotheses. The ceremonies that took place both inside and outside the telesterion probably related to the myth of the two goddesses. It is known that the initiates, bearing their torches, imitated Demeter who wandered with her torches in the search for Persephone. Several ceremonies comprised the use of legomena, short liturgical formulas and beseechments. Hardly anything is known of the rites that took place on the second day in Eleusis. It is likely that the apex of the initiation was reached during the night, a supreme vision, the epopteia, accessible only to those who had

been initiated for at least a year. The following day was devoted particularly to the rites and libations for the deceased; the next day, the ninth and last day of the ceremony, the initiates returned to Athens." [112]

We may therefore only *deduce* what happened inside the sanctuary; we may hypothesise that the initiates, *remodernising* the legend of Demeter, were placed mystically in the condition to receive the revelation that was transmitted by the *dromena*, the *legomena* and the *deiknumena*.

The *dromena*, in substance, were the dramas, with the hall in which the Initiation took place being arranged as an actual theatre, a square atrium with steps at each side.

The *dromena* were accompanied by a verbal revelation, the *legomena*. These consisted probably of secret formulas (*aporrheta*) for recognition, actual *laissez-passers* (*symbola*). The *legomena* however had a rather limited importance; indeed, in the words of Aristotle: *"Initiates do not need to understand anything; rather, they undergo an experience and a disposition – become, that is, deserving."*

Indeed, all ancient authors agree that the essential moment of the revelation consisted in a "vision" or "illumination". This was the privilege of those who had reached the highest initiatic degree, known as *epòptai* — "those who have seen". The 'objects' that were thus "revealed", or *deiknumena*, were no other than the mysterious sacred objects (*hiera*) mentioned above: the hierophant, as also mentioned previously, was literally *"he who displayed the sacred objects"*. The historian Puech refers to this rite *"it is still inscribed on the map of the Initiation Hall: at the centre of the square 'stage' is Anaktoron, a closed chapel in which the sacred objects were deposited throughout the year, and, in occasion of the ceremonies, the hierophant appeared on the threshold to display the same in the burning light of the torches."* [113]

The Common Elements

Albert Mackey, renowned North American historian and expert in twentieth-century Freemasonry, is, like Leadbeater before him, in no doubt as to the "direct" influence of the Mystery Societies on Freemasonry. Despite the numerous distortions, several of his notes are of interest:

"The candidate was at first called an aspirant, or seeker of the truth, and the initial ceremony which he underwent was a lustration or purification by water. In this condition he may be compared to the Entered Apprentice of the Masonic rites, and it is here worth

112 Mircea Eliade, *Storia delle credenze e delle idee religiose*, Sansoni Editore, Florence 1990, page 322. Original title: *Histoire des croyances et des idées réligieuses*, Payot, Paris 1975.

113 Henri-Charles Puech, *Le religioni nel mondo classico*, Mondadori, Milan, 1992, pages 95-96.

adverting to the fact that all the ceremonies in the first degree of masonry are symbolic of an internal purification. In the lesser Mysteries the candidate took an oath of secrecy, which was administered to him by the mystagogue, and then received a preparatory instruction, which enabled him afterwards to understand the developments of the higher and subsequent division. He was now called a Mystes, or initiate, and may be compared to the Fellow Craft of Freemasonry. In the greater Mysteries the whole knowledge of the divine truths, which was the object of initiation, was communicated. Here we find, among the various ceremonies which assimilated these rites to Freemasonry, the aphanism, which was the disappearance or death; the pastos, the couch, coffin, or grave; the euresis, or the discovery of the body; and the autopsy, or full sight of everything, that is, the complete communication of the secrets." [114]

Mackey then goes on to list several common elements found in both the Ancient Mysteries and the rituals of Freemasonry. The symbol of the *Sun*, the first to be examined by the author, is indeed present in the Egyptian Mysteries of Osiris and Herodotus, likewise an initiate; Mackey maintains that the Egyptian ceremony consists in the ritual *representation* of a sun god who has descended to earth and been murdered by Typhon, the symbol of darkness. In the Celtic Mysteries of the Druids, the temple of initiation was oval, representing an egg (the symbol of the world); circular, as the circle was also used to symbolise the universe; or cross-shaped, representing the four founding elements of the universe. In the Greater Eleusinian Mysteries celebrated in Athens the temple of initiation symbolised the universe, with one of the officiates representing the *Sun*. The symbol of the *Sun*, as we know, represents one of the *Minor Lights* inside the Masonic temple.

An additional common element between Masonic rituals and the rites of the Ancient Mysteries is identified by Mackey if the rite of "Discalceation", with the author stating:

"The rite of discalceation, or uncovering the feet on approaching holy ground, is derived from the Latin word discalceare, to pluck off one's shoes. In the days of Moses, we learn from that passage of Exodus where the angel of the Lord, at the burning bush, exclaims to the patriarch, 'Draw not nigh hither; put off thy shoes from off thy feet, for the place whereon thou standest is holy ground.' (Ex. III, 5). Pythagoras said to his disciples 'Offer sacrifice and worship with thy shoes off' (Giamblico, Life of Pythagoras). The rite of discalceation is, therefore, a symbol of reverence. It signifies, in the language of symbolism, that the spot which is about to be approached in this humble and reverential manner is consecrated to some holy purpose." [115]

114 Albert G. Mackey, *Massoneria Antica e Moderna*, Atanòr, Rome, 2009, pages 34-35. Original title: *The Symbolism of Freemasonry*.

115 Ibid. page 83.

The Symbolism of the Gloves

As mentioned previously, prior to commencing the ceremony, ablutions and various purification rituals were necessary to the initiate who was preparing to undergo the mystic ritual.

In the Masonic ritual this function was carried out allegorically at the moment when the Freemason was asked to put on his Gloves, Gloves that had to be rigorously "white", to represent a symbol of interior and exterior purity. They serve to remind the initiate that his hands should always remain free of blemish.

In a Masonic context the most ancient reference to the symbolism of Gloves is observed in the widely acknowledged *Natural History of Staffordshire* published in 1686 by Robert Plot.[116] In the volume written by Plot, following a brief introduction on

116 With reference to this important volume, Yasha Beresiner, Librarian of the Regular Grand Lodge of Italy, writes: "Robert Plot (1640–96) was born in Kent and received a BA degree from Oxford University in 1661, an MA in 1664 and a Law degree in 1671. In 1677 he was elected a Fellow of the Royal Society and became Secretary in 1682. He was responsible for the publication of Nos. 143 to 166 of *The Philosophical Transactions of the Royal Society*. In 1683 Elias Ashmole appointed him as the first keeper of his museum, the now well known Ashmolean Museum and Bodleian Library in Oxford. Although there for just seven years, Plot acquisitioned a vast collection of what were considered natural curiosities, many of which he had described in both his histories of Oxfordshire and Staffordshire. These objects are still today preserved in the Ashmolean Museum. He did not complete his life ambitions to write, as he intended, the Natural Histories of Kent and Middlesex for which several extensive MSS survived him. He achieved many more distinctions before his death on April 30th 1696. Robert Plot was not a Freemason.

His love was the study of natural history and this is reflected in his publications, including the folio size *Natural History of Staffordshire* printed in Oxford in 1686, the subject of this article.

The references to Masonic customs as described in the text are easily recognisable in today's terms. The importance given to this early text is reflected in the study and analysis that has been undertaken by many prominent Masonic scholars in the past such as Gould,[1] Dring[2] and Knoop, Jones & Hamer,[3] amongst others. Thus we find that the content of the text reflects our own understanding and knowledge of Masonic practices.

The views expressed by Plot are clearly divisible into

a) statements of fact as to the practices of the members of the fraternity, which can be treated as trustworthy and

b) those that may be interpreted as his opinion and which are, at times, faulty and biased by his negative views of the fraternity. An instance is his quote regarding Masonic secrets when he states:

...I have reason to suspect are much worse than these, perhaps as bad as this History of the craft it self than which there is nothing I ever met with, more false or incoherent. (§86 line 16)

His most consequential statement, however, lies in his mention of *'large parchment volum they have amongst them, containing the History and Rules of the craft of masonry'* (§85 line 5). Although mention of freemasonry has been recorded since the 16th century, this is the first and earliest reference we have to what are now known as the *Old Charges of the British Freemasons.*[4] Notwithstanding the fact that some fifteen *Old Charges* have been identified prior to the publication date of the *Natural History of Staffordshire* in 1686 there is still no known copy of any earlier *Old Charges* in which all of the details given by Plot can be found.

Accepting the fact that much of Plot's statements are true and correct as evidenced by other sources, the question still remains: where did Plot get his information?

Plot's Sources:

Specific statements by Plot have been identified and sources traced to earlier manuscripts, as for instance his reference to '*...the candidates present with gloves, and so likewise to their wives, and entertain with a collation*

Footnote continued overleaf

the traditional legend of the origins of the *Society of Free Masons*, it mentions how in this context there was a custom to give candidates two pairs of gloves, one for them and one for their wives, with the chapter concerned describing this ancient custom of Freemasonry as follows:

"To thefe add the Cuftoms relating to the County, whereof they have one, of admitting Men into the Society of Free-mafons, that in the moorelands of this County feems to be of great requeft, than any where elfe, though I find the Cuftom fpread more or lefs all over the Nation; for here I found perfons of the moft eminent quality, that did not difdain to be of this Fellowfhip.

Nor indeed need they, were it of that Antiquity and honor, that is pretended in a large parchment volum they have amongft them, containing the Hiftory and Rules of the craft of mafonry. Which is there deduced not only from facred writ, but profane ftory, particularly that it was brought into England by S^t^. Amphibal, and firft communicated to S^t^. Alban, who fet down the Charges of mafonry, and was made paymafter and Governor of the Kings works, and gave them charges and manners as St. Amphibal, had taught him. Which were after confirmed by King Athelftan, whofe youngeft fon Edwyn loved well mafonry, took upon him the charges and learned the manners, and obtained for them of his Father a free-Charter. Whereupon he caufed them to affemble at York, and to bring all the old Books of their craft, and out of them ordained fuch charges and manners, as they then thought fit: which charges in the faid Schrole or Parchment volum, are in part declared: and thus was the craft of mafonry grounded and confirmed in England. It is alfo there declared that thefe charges and manners were after perufed and approved by King Hen. 6. and his council, both as to Mafters and Fellows of this right Worfhipfull craft (Ex Rotulo. membranaceo penes Camentariorum Societatem.)

according to the Custom of the place:'(§86 line 3). This has been sourced to Schaw Statutes of 1599 and Elias Ashmole's diary entry dated 10 March 1682,[5] respectively. Robert Plot's close association with Elias Ashmole and the latter's immediate entourage of Freemasons may well have been an opportunity for Plot to get an insight into some aspects of the Craft. Much of his information may have also come from the four page 'questionnaire' which was sent out by Plot to the residents in Staffordshire prior to his journey to write his History. The ninth of the ten headings on the form related to all matters 'Concerning Arts' in which he asked for information on trades peculiar to the locality, assuring the contributor that '*...this design desires not to dive into the mystery of any Trade, but only to represent matter of fact...* [6] The responses may well have included references to Freemasonry and the activities of the fraternity as later described by Plot in his own words in his tome. Sadly, there appear to be no surviving examples of the responses.

As to the *Old Charges*, suggestions that Plot actually had access to the Sloane MS of 1646 have been dismissed on the grounds that more would have been made by Plot had he had such access and that, in any case, the Sloane MS was likely to be of a much later date previously thought[7]. The closest *Old Charge* to the text cited by Plot is the William Watson MS No.2[8] attributed to the 17th century, in which the history of the Craft appears very similar, though Plot did not use sufficient excerpts from the *large parchment volum* he mentions, to allow fuller comparison, both of which can be traced to the 15th century Cooke manuscript. There is a possibility that Plot saw and used the Wilson manuscript, although this too has been put into doubt by Bro Begemann[9]. There is no doubt that Plot's text is written in his own words and not transcribed from any other document.

Into which Society when any are admitted, they call a meeting (or Lodg as they term it in fome places) which muft confift at left of 5 or 6 of the Ancients of the Order, whom the candidats prefent with gloves, and fo likewife to their wives, and entertain with a collation according to the Cuftom of the place: This ended, they proceed to the admiffion of them, which cheifly confifts in the communication of certain fecret fignes, whereby they are known to one another all over the Nation, by which means they have maintenance whither ever they travel: for if any man appear though altogether unknown that can fhew any of thefe fignes to a Fellow of the Society, whom they otherwife call an accepted mafon, he is obliged prefently to come to him, from what company or place foever he be in, nay tho' from the top of a Steeple, (what hazard or inconvenience foever he run) to know his pleafure, and affift him; viz. if he want work he is bound to find him fome; or if he cannot doe that, to give him mony, or otherwife fupport him till work can be had; which is one of their Articles; and it is another, that they advife the Mafters they work for, according to the beft of their skill, acquainting them with the goodnefs or badnefs of their materials; and if they be any way out in the contrivance of their buildings modeftly to rectify them in it; that mafonry be not difhonored: and many fuch like that are commonly known: but fome others they have (to which they are fworn after their fafhion) that none know but themfelves, which I have reafon to fufpect are much worfe than thefe, perhaps as bad as this Hiftory of the craft it felf; than which there is nothing I ever met with, more falfe or incoherent." [117]

Today, with a few rare exceptions, the custom practised initially by the ancient English speaking Freemasons of giving two pairs of gloves to the initiate, the second as a gift for their wives, has been almost completely lost.

The "Pass Word" and the Mystagogue-Deacon

On returning once again to the *legomena*, actual *laissez-passers*, we may, in a parallelism with the Masonic ritual, identify these "secret words" communicated to the *mystai* with our "Pass Words" that permit Freemasons to accede to a higher Degree.

The identification of the *legomena* with the "Pass Words" used in the Eleusinian rituals is underlined by the scholar Marion Giebel:

"The initiation formula is the 'sacred basket'. This rite is correlated to the 'pass word' (Synthema) handed down to us by the Christian author Clemente Alessandrino who uttered all mysteries on admittance to the sacred place of initiation: 'I have fasted, I have drunk Kykeon, I have taken (something) from the cist (a lidded container), I have handled it, I have placed it in the Kalarhos (an open basket) and moved it once more from the basket to the cist.'" [118]

117 Robert Plot, *The Natural History of Staffordshire*, Oxford, 1686, pages 316-317.

118 Marion Giebel, op. cit., page 37.

It is a known fact that the "Pass Words" currently in use in Freemasonry are of Jewish origin; however, several scholars maintain that these have *replaced* the "original" pass words of Greek origin, linked in particular to the Mystery societies. Among the supporters of this theory, the most renowned is W. Hutchinson who, in his *The Spirit of Masonry* envinces how the "Pass Words" used in the passage from the 1st to the 2nd Degree, and from the 2nd to the 3rd Degree were, in his opinion, of clearly Greek origin.[119] The theory, shared by other scholars of Freemasonry, among them the Italian Arturo Reghini, was based on the assumption that in eighteenth-century England the inclusion of references in the ritual to Osiris, Dionysus, Mithra, Demeter or other heathen gods would have provoked the intolerance of the Christian ecclesiastical authorities and, for this reason, the original words were replaced with references to the Old Testament.

The Swiss scholar Oswald Wirth is of a different opinion, identifying in the "Pass Word" used in the 2nd Degree of the Masonic ritual a clear reference to the Mysteries of Ceres and their agricultural symbols, seeing in the Eleusinian initiatic death the allegory of the grains of wheat that die in the winter to be subsequently reborn in the spring, vigorous and thriving.[120]

The theory of the Greek origins, or rather the "mystery" origins of the "Pass Words" present in Masonic rituals, has obviously been rejected by the overwhelming majority of English speaking scholars who, although supporting the English origins of the "Pass Words", only date their first appearance to the early decades of the eighteenth century, some time therefore after the birth of the "speculative" or, if we wish, "non-operative" Freemasonry. To find the first emergence of the "Pass Word" in printed matter, we will have to wait until 1760, when these were used for the first time in the catechism *Three Distinct Knocks*.[121]

119 W. Hutchinson, *The Spirit of Masonry*, London, 1943, page 158.

120 Oswald Wirth, *Le Livre du Compagnon*, Librairie Maçonnique & Initiatique, Paris, 1911, page 84.

121 A.C.F. Jackson, *Masonic Passwords*, AQC Vol.87, 1974, Pages 106-112. Jackson, one of the most prestigious members of the historic Research Lodge in London, Quatuor Coronati, stated that: "The earliest appearance of Masonic 'Passwords' in print in England was in the exposure *Three Distinct Knocks*, first published in 1760. It claimed that in those days the prospective Fellow Craft, at the beginning of that degree, was entrusted with a password; a word taken from Chapter 12 of the Book of Judges. The prospective Master Mason was similarly entrusted with a word which came from Chapter 4 of the Book of Genesis. If the password had been in use in the earliest period of non-operative Masonry, one might expect that there would be some reference to them in the comparatively large number of Masonic documents of that period still extant. This, however, is not the case. Passwords, identifying an individual as a mason possessing a certain degree, would not have been necessary when there were only one or two degrees; in the case of non-operative, both usually given on the same noght. This broadly limits their earliest inception in the period of the development of the Trigradal System. The suggestion that passwords originated during the third decade of the 18th century has much to recommend it. It is immaterial in which country they started. They may have originated among

The Secret, the Epòpteia

Participation in the culmination of the Eleusinian ritual, known as the *epòpteia,* was not permitted until one year after taking part in the Greater Mysteries. This referred to one of the three stages that indicated the "revealed objects", naturally visible only to those who had been admitted to the ceremony, i.e. the *epòptai.*

The apex of the *epòpteia* was reached when the *mystai*, on having their blindfolds removed and under a blinding light were "shown" the "secret" object, purportedly a cut *ear of wheat* representing the complete life cycle.

The *epòpteia*, which could be translated by the term "contemplation", and consequently denotes the *epòptai* as "contemplators", corresponds therefore to the "revealing of the secret" concealed in the ritual. This secrecy was specifically coded in the *Hymn to Demeter* and was underlined by two adjectives, *arrheta* and *aporrheta.*

Although the terms denote respectively "the unutterable" and "the prohibited", *arrheta* and *aporrheta* appear to be used interchangeably, almost as though they were synonyms, even at times referring to the same Mysteries. The secret was revealed by means of words and gestures, rituals and sacred objects that were shown to the adepts. Generally speaking, however, the *arrheta* or *aporrheta* permeated the entire ritual ceremony, frequently synthesised, as mentioned previously, in a sort of "tripartite formula", the "things shown", an action corresponding to the displaying of "sacred objects", the "things done", the ritual activities, and the "things said", that may have coincided with the reciting of a "sacred" story using a ritual form.[122]

The dynamics applied in the rite underline therefore how the purpose of the Eleusinian initiation was not aimed at "salvation", with no expectations of eternal life; on the contrary, the ceremony resulted in an actual "ontological change", a mutation of "state", not to be confused with "status", a change elicited by an *active-realisatory metaphysical* dynamic rather than a quiescent and quietist one. The knowledge to be invoked by the *mystai*, therefore, is of a super-individual, super-rational, intuitive and discursive *metaphysical* nature.

One of the major experts of the Ancient Mysteries, Walter Burkert, described the place in which the ritual was performed, the Eleusinian sanctuary, thus:

the specialist lodges working the Third Degree, either in England or Ireland; but it is unlikely they started in Scotland. But, wherever they started in the latter half of the decade, by 1730, many lodges in England, Ireland and some in Scotland would have had them in their ceremonies or at least known of their existence, while lodges formed on the Continent under British patronage would gradually be adopting them also. It therefore follows that passwords, as such, would not have been one of the causes of complaint by the Antient Mason in connection with the changes in the Landmarks of the 1730s, as the manner of communicating them appears to have been less."

122 Paolo Scarpi, op. cit., Page XVIII.

"In the centre was the 'Anàktoron', a rectangular, oblong, stone construction with a door at the end of one of its longer sides; there the throne of the hierophant was placed; he alone might pass through the door into the innermost part of the construction... There was no true entrance to the nether world, no chasm, no possibility of acting out a journey into Hades. The great fire under which the hierophant would officiate obviously burned on top of the Anàktoron.

"It is remarkable that the concept of 'immortality' is never mentioned in connection with Eleusis. Death remains a reality, even if it is not an absolute end, but at the same time a new 'beginning'. There is another kind of 'life', and this, at all events, is good. Attention has been drawn to the saying from St. John's Gospel that a grain of corn must die if it is to bring forth fruit. The ear of corn cut and shown by the hierophant can be understood in this way." [123]

We should now therefore ask ourselves what was meant by mention of the "secrets" present in the Eleusinian rituals.

André Motte is of the opinion that there is a vestige of "esoteric" content to be transmitted beneath the term "secrets", no doctrinal teachings; the "secret" is merely a "vision" which was meant to produce an *emotional* reaction featuring mystic connotations. He writes:

"The singular use of the term 'secret' should make us think of a knowledgeable and esoteric doctrine communicated to the initiates during the course of the ceremony. Actually, there is no documented proof that this indeed occurred. It is known that the legòmena were present, several 'things said', and undoubtedly the priests and mystagogues were given the task of guiding and instructing the candidates for initiation. However, the teachings were not meant to be in an elaborate and knowledgeable form...Moreover, the mysteries were largely comprised of dròmena, 'things done', and deiknùmena, 'things shown'. Initiation was achieved by means of a symbolic vision, a sort of active contemplation, as underlined by the frequently reiterated formulas proclaiming the beatitude of the initiate: 'Blessed is he who sees the mysteries!' The word epoptéia, indicating the highest degree of initiation, is linked to a root capable of 'seeing', 'contemplating'... At the heart of the mystic experience is thus the idea of a beatified vision; by means of the objects contemplated, that sensitised the efficacious presence of the deities and invoked unity, the initiates acquired a sort of vital knowledge capable of transforming their very existence." [124]

The meaning and the content of the "secret" in the Eleusinian Mysteries is described in minute detail by the renowned Italian scholar Dario Sabbatucci, who went far beyond

123 Walter Burkert, *La religione greca*, Jaca Book, Milan, 1983, page 518.

124 André Motte, *Silenzio e Segreto nei Misteri di Eleusi*, in *I Riti di Iniziazione*, Julien Ries (ed), Jaca Book, Milan, 1989, pages 149-150.

the definition of "beatified vision" referred to by Motte, ruling out the possibility that the secret could be of a doctrinal nature (a revelation), and was left with no choice but to move into *ritual action*. To this aim, Sabbatucci distinguished a "functional" secret intended to defend the Eleusinian Mysteries from being repeated elsewhere, and a "formal secret" extended throughout the entire complex, and thus comprising the "functional secret". In the new mystic initiation, at variance with the ancient tribal initiation which was aimed at constituting a company of initiates, the secret was only meant to circumscribe the spatial and temporal *punctum* (Eleusis and several days in the month of Boedromion) in which the mystic miracle could take place.[125]

Sabbatucci emphasises how numerous scholars have expressed their marvel at how the secrets of Eleusis have been so well preserved throughout the centuries, with the exception of the few comments made by Saint Clement of Alexandria and Hippolytus of Rome. The reply given by Sabbatucci to this anomaly, whose view I share fully, is that possibly nothing was revealed as there was objectively nothing to reveal. *"In other words"* explained Sabbatucci, *"the true secret was represented by a subjective mystic experience that would not have been deemed credible, nor even communicable by others. This experience maintained its validity, as a secret to be guarded, as long as one believed in it."* [126] This is an explanation which, in my opinion, fits perfectly with the personal experience of a Freemason, whose wholly "inner secret", and for this reason incommunicable, may be discovered solely by means of a *spiritual realisation*.

Thus, the "secret" referred to in the Eleusinian Mysteries comprised in a *personal* and *metaphysical* dynamic which as already stated is prevalently, incommunicable, and, continues Sabbatucci, when Hippolytus states that during the Mysteries *"the mighty, marvellous and perfect secret was shown in silence to the epopts, a reaped ear of corn"*, the Christian theologist reveals the Eleusinian secret not so much as by the showing of the ear of corn, but rather by describing the sense of "mightiness", "marvel" and "perfection" the initiate experienced during this phase of the rite, therefore in a state *modified* by the mystic experience. The same things occurs when Saint Clement of Alexandria, on referring to the Eleusinian *synthema*, the ritual formula that transformed the initiate, does not actually reveal any secret, but merely gives a more detailed description, describing the *animus,* the innermost feelings. In the words of Sabbatucci, all these aspects underline the entitlement of the Eleusinian experience to be rightfully included on the list of *mystic* phenomena, and, I wish to add, if correctly performed, the Masonic ritual is characterised by the same dynamic and the same aim.

125 Dario Sabbatucci, *Saggio sul Misticismo Greco,* Edizioni dell'Ateneo, Rome, 1965, page 143.
126 Ibid. page 145.

In a comparison with Freemasonry, it may be concluded therefore that the "mystic secret", in the same way as the "initiatic secrets", removes the candidate to a new spatial and temporal dimension and effects an ontological change, as opportunely referred to by Mariano Bizzarri: *"In the field of the initiatic pathway, there are truths that have to be experienced sub specie interioritatis, promoting a fusion between acquaintance and acquaintanced that alone will lead to illumination, i.e. to a pure intellectual understanding in the absence of intermediaries based exclusively on one's own personal capacity of intuition. For this reason the Masonic secret is not only incommunicable but is likewise inviolable."* [127]

The Symbolism of Light

I shall return subsequently to discussing this important symbolic aspect, in the chapter focusing on the similarities between Masonic symbology and Neoplatonist thought. Indeed, Light has long been viewed as the symbol *par excellence* of Truth and Knowledge. At the moment in which the candidate states he is seeking Light, he is hoping to achieve the *intuitive awareness* that will lead him away from the shadows of moral and intellectual ignorance and guide him as close as possible to knowledge of the Divine which is He.

In reference to the symbology of Light in the Mystery Societies, Albert Mackey writes:

"In the Mysteries of every nation, the candidate was made to pass, during his initiation, through scenes of utter darkness, and at length terminated his trials by an admission to the splendidly-illuminated sacellum, or sanctuary, where he was said to have attained pure and perfect light, and where he received the necessary instructions which were to invest him with that knowledge of the divine truth. Light, therefore, became synonymous with truth and knowledge, and darkness with falsehood and ignorance. Death and the resurrection were taught in the Mysteries, as they are in Freemasonry. The initiation was the lesson of death. The full fruition or autopsy, the reception of light, was the lesson of regeneration or resurrection. Light is, therefore, a fundamental symbol in Freemasonry and contains within itself the very essence of Speculative Masonry, which is nothing more than the contemplation of intellectual light or truth." [128]

It should however be borne in mind that in the Masonic Initiation ceremony the thing that is "returned" to the Initiate is still a "material" Light, the "spiritual" Light, the "true" Light will only be imparted subsequently in the Third Degree, at the fundamental moment of his "initiatic death".

127 Mariano Bizzarri, *La Via Iniziatica: Introduzione alla Libera Muratoria*, Atanòr, Rome, 2002, page 37.
128 Albert G. Mackey, op. cit., page 98.

Death Unto Oneself

In the Third Degree of Freemasonry, in the legend narrating the allegory of the Death of Hiram, we may observe the most important analogy between Masonic ritual and those of the ancient Mystery societies, the so-called "initiatic death". The discovery of the body of God or of the "sacred" Archetype recounted in the Eleusinian Mysteries and its recovery from the ground to be honoured in a sacred place, occupies a key role in both the rituals practised by the Mystery societies and in Freemasonry.

The aim of the "initiatic death" is to *die unto oneself* in order to unleash the Divine that is within; as stated by Guido De Giorgio *"tradition implies that on finding himself, Man finds Him, finds God, but dictates than man should die on finding himself as he must retrace the pathway to the chasm created by his fall, he must kill ignorance, abolish it, turn it into wisdom, turn his death into his very life, in which his inner awareness is awareness of God".*[129]

Likewise, the *mystai*, in the same way as a Freemason when "enacting" the Myth of Hiram Abif, are "subjected" to something during initiation, although it is not necessarily true that the initiate is invariably subjected to the same fate as his god, the *first initiate*. The "sufferances" are correlated therefore to the aspect of initiation, in the same way as the overcoming of the *fear* of death may be experienced and interpreted as anticipation, but above all *overcoming* of death itself. In the course of the ceremony of the "initiatic death", the *myste*, the initiate, lives the sacred story of his deity; he relives the story in a borderline situation during which he opens up to the experience of a relationship that overcomes his human life, and in which he will live as a "new man".[130]

To this regard, another interesting parallelism between the Mystery societies and Freemasonry has been proposed by the English scholar Duncan Moore who, citing the volume published on the Eleusinian Mysteries by Hippolyto Joseph da Costa, entitled *The Dionysian Artificers,* and in referring to these Mysteries, writes:

"First of all the statement that 'The aspirant for these mysteries was not admitted a candidate till he had arrived at a certain age, and particular persons were appointed to examine and prepare him for the rites of initiation' rings true of Masonry. We only admit mature individuals over 21 and of good character. Going on to the second paragraph we learn that 'those found worthy of admittance were then instructed by significant symbols in the principles of society' – this sounds like a peculiar system of morality, veiled in allegory and illustrated by symbols! The dark room called the mystical crape may not be familiar to English Masons but, in the chapter on the first Degree we refer briefly to the Initiation ceremony in Continental European Scottish Rite Masonry in which it is a familiar concept. In the next paragraph we really are on familiar ground where da Costa

129 Guido De Giorgio, *La Tradizione Romana*, Mediterranee, Rome, 1989, page 95.

130 Marion Giebel, op. cit., page 28.

says 'when introduced, the holy book was brought forward, from between two pillars or stones, he was rewarded by the vision: a multitude of extraordinary lights were presented to him, some of which are worthy of particular remark'. This says to me that he was blindfolded, stood between two pillars and took an obligation on a holy book. On restoration to light he is shown extraordinary lights. We do not know the precise symbolism involved, but it would be fair to assume, at least to some extent, that it would be similar, if not identical, to our own. All the things in the final paragraph are familiar to us, when you think about it. 'He stood on a sheep skin' – the lamb has been since time immemorial the universally accepted emblem of purity and innocence – and at one time English Masonic aprons were made from sheepskin and some still are. It should be noted that the inclusion of the sheep in the Eleusinian mysteries was also connected with the Zodiac sign of Aries which we will look at later. The candidate also wore a sheep skin and a veil of purple – the significance of that regal colour being also well known to us. The spotted or variegated mule skin we may not know about, except inasmuch as the word 'variegated' is applied in the Lecture on the First Degree Tracing Board to the Chequered Pavement in our lodges. But we are told what the mule skin symbolised: 'the rays of the sun and stars'! These are familiar decoration on Masonic ceilings. Lastly, if we consider that the candidate is being instructed by three people, we can draw a parallel with the master and his two Wardens because the first is the 'revealer of sacred things', the second represents the Sun and the third the Moon!" [131]

As can be observed, More, in spite of conveying an interesting, albeit somewhat fantastical representation of the Eleusinian Mysteries, on being required to enter into the fine detail of the Mysteries, is not capable of grasping the *esoteric* and *initiatic* value, focusing stoutly, as do many English authors, on a merely *moralistic* vision of Freemasonry, concluding that:

"I suppose the fact that the Eleusinian Mysteries introduced a legend into their ceremonies is a point of similarity with Masonry, given that we have the legend of Hiram Abif in our Third Degree. In both instances it is the use of a fictional symbolism, in our case to teach a moral lesson." [132]

On viewing the "initiatic death", the fulcrum of all initiatic rituals and the heart of the initiatic pathway in Freemasonry, as a "moral" teaching, it is clear that the beholder has not understood the exquisitely initiatic characteristics of either Mystery societies, and above all of Freemasonry. If Freemasonry were only a system of morals there would be no need for a ritual representation similar to that of the "initiatic death", and even less of enacting the allegory of the death of the architect Hiram Abif.

However, numerous scholars on an international level lend ample "initiatic" emphasis to the Masonic pathway, among whom the English author Julian Rees

131 Duncan Moore, *A Guide to Masonic Symbolism*, Lewis Masonic, Hersham, 2009, page 25.
132 Ibid. page 23.

describes most effectively the *esoteric* connotations present in the ceremonies of passage from the 1st to the 3rd degrees and, in referring to the "initiatic death" writes:

"As the first two degrees dealt with birth and life, so this degree dealt with one of the great mysteries to which we shall one day be subject: the mystery of death. Here, as you know, we dealt not so much with physical death, but the death of the material side of the self, to be reborn at a higher level of consciousness. This was an echo of the first degree, where we sought to subdue the material senses and physical passion, in order to attain to moral growth, rebirth in a sense now familiar to you. In another sense, we have here a sublime application of the Rule of Three – the first degree as the active principle, the second as the passive, both of them co-ordinated and given form and meaning by the third degree. Your rough ashla is well on the way to emerging as a perfect ashla, but this degree was to impart to you something much more profound – the culmination of the knowledge and understanding of your own nature, and your knowledge of, and oneness with, God." [133]

In Masonic ritual therefore there is a wide range of symbols and allegories which, by reaching beyond morality, relate exclusively to the metaphysical. Among these the allegory of the "initiatic death" is one of the most important; its purpose, as mentioned previously, is to provide an allegorical representation of the definitive killing of the *ego*, started in the 1st Degree, continued in the 2nd Degree and finally concluded in the 3rd Degree. In this regard, I concur with Mariano Bizzarri, who states:

"Freemasonry does not represent a pathway to moral perfection, although this latter aspect may be implicated, we might say necessarily, in spiritual realisation. The explanation that we wish to convey is that initiation itself presents no "social", "philanthropic", and even less so "ethical" features". [134]

The problem of an excessive "moralisation" of Freemasonry has invariably resulted in controversy, particularly among Italian scholars, and not only in recent years. At the beginning of the twentieth century Arturo Reghini wrote as follows:

"In the Anglo-Saxon countries, following the prevalently moralist trend assumed by Protestantism, which should be better suited to be known as Moralism, every effort is made to emphasise the exquisitely moral character of Masonic initiation, the death of vice and the birth of Masonic virtues... To be gratified by this moralist interpretation of the Masonic allegory almost always implies the need to sacrifice, misunderstand or at least distort the universal, non sectarian, esoteric character of the Order; and it is incredible to think that so much enthusiasm can be gained from having Freemasonry don the white suits of the First Communion and wallowing in morals up to one's knees... The ancient Masonic tradition,

133 Julian Rees, *Making Light, A Handbook for Freemasons*, Lewis Masonic, Hersham, 2006, page 90.

134 Mariano Bizzarri, op. cit., page 129.

and the inspiration for ceremonies of the Pagan Mysteries demonstrate how the true sense of Masonic allegory is metaphysical, given by an effective spiritual palingenesis." [135]

There is no doubt that in Masonic rituals the *esoteric* component first became dominant, using symbols and allegories (the *tools of the craft* first and foremost) only at the start of the eighteenth century. It may thus be concluded that although Freemasonry was mainly developed initially as a system of morals, it undeniably *evolved* into a true "initiatic Order", and the retrospective introduction of the Legend of Hiram is proof of this. Naturally, throughout its transformation and evolution, morals have continued to play a key role in Freemasonry.

To return to the issue of an "initiatic death", the culmination of all initiation rites, Mircea Eliade in his famous work *Birth and Rebirth* underlines the effect of the personality of the initiate, which is capable of eliciting a true ontological change:

"The majority of the initiatory ordeals implies, in a more or less transparent manner, a ritual death followed by a resurrection or a rebirth. The central moment of all initiatory rituals is represented by the ceremony symbolising the death of the neophyte and return to the fellowship of the living. But he returns to life a new man who assumes a new mode of being. Initiatory death signifies the end of childhood, of ignorance, and of the profane condition… All the rites of rebirth or resurrection, and the symbols that they imply, indicate that the novice has attained to another mode of existence, inaccessible to those who have not undergone the initiatory ordeals, who have not tasted death." [136]

The Masonic legend of the death of Hiram, in addition to representing the "initiatic death", may likewise be interpreted as an allegory of the death of *Tradition*, in constant danger and which must absolutely be prevented; in this regard, an important scholar of traditions, Oswald Wirth, writes:

"Hiram lives again because Initiatic Tradition cannot be lost; this veiled light that at times seems to extinguish can only undergo the briefest of eclipses. Enclosed within dirty lamps it has reached us in an almost unrecognizable form. In the course of lengthy centuries of incomprehension Hiram slept, but has awoken since his adepts approached the tomb of the dead letter to take the inanimate corpse upon themselves. He who perceives breathes life into the dead of spirit, the victims of incomprehension. Misunderstood, Initiation may be practised as a form of cult that perpetuates rites and transmits symbols; Freemasonry has done no better thus far: it was an initiatory play, appealing to the elder youths who were amused by the enactments. Of which they were able to grasp only vaguely the significance.

135 Arturo Reghini, op. cit., pages 92-94.

136 Mircea Eliade, *La Nascita Mistica: Riti e simboli d'iniziazione*, Morcelliana, 1974, pages 12-13. Original title: *Birth and Rebirth, Rites and Symbols of Initiation*, Harper & Row, New York, 1958.

But the adolescent no longer plays with childish pastimes; on becoming serious and no longer lingering among the things of youth, he strays from Tradition if this is no longer vital but languishes as a corpse without a soul, as a hollow shell or an empty container." [137]

In the "initiatic death" therefore, we are faced with the *purpose* of Freemasonry as an "Initiatic Order" and "form"of *Tradition.* Throughout the Masonic pathway there is no sin to redeem, no soteriological connotations of salvation, the Truth for a Freemason, the quest for the profound essence of being, is never located "behind", but invariably "ahead".

Demofonte, the First Initiate

As mentioned previously, The Homeric *Hymn to Demeter* refers to two types of initiation; specifically, the book explains the foundation of the Eleusinian Mysteries both as the *reunion* of two goddesses and as the consequence of the failed *immortalisation* of Demofonte. The story of Demofonte may be compared with the ancient myths focusing on a tragic error which, at a certain time in primeval history, removed the possibility of man becoming immortal. In this case, however, there was no mistake, and it was not through the fault of a mythical forefather that the condition of immortality was lost to him and his descendants.

In narrating the episode, Mircea Eliade states:

"Demofonte was not a primeval personage; he was the last-born son of a king. Demeter's decision to immortalise him may be interpreted both as a desire to 'adopt' the child (as a consolation for the loss of Persephone), and to seek revenge against Zeus and the gods on Mount Olympus. Demeter was transforming a man into a god. The goddesses were empowered to bestow immortality on man, and the flames, with the burning of the neophyte, were among the most widely applied methods of achieving this aim. On being interrupted by Metanira, Demeter did not conceal her disappointment in the stupidity of men. The hymn however does not in any way allude to an eventual generalization of this technique of immortalization: to fusion, i.e. an initiation by fire aimed at transforming men into gods.

Only following her failure to immortalise Demofonte did Demeter disclose her identity and demand that a sanctuary was built in her honour. And she imparted her secrets only subsequent to her reunion with her daughter. The mystic initiation was clearly diverse from that which had been interrupted by Metanira. The subject initiated to the Mysteries of Eleusis did not achieve immortality; a great fire illuminated the sanctuary of Eleusis but, although several examples of cremation have been reported, it is highly unlikely that the flames were directly implicated in the rites of initiation." [138]

137 Oswald Wirth, *I Misteri dell'Arte Reale*, Atanòr, Rome, 1996, page 173.

138 Mircea Eliade, *Storia delle Credenze e delle Idee Religiose*, Vol.I, Sansoni Editore, Florence, 1990, pages 318-319.

Eliade continues to narrate the process of immortalisation, not grasping however, in my opinion, the *additional* allegory present in the act. Indeed, the episode in which Demeter attempts to transform Demofonte into a god reveals, more than the intention to bestow immortality on the man, the *allegory* of man possessing the *potential* to return to the Divine within him. Demeter wishes to achieve a "change in state" in Demofonte, an ontological change which, thanks to the ill-timed interruption by the child's mother, Metanira, fails, although success is deemed "possible". Thus, Demofonte became the "first initiate", the first human being to approach, by means of Demeter's intervention, the Deities, a "Gnosis" that was intended to lead to a *deification. "Ignorant men, senseless, who cannot even see your fate of fortune or misfortune!"* exclaims Demeter on being prevented from completing her "work". By these words, Demeter tries to tell men that they are *capable* of imitating the gods and becoming, by means of the appropriate Knowledge, just like them.

The goddess, discovered in the course of her terrible and mysterious activity, speaks in mystical tones of the ignorance of mortals. If they were aware of the existence of good and evil they would understand the significance of the process, mortal only in appearance. The significance – good concealed within evil – in this case is immortality. This is beyond any trace of doubt. It is superfluous to underline, maintains Kerényi, that the procedure carried out by Demeter was not of an "anthropomorphic" nature: *"To be placed in the flames and still be alive, even to achieve immortality, is not a human fate. The goddess has surpassed all human limitations."*[139]

Indeed, Demeter *allegorically* plunges Demofonte into the fire of Knowledge, and the Temple that she demands be erected in her name is aimed at teaching man the Mysteries that will lead them to the Knowledge of themselves.

The description of the episode provided by the scholar Paolo Scarpi is noteworthy:

"The episode of Demofonte represents the apex, in a certain sense ambiguous, of the tale narrated in the hymn. This failed attempt to render the son of Celeus and Metanira immortal possesses all the features of a ritual of entrance or aggregation, and Demeter would have had to move Demofonte from the human to the divine world which was out of reach for man. In Demeter's intentions this corresponds to a purely Olympian logic: immortality is a privilege bestowed on the gods and cannot be shared by man. From a certain point of view Demofonte may be seen as the 'first initiate' – there are however no elements to lead us to maintain that this episode represents an action of the obscure ritual of 'the boy in the fireplace'. Whilst in the hymn Demeter, following the interruption by Metanira, places the child on the ground to be assisted by the sisters, in the

139 Károly Kerényi, *Prolegomeni allo studio scientifico della mitologia*, Bollati Boringhieri, Turin, 1972, page 170.

paraphrasing of Orphism and the Pseudo-Apollodorus variant Demofonte dies. However, whether Demofonte dies – and in this case he 'dies' respect to the state he was in prior to his passage through the flames – or not, his exposure to the flames in the fireplace implies a transformation, a 'burning' that changes him into a member of the human culture; at the same time death, unavoidable, is seen as a choice exchanged with a series of privileges linked to the practising of rituals, and thus removed from nature and inserted into culture. In this way even death is tamed." [140]

The Eleusinian Mysteries, as mentioned, were readily accessible to foreigners, slaves and women, and not reserved solely to men having the status of "citizens" of Athens, thereby demonstrating their intimist intent, and relating to the person as an "individual". However, as Sabbatucci rightly perceives, this situation was the *natural* outlet for a characteristic trend of the cult which could be revealed by the abolition of all differences between man and man, and through the elaboration of a new concept of humanity. However, he once again points out that these should not be viewed as the ultimate *aim* of the cult: *"It was certainly not the materializing of a 'humanistic' ideology, or a concentration of men as 'equals' or 'brothers' that produced the Eleusinian Mysteries, but rather the contrary, if we are to believe the reality of the issues defined above as a point of arrival, and which in no case may be defined as a starting point. The Eleusinian 'humanistic' thus seems to be more of an instrument than a destination; it could be defined as functional, or even unnecessary, not conclusive, not absolute, but rather contingent, dialectic and relating to the performance of the Eleusinian cult. We are therefore in the midst of a mystic phenomenology: in Eleusis there was no catechisation and neither was the initiate exalted in the name of an ideal human brotherhood, but this brotherhood was achieved involuntarily when he accepted to undergo a rite in which he would be asked to give up his individuality."* [141]

Thus, the Eleusinian Mysteries feature the same form of *misunderstanding* that occurred with Freemasonry, with the ultimate product being confused with the entire programme, the aim.

The analogies with the historic development of Freemasonry are of particular interest. I have mentioned previously how Freemasonry subsequently transformed from an "Initiatic Society", degenerating into a fraternal association of mutual assistance that would have found the height of expression in the Obediences strongly bound to the ideals of Liberty, Equality and Fraternity.

Another point underlined by Sabbatucci is how the Eleusinian initiation represented a sort of *parenthesis* in the course of the everyday life of the Greek citizens, as, at the end

140 Paolo Scarpi, op. cit., page 444.

141 Dario Sabbatucci, *Saggio sul Misticismo Greco*, Edzioni dell'Ateneo, Rome, 1965, page 129.

of the ceremonies, the initiates returned each to his own city to take up, at least under a judicial and religious profile, his place in the world.[142] The guarantee of the absolute adherence of the initiate to the order of the State was assured, with this attitude likewise being observed in the principles of Freemasonry, the *Constitutions* of which address this issue in an entire chapter "The Charges of a Freemason" under the heading "Of the Civil magistrates, supreme and subordinate" which clearly convey how a Freemason should be: *"A Mason is a peaceable Subject to the Civil Powers, wherever he resides or works, and is never to be concern'd in Plots and Conspiracies against the Peace and Welfare of the Nation, nor to behave himself undutifully to inferior Magistrates."* [143]

Mithraism

The term "Roman Mithraism" is intended to denote a form of mystic spiritualism that in the world of the Roman Empire assumed a particular degree of originality as it used a series of materials of various origins from the reigns of Iran and Babylon to the syncretism of the Hellenic world, placing the same into a new fabric in which each element took on a new significance and new functions.

Mithra is an ancient god from the Indo-Iranian pantheon who afforded protection over contracts and negotiations and oaths, which, in late Antiquity was to characterise its followers as an epithet. Without a shadow of doubt pre-Zoroastrian Iran and subsequent cultural transformations were the cradle from which the *initiatic-esoteric* cult was devolved during the Roman Empire to the god Mithra.

The wide diffusion of Mithraism among the Roman legionnaires may lead us to suspect an origin linked to possible cultural and *initiatic communities* of men founded on aristocratic and warlike ethics. Secret and initiatic, Mithraism seems to have been organised hierarchically in grades which were gained by means of a complex system of *rites of passage*. There were seven degrees, a symbolic transfiguration of the seven celestial spheres where each degree corresponded to a planet. By passing from one to the next and reaching the last degree the follower of the god succeeded in entering the super-worldly universe according to a design evoking an ascent of the soul through the planetary spheres of the *Corpus Hermeticum*, in which the outcome was "deification".

The followers of Mithra were likewise promised this same outcome, as can be observed in the "prescription for immortality" present in the Mithraic ritual contained in the *Great Magical Papyrus* published in Paris. Officially transformed into a public cult by Aurelian in the year A.D.274, the date to be used in celebrating the birth of the god

142 Ibid. page 132.

143 Constitutions and Regulations of the Regular Grand Lodge of Italy, 1993, pages 23-24.

was established as December 25th, the *Natalis Solis Invicti*, following which Mithra, identified with the *Sun*, became the undefeated god *par excellence*.[144]

As essential part of the Mithraic rite was the *tauromachy*, the ritual killing of a bull by a god bearing the semblance of an adult man. This ritual represented an "initiatic birth" at a higher degree, as well as a passage to a second level more meaningful than that symbolised by the Sun child born from rock. In other words, the two symbols could allude to two different stages of initiation, one relating to the Lesser Mysteries and subsequently to the Greater Mysteries. In the Mithraic ritual the fundamental element is the desire of the initiate to *imitate*, by means of a mystic-magical action, the god that *dies* and is *resurrected*.

An interesting version of Mithraism as an inner experience, seen from a metaphysical point of view having as its ultimate aim a true ontological change of state, is proposed by Julius Evola[145] in a renowned essay published in *Ultra*,[146] the journal of the Independent Theosophical League of Rome, edited by Decio Calvari. The document represents the only ritual from the Ancient Mysteries that has been handed down in an integral condition.

In his essay Evola presents Mithraism in a new perspective, as a "realization of Self", an inner process of spiritual *self-realisation* as illustrated in the doctrine of the Mithraic Mysteries. Evola therefore does not view the Mysteries as a mere doctrine underlying an "ascent" to the divine, but also from the point of view of the Mithraic adept in his journey through the "passing of levels", in undertaking a process of gradual simplification and denudation of Self, of freeing himself from the bonds of the body and attachment to material things, thus rediscovering Self, i.e. the divine spark, the original identity which, in an ordinary condition, would be buried underneath layers of waste.[147]

The entire Mithraic pathway is seen by Evola as an integration of the conscious principle required to cross a series of phases and "states", of trials, to achieve a *spiritual realization* and approach one's union with God, a pathway which, as we will see, is remarkably similar to that of Freemasonry. *"To be initiated,"* writes Evola, *"is to free oneself from the "stone" and achieve a state of awareness that is no longer conditioned by the body."*[148]

Numerous Masonic symbols have been inspired by Mithraism. The *Mystic*

144 AAVV, *Le Religioni dei Misteri*, Paolo Scarpi (ed), Introduction, Fondazione Valla, Mondadori, 2002.

145 Fabio Venzi, *Julius Evola e la Libera Muratoria*: *Una verità scomoda*, Settimo Sigillo, Rome, 2010, page 42.

146 Julius Evola, *La via della realizzazione di sé secondo i Misteri di Mithra*, *Ultra*, No. 3, June 1926.

147 Stefano Arcella, Introduction to Julius Evola, *La via della realizzazione di sé secondo i Misteri di Mithra*, Fondazione Julius Evola, Controcorrente Edizioni, Naples, 2007, page 12.

148 Julius Evola, *Idealismo, occultismo e il problema dello spiritismo contemporaneo*, Ultra, number 6, December 1923.

Ladder, for example, in Freemasonry signifying the theological ladder that connects the heavens to the earth, and which Jacob saw in his vision, was widely diffuse in the ancient religions and was thought to have seven steps or rungs. In the Mithraic Mysteries in Persia, comprising seven stages of initiation, a high ladder with seven rungs (or gates), each of which was devoted to one of the planets, which in turn represented the metals, was erected in the Temples (or caves). The highest rung represented the Sun and, starting from the bottom-most rung and ascending, were situated Saturn, represented by lead, Venus by tin, Jupiter brass, Mercury iron, Mars a base metal, the Moon silver and the Sun gold. The entire ladder symbolised the sidereal progress of the Sun throughout the universe.[149]

The previously mentioned controversial Charles Leadbeater belonged to the Theosophical Society, and in the very year that Evola published his essay on Mithraism in the Journal *Ultra*, he printed a famous text on Freemasonry in which he hypothesised a direct descent for the Mithraic Mysteries perpetuated through the *Collegia Fabrorum.*[150]

In this regard, Leadbeater writes that *"twenty of the Mithraic temples still remain and show certain points of resemblance to our Masonic Lodges. The temple was rectangular with a raised platform at the east end, often apsidal in form. Continuous benches ran along its walls on the longer sides for the accommodation of the Brethren, and the ceiling was made to symbolise the firmament".*[151]

Moreover, Leadbeater opines how the Mithraic system of rituals, similar to Freemasonry, was made up of seven degrees, although, he underlines: *"It is not easy to trace exact correspondences between these seven stages and our degrees, because of the difference between the systems. The Corax is fairly parallel with the Entered Apprentice and the Cryphius and Miles with the Fellow Craft, the latter being distinguished from the former by additional which may not inaptly be compared with that of the Mark Degree. These three classes together were regarded to some extent as servitors; the next stage, Leo, was the first whose members were called 'participants' and were*

149 Albert G. Mackey, *Massoneria Antica e Moderna*, Reprint, Atanòr, Rome, 2009.

150 Charles Webster Leadbeater (1854–1934) a key representative of the Theosophical Society founded by Helena Petrovna Blavansky, a close collaborator of the English writer Annie Wood Besant who became President following the death of the founder. He was a controversial figure, an Anglican priest, a mystic clairvoyant who wrote a series of books based on his extrasensory experiences; he was accused of immorality and homosexuality and expelled from the Society in 1906, to be subsequently readmitted in 1908 following the election of Ms. Besant as President. He discovered the 14-year-old Indian Jiddu Krishnamurti who Leadbeater maintained was the incarnation of the future Messiah. He was initiated in the Ancient and Accepted Scottish Rite of Freemasonry. He wrote numerous essays on Freemasonry, in addition to the previously cited *Glimpses of Masonic History*, among which is *The Hidden Life in Freemasonry*.

151 Charles W. Leadbeater, *La Massoneria e gli Antichi Misteri*, Atanòr, Rome, 1926, page 140.

admitted to the Mithraic sacrament. We may consider the three stages of Leo, Perses and Heliodromus as divisions of the Master Mason Degree; the first gave access to the full fellowship of the Mithraic brotherhood; the second passed him who received it through a most impressive ceremony in the course of which he was symbolically slain and raised to life in the honour of Mithra; and the third put him in possession of additional knowledge equivalent to that which is supposed to be given to us in the Holy Royal Arch; for only when he had that knowledge of the name and qualities of the deity was he fitted to go forth as a messenger of the Sun to bear his strength and life through the world. The Pater corresponded to our Installed Master who alone can confer the various degrees and pass on the succession to posterity." [152] In this analogy proposed by Leadbeater, the Most Worshipful Master would therefore correspond to the Pater, the supreme initiatic grade that designates supreme sacerdotal authority, the spiritual guide of the affiliates, he who directs the liturgy according to the regulations imparted by tradition and monitors compliance.

Masonic historiography is somewhat sceptical towards the theory of Mithraic descent of Masonic rituals with any degree of credibility, with contrasting versions still being present today.[153]

152 Ibid. page 141.

153 As an example Wynn Westcott in *The Resemblances of Freemasonry to the Cult of Mithra*, in AQC, Vol.XXIX, 1916, writes: "Many writers have exercised their ingenuity in finding points of resemblances between Freemasonry, its ideal and ceremonies, and certain older institutions whether religious or civil. Some have gone beyond the assertion of resemblances and have declared that Freemasonry, as we know it to-day, has descended from these institutions, or has been beholden to them for its inspiration and for many peculiarities of doctrine and procedure. Freemasonry has been affiliated by essayists to the Ancient Mysteries of Egypt and Greece, to the Collegia of Rome, to the Essene Brotherhood and to the Culdees of old, as well as to the much later Vehm-Gerichte of Westphalia, the Steimetzen, the Trade Guilds, the French Compagnonage and the Rusicrucians; even our origins from the Celtic Druids of Britain and Normandy has been inferred. In this note upon the Cult of Mithra (Persian), Mithras (Greek) or Mitra (Sanscrit), the 'Genius of the Heavenly Light', I shall show that this ancient Persian religion spread in the course of time to Europe, and has left its trace in ruined temples and sculptures, which have been *found* in Italy, Germany, France, and even in England. This institution made use of secret temples and mysterious ceremonial of a religious and moral nature, was of pre-Christian origin, and had as part of its system a mode of progress by grades or stages, each with its mystical and symbolic name, available for its devotees, but there does not appear to me to be any basis for the suggestion that the origin of Freemasonry had any relation to it, for almost all that is known of Mithraism is quite recent discovery, due to archaeological and architectural research among the ruins of many countries." Also worthy of note: Count Goblet D'Alviella, Mithraic Rites, in AQC, Vol.XIII, 1900: "It is well known that these mysteries offer striking analogies with much that is found in Free-Masonry: their celebration in grottoes or covered halls, which symbolised the Universe and which in dimension, disposition and decoration, presented a strict counterpart to our Lodges;—their division in seven degrees conferred by initiatory rites wonderfully like our own;—their method of teaching, through the same astronomic symbolism, the highest truths then known in Philosophy and Morals;—their mystic bond of secrecy, toleration, equality and brotherly love."

3. Hermeticism

The second *Traditional* "form" which inspired the Masonic thought that I am going to examine is Hermeticism.

Hermeticism can be defined as a philosophical and religious movement that formed itself between the second and third centuries A.D. during early Christianity, featuring Oriental influences deriving from the Gnostic representation of Platonist, Neoplatonist and Stoic Greek philosophy. This fascinating doctrine represented the first historically documented example of interaction between the Greek Rationalist tradition and oriental knowledge as a form of revealed knowledge.

It essentially reintroduced the same dynamics that led to the birth of Mystery societies; Hermetic doctrines, in fact, were developed because of the dissatisfaction of pagans looking for answers to the meaning of life that religion had long since failed to provide.

Indeed, as explained by the historian Frances A. Yates who focused on Renaissance thought, Hermeticism turned *"to other ways of seeking an answer, intuitive, mystical, and magical. Since reason seemed to have failed, it sought to cultivate the Nous, the intuitive faculty in man. Philosophy was to be used, not as a dialectical exercise, but as a way of reaching intuitive knowledge of the divine and of the meaning of the world, as a gnosis, in short, to be prepared for by ascetic discipline and a religious way of life. The Hermetic treatises, which often take the form of dialogues between master and disciple, usually culminate in a kind of ecstasy in which the adept is satisfied that he has received an illumination through contemplation of the world or the cosmos, or rather through contemplation of the cosmos as reflected in the Nous and gives him spiritual mastery over it, as in the familiar Gnostic revelation or experience of the ascent of the soul through the spheres of the planets to be immersed in the divine."* [154]

According to Yates, Hermeticism thus presented itself as a true Gnostic experience, if a gnosis that is not *only* knowledge to be imparted, but also and above all "heightening of awareness", at times represented as a sudden *illumination* (especially clear in the books of *Poemandres* and *Kore Kosmou*). Hermetic gnosis would thus represent both a religious practice and a knowledge aspiration, aimed at dispersing that veil of ignorance that prevents us from reuniting with our divine side; the main objective would be a quest for unity and foundation of all things, which can also be found, as we are all aware, in the dynamics of Masonic gnosis.

Freemasons' documents contain very few direct references to Hermeticism, or rather, to the figure of Hermes Trismegistus. Hermes' name, indeed, is only just mentioned in a number of copies of the *Old Charges*, the first of which, in chronological order, is the

154 Frances A. Yates, *Giordano Bruno e la Tradizione Ermetica*, Laterza, Bari, 1998, pages 16-17.

Cooke Manuscript (1410). This, the second oldest Masonic document after the *Regius Poem* (1390), describes, with reference to the biblical story, although revisited, how Hermes together with Pythagoras discovered the pillars on which, before the Great Flood, Lamech's sons carved the Arts and Sciences known at the time.

In the *Sloane Manuscript 3848* (1646) Hermes is once again mentioned with regard to the famous pillars erected by Lamech's sons:

"...and these children did knowe that god would take vengeance for sinne eather by fire or water; Wherefore ye writ ye Sciences wch weare found in 2 pillars of stone; yt ye might be found after the flood; The one stone was called Marble that cannot burne with fire; The other was called Letera that cannot drowne with water; Hermenes that was sonne to Cus, & Cus was sonne to Shem wch was son of Noath: The same Hermenes was afterwards Hermes; the ffather of wise men, and hee found out ye 2 pillars of stone where ye Science weare written, & taught him forth."

Hermes is also discussed in the *Spencer* (1726) and *Cole Manuscripts* (1728), whereas his figure is replaced by that of Euclid in the *Inigo Jones Manuscript*, dating back to 1725.

The Origins of Hermeticism and its Historical Placement

The meaning and origins of the term "Hermeticism", which thinkers from the Renaissance erroneously thought derived from a figure that had supposedly lived in ancient times, Hermes Trismegistus, are represented within literature with a precise historical and cultural placement; Frances Yates summarises the characteristics of this literature as follows:

"The Egyptian God, Thoth, the scribe of the gods and the divinity of wisdom, was identified by the Greeks with their Hermes and sometimes given the epithet of 'Thrice Great'. The Latins took over this identification of Hermes or Mercury with Thoth. A large literature in Greek developed under the name of Hermes Trismegistus, concerned with astrology and the occult sciences, with the secret virtues of plants and stones and the sympathetic magic based on knowledge of such virtues, with the making of talismans for drawing down the powers of the stars, and so on. Though cast in a pseudo-Egyptian framework, these works have been thought by many scholars to contain very few genuine Egyptian elements. In any case, however, they were certainly not written in remotest antiquity by an all-wise Egyptian priest, as the Renaissance believed, but by various unknown authors, all probably Greek, and they contain popular Greek philosophy of the period, a mixture of Platonism and Stoicism, combined with some Jewish and probably some Persian influences. They are very diverse, but they all breathe an atmosphere of intense piety." [155]

155 Frances A. Yates, op. cit., page 14.

The latter is a dominant characteristic in Hermetic writings, one of their essential peculiarities; the single treatises making up the *Corpus*, in fact, although influenced by different learning traditions and inspired by Hellenistic traditions, essentially remain *religious* pieces of writing, apparently confused and contradictory testimonies of a continuous and persistent quest for the *divine*.[156]

One of the most controversial issues regarding the texts that make up Hermetic literature concerns their sources. As previously mentioned, despite the fact that the choice of the main characters of dialogues in the different treatises was inspired by Egyptian mythology, Hermes-Thoth, Asclepius-Imhotep, Amun, Isis and Horus-Ptah (in the *Kore Kosmou* treatise), very few elements actually recall Egyptian culture, leading us to think that its real sources belong not to Ancient Egypt but rather to the popular Greek philosophical thought.

Hermetic literature is usually divided into philosophical Treatises (*Corpus Hermeticum*, *Asclepius*, *Stobaeus Fragments*) and alchemical and magic literature (*Picatrix* and others), defined by the historian of classical thought André-Jean Festugière, as "popular" Hermeticism. In this regard, in what is considered the ultimate work on the subject, *La Révélation d'Hermès Trismégiste,* Festugière informs us:

"Towards the end of the Hellenistic period and under the Empire a certain amount of revealed knowledge was spread throughout the Greek-Roman world and attributed to either Persian Magi (Zoroaster, Ostan, Hystaspes), or a Greek god (Thoth-Hermes), or the Oracles coming from Chaldea (Chaldean Oracles), or even to Greek prophets and philosophers who, more than anyone else, had come close to divine truth, seeing as Pythagorism and Orphism both flourished again at that same time. Among the revealed knowledge the one bearing Hermes Trismegistus' name is one of the most significant both in terms of the number of written works that were handed down to us and the role played by this literature. We usually know and study anything dealing with philosophy and theology. Egyptian Hermes however took an interest in several other fields: astrology, alchemy, magic, and this Hermeticism that could almost be defined as 'popular', far from being a secondary and late branch of the Hermetic revolution, is, on the contrary, the most ancient production, which gave its form to and largely acted as a model for Erudite Hermeticism."[157]

Magic-alchemical Hermetic literature should therefore not only not be considered inferior to "erudite" Hermeticism, but should even be *inspired* by the latter. It is the latter trend of Hermeticism that, starting from the second century A.D., inspired the alchemical movement mainly represented by Zosimos' texts (A.D.300), in which the technique of transmutation of metals had already been translated into an *allegorical* process of internal transformation.

156 Giovanni Filoramo, *Introduction to La Pupilla del Mondo*, Marsilio, Venice, 1994, page 10.

157 A-J. Festugière, *La Révélation d'Hermès Trismégiste*, Gabalda, Paris, 1944.

As emphasised by Pinella Travaglia: *"In the Arab world, a true philosophical knowledge basing its peculiar character on the principles of transmutation and the understanding of the raw materials representing its foundation was established under Hermes' name. More than a club or a sect, in this case Hermeticism therefore defined the philosophical meaning of a knowledge that never lost its relationship with praxis but also developed an original synthesis with philosophical traditions. A significant example of the latter synthesis is the Kitab sirr al-haliqa (The Secret Book of Creation), in which the first recognised brief text of Arab alchemy, Al-lawh alladì kana min al-zumurrud (The Emerald Tablet), also known to the Latins as the Smaragdine Tablet, can be found. The Secret Book of Creation, written in Arabic in the 8th century, played a significant role in the later Arab and Latin traditions, having been translated by Ugo di Santalla in the first half of the 12th century and entitled De secretis naturae. Only by reading both texts can one appreciate to what extent and how the alchemical phenomenon was considered valid in that context based on precise cosmological and philosophical prerequisites: the latter represent the contents of the Secret Book of Creation, whereas operational practices are summarised in the Smaragdine Tablet, the Secret Book of Creation presents all the elements that Festugière had identified as characteristic of Hermetic literature: 'literary fiction' that defines a way of transmission of said knowledge (the discovery of a book or a stele in the underground or in a cave); the revelation of secret knowledge, attributed to Hermes, regarding the occult properties of things and thus their initiatic character."* [158]

The vision of the world on which "magical" written works are based does not differ from the more organic and elaborate one of philosophical works; indeed, they both feature the doctrine of universal *sympatheia* of things according to which mysterious links unite and connect all the elements in the animate and inanimate cosmos. This gives rise to the conception of a unitary, animate and lively cosmos crossed and supported by divine energy, the unitary foundation of the multiplicity of things.[159]

Controversy still reigns on the subject, characterised by often contrasting opinions; even an expert on the subject such as Mircea Eliade contributes to increasing the confusion on the definition of treatises, classifying the *Asclepius* and *Kore Kosmou* as part of "popular" Hermeticism whereas they were usually recognised as being part of the so-called 'philosophical' Hermeticism and stressing that:

"Popular Hermeticism written works have played a prominent role in the Imperial era. In this amorphous corpus of magic recipes and treatises on natural magic and occult sciences, ideas typical of erudite literature are often to be found: in the Kore Kosmou the creation of souls is portrayed as an alchemical process; the closing prayer in the Asclepius can also be

158 Pinella Travaglia, *Ermetismo e Alchimia: Esoterismo*, Einaudi, pages 116-117.

159 Giovanni Filoramo, op. cit., page 17.

found in Greek, in a magic recipe. The importance of this popular Hermetic literature should not be underestimated, as it inspired and enriched Pliny's Natural History; its cosmology and its guidelines (the doctrine of sympathy and correspondence, particularly the correspondences between macro and micro-cosmos)".[160]

In any case, whatever the division between the two types of literature may be, underestimating the literature of so-called "popular" Hermeticism would prove a major mistake, especially seeing as true masterpieces of esoteric thought are classified among the texts making up the above literature. Establishing a strict dichotomy between the two literatures should at the very least be an arbitrary operation and keeping the two branches apart would actually be impossible, for the simple reason that, in many works, the "philosophical" and "magic" thoughts are virtually inextricable.

The leit motiv of the treatises forming the *Corpus Hermeticum* is the description of the ascent of the soul through the planetary spheres, finally reaching the divine. Hermes is portrayed playing different roles in different texts, sometimes a god, sometimes a disciple or a *Nous* intermediary or Divine Intellect, sometimes a simple wise man.

Treatises with the largest initiatic content are, in my opinion, the 1st and 13th of the *Corpus Hermeticum*, and the treatise known as the *Ogdoad*, whose content will be briefly discussed together with the *Asclepius* and the *Kore Kosmou*.

The Rediscovery of Hermeticism in the Renaissance

Hermeticism was rediscovered during the Renaissance thanks to the Neoplatonist movement, of which it represented a component of fundamental importance. As already discussed, until Casaubon's discovery in 1612, Hermes Trismegistus was considered a historical figure, a part of the *Prisca Theologia* that Renaissance Neoplatonism regarded as the essential core of its thought. Pico della Mirandola and Marsilio Ficino had no doubts on the historical figure of Hermes Trismegistus as already in the second century a number of authors, among whom was the apologist Lattanzio, regarded Hermes Trismegistus as a wise man inspired by God, interpreting a number of Hermetic prophecies as presages of the birth of Jesus Christ.

Whereas with Marsilio Ficino a certain harmony between Hermeticism and Hermetic magic on one side and Christianity on the other was re-established, with Giovanni Pico della Mirandola Hermetic magic and Jewish Kabbalah were used to confirm the divinity of Christ. The unforgettable opening of the *Oration on the Dignity of Man* by Pico, *"A great miracle, Asclepius, is man…"*, inspired by the *Asclepius* Treatise

160 Mircea Eliade, *Storia delle Credenze e delle Idee Religiose*, Vol.II, Sansoni Editore, Florence, 1980, pages 197-198.

(*"A great miracle, Asclepius, is the human being, worthy of respect and honour"*), represents the most wonderful example of how Hermetic written works made a forceful comeback.

Eugenio Garin, the leading Italian Renaissance historian, confirms the great influence exercised by the rediscovery of Hermetic treatises on thinkers of the time:

"In the 1400s the new image of man gained awareness and characteristic dimensions under the sign of Hermes Trismegistus, and now modelled itself on the guidelines determined in Hermetic books. Now, much as it might be legitimate, and even necessary, to establish a clear distinction between the Poemandres and the Asclepius and theological works on one side, and the countless magic-alchemical treatises on the other, it is also true that the thin and deep underground tie joining the former and the occult, astrological and alchemical tradition of the latter (this was clearly emphasised by Festugière) should not be forgotten. The agreement lies in the idea of a universe that is entirely alive and made up by hidden correspondences, occult sympathies and pervaded by spirits. The beautiful opening passage of the Asclepius, which had already tried to seduce the old Fathers of the Church, once again resonated solemnly: 'great miracle is man, worthy of honour and veneration'. Even before that the divine Marsilio turned these words into Latin, and his friend Tommaso Benci from Latin into Tuscan, the strict humanist Salutati bowed to him; the moderate Giannozzo Manetti commemorated him through Lattanzio; in the end Ficino turned it into an appeal and a programme. The tradition of the Poemandres crossed not only Italy but Europe too; it redeemed the underground and mysterious Hermetic doctrine; it turned into a new cult. According to Pico the miraculous character of man lies in his peculiar suspension right in the middle of the definite reason of things, meaning that somehow nature, all beings, all finite reasons depend on his decision." [161]

Hermeticism thus experienced a great comeback from the Late Middle Ages to the end of the 18th century and its influence not only manifested itself in Italian Neoplatonists and Paracelsus, but also across the Channel: its presence will be found in the works of English alchemist John Dee, Elias Ashmole, Robert Fludd and even, as we will observe later, in scientist Isaac Newton.

Hermeticism in Freemasonry Studies

The study of the influence of Hermetic thought on Freemasonry often leads to controversial conclusions. Furthermore, whereas on the European mainland there was never a shortage of studies on the subject, the English speaking Masonic historiography, on the contrary, always somewhat disregarded the Hermetic thought. Curiously, in the documents of the famous *Quatuor Coronati* Research Lodge in London, mentioned several times in this book, an article on Hermeticism made its appearance, with other

161 Eugenio Garin, *Medioevo e Rinascimento*, Laterza, Bari, 1998, pages 144-145.

esoteric articles, in 1886, in the first issue of the journal entitled *Freemasonry and Hermeticism*[162] by the Rev. A.F.A. Woodford; strangely, it was over a century later that another article on the subject was published, *Freemasonry, Hermetic Thought and the Royal Society of London,*[163] dated 1996, written by Michael Baigent, which highlights a clear change within the renowned English Research Lodge, moving from initial *esoteric-initiatic* studies towards purely, or rather exclusively, *historical-documentary* ones.

Baigent's text offers interesting cues confirming the theory of an influence exercised by the Hermetic thought on Freemasonry; indeed, the author highlights symbolic limks between Freemasonry and Renaissance Hermeticism, with significant references to the symbolism of the Royal Arch, stating:

"Modern Masonic ritual and symbolism has inherited much of importance from this tradition: the Architect of the Universe, as is well known, is first mentioned by Plato in his Timaeus, a work of particular significance to Renaissance Hermeticism. The all-seeing eye, or the tetragrammaton, within a blazing triangle, a symbol common in Freemasonry since the eighteenth century, was widely used to illustrate Hermetic texts of the fifteenth, sixteenth and seventeenth centuries. It symbolised the triple expression of the one Deity from which all life and form radiated.

The Royal Arch, that repository for much early material, contains a particularly clear example of Hermetic symbolism: the two interlocked triangles, the so-called hexalpha, which has been so prominent on its jewels since the earliest known example of 1766. This symbol has long been common in Hermetic circles: it represents the dynamic significance of macrocosm and microcosm – the triangle of heaven reaching downwards, that of man reaching upwards. This is the Hermetic symbol par excellence. It seems an inescapable conclusion that, at some point, Freemasonry absorbed material from the Renaissance Hermetic tradition. Material which altered its nature and which provided a basis both for its later ritual and its moral symbolism."[164]

Baigent later discusses what is referred to as Elias Ashmole's "Hermetic" initiation, a subject already discussed in a previous chapter, not to be confused with his "Masonic" initiation, carried out five years earlier, in 1646, which is regarded as the first documented initiation of a "speculative" Freemason. In this regard Baigent explains: *"In the introduction to his Theatrum Chemicum Britannicum he states that the alchemist, 'rejoyceth not so much that he can make Gold and Silver as that he sees the heavens open'. My reason for dwelling upon this is that I wish to make it clear that all mention of 'Hermetic' or 'Alchemical' works are essentially describing equivalents, that is, they both refer to the same perspective upon reality; texts using either term are, so to speak, synoptic. Elias Ashmole famously received his initiation into*

162 Rev. A.F.A. Woodford, *Freemasonry and Hermeticism*, AQC Vol.I, 1886.

163 Michael Baigent, *Freemasonry, Hermetic Thought and the Royal Society of London,* AQC Vol.109, 1996.

164 Michael Baigent, op. cit., page 155.

Freemasonry at Warrington, 16 October 1646 at 4.30 in the afternoon. His hermetic initiation came five years afterwards. What can we deduce from this? Surely, given his comment, it is that whatever he received in his Hermetic initiation was something other than that which he had received in his Masonic initiation. Such was his desire for Hermetic knowledge that, after the latter, he had continued searching for another five years. It is, then, reasonable to conclude that speculative Freemasonry of the type mentioned by Ashmole in 1646 did not contain anything of hermetic importance, even though Ashmole, given his life-long dedication to Hermetic philosophy, might well have had the expectation of learning something of that sort. As I have argued with my examination of Elias Ashmole's Hermetic initiation, 1651 would appear to provide the earliest possible date for the inclusion of the Hermetic strand into Freemasonry".[165]

Yet again in a British context, the opinion of the renowned English scholar Tobias Churton, expert in Gnostic Studies, who, in his book *Freemasonry: The Reality*, described an interesting parallelism between Hermeticism and the Three Degrees of Freemasonry, appears noteworthy:

"Masons today might look to the tragic drama that is enacted in the third degree and contemplate the meaning of the 'lost secrets' or 'Lost Word'. A tragedy has occurred. The original unity has been lost. Therefore, the aim of the most essential Hermetic philosophy is to re-awaken the gnosis that resides in man as his immortal component, the knowledge of the original divine nature. Surely, this Hermetic philosophy makes perfect sense of the three degrees, as we currently know them. We begin with purification – the candidate enters the cosmos in a poor benighted, blind state. A door is opened to him; he learns the call of his neighbours upon his heart and the presence of a larger universe than his unenlightened, or unopened, self.

As a fellow, he approaches illumination – he learns the seven liberal arts (geometry, grammar, logic, music, mathematics, rhetoric, and astronomy), these pillars of arts and sciences vouchsafed by Hermes' legendary discovery of antediluvian wisdom.

Thirdly: benediction of the spirit – transformation. He learns how to die, and that to know how to die is to know how to live. Through the veil, beneath the Arch, beyond the pillars is eternal life." [166]

A comprehensive definition of Hermeticism from a Masonic point of view is undoubtedly offered by scholar Mariano Bianca, who in this regard states that: *"It can be said that Hermeticism is an esoteric theologisation of Plotinus' philosophy expressed in the Enneads with the addition of elements of Egyptian culture and the introduction of the notion of initiation, Nous or Supreme Intellect, which cannot be related to a personalised deity. Hermeticism is not a synonym for Esotericism and Hermetic thought can be considered a specific Esoteric conception: this*

165 Michael Baigent, op. cit., pages 157-158.
166 Tobias Churton, *Freemasonry: The Reality*, Lewis Masonic, Hersham, 2007, pages 133-134.

is the case particularly because it revolves around the notion of initiation, meaning that access to the dimension of the invisible and beyond does not cross through theological dogmas and attitudes of faith, but rather through the commitment of single persons, perhaps even with a revelation, which takes place through a learning practice. Access to this dimension is thus not granted to man but can be referred to as Noetic because it is based on the use of human intellect."[167] It is clear that Bianca's thesis is centred around the concept of *Nous*, as he continues:

"Working to the Glory of the Great Architect of the Universe implies that one is able to do so, with adequate instruments, meaning that man possesses these instruments and that the latter are of the same nature of what one wants to know: this instrument is the intellect that characterises the Noetic-Gnostic conception of Hermeticists and that represents the central core of Masonry. It should then be emphasised that the divine essence of man lies in the fact that he shares the Nous in the strict sense that the man's intellect is of the same nature as the Nous as the first and organising principle of the cosmos in the above-mentioned meaning" subsequently reaching the conclusion that "Hermeticism and Masonic doctrine are both of Noetic nature." Indeed, "The learning or Gnostic valence of the Hermetic doctrine is also the element that characterises the Masonic Esoteric method: for the Masonic doctrine the core of all intellective and practical activities is man, or rather the single individual, but the latter is a being endowed with intellect, which, although of an ultra subjective nature, is the only thing that allows him to investigate by himself, the reality surrounding him and the dimension of the invisible and beyond."[168]

Did Hermetic Communities Actually Exist?

Numerous scholars, among them Reizenstein and Geffcken, and subsequently Fowden, viewed Hermeticism as a true *religious brotherhood*, with its rituals, symbols and liturgy. In this community the *Corpus Hermeticum* was used to represent their Sacred Scriptures.

This hypothesis was however strenuously rejected by Festugière on the basis of the fact that the presence in the hermetic movement of two substantially opposed Gnostic doctrines, in his opinion virtually impossible to reconcile, would have hampered the development of a joint community. Moreover, in Festugière's opinion, the documents available provide no evidence of any form of *hierarchical* organisation or of a progressively initiatic system.

We have previously seen the questionability of practising within a rigid doctrinal dichotomy between the two hermeticforms; personally I would therefore not exclude *a priori* the possibility that the followers of Hermeticism may have been organised in communities. Indeed, it is an acknowledged fact that they gathered in a sanctuary and

167 Mariano Bianca, *Ermetismo noetico e dottrina massonica*, in *Le radici esoteriche della Massoneria*, Atanòr, Rome, 2001, page 16.
168 Ibid. pages 20-23.

adhered to the rule of silence, maintaining the secret as to the revelations received, and let us not forget the representation of a baptism in a basin, cited in several texts, which resembles the customs used previously by Mystery societies.

The aims of these groups, if they indeed existed, were to seek a Divine *intuition* without resorting to the intervention of a religion contemplating a personal god, practically relying on a totalitarian understanding of the Universe.

With regard to the existence of hermetic communities, A.D. Nock, who together with Festugière compiled possibly the most famous edition of the *Corpus Hermeticum,* writes in the Preface:

"But did a Hermetic religion or Hermetic clique ever truly exist? We have often asked this question, and this issue is in many ways similar to those raised by Orphism. In both cases it is certain that a sacred literature existed; in both cases there is a 'lifestyle', specific forms of prayer and praise to god, in both cases there is a conscious separation from the earthly world, in both cases there are individuals who assign considerable value to the 'Pathway' and in seeking to communicate this to other men and thus render them similar. There are however several differences: Hermeticism does not comprise purifications, ceremonies that cleanse the individual from sin, or certain practices aimed at producing a divine epiphany which are frequently associated with Orpheus in later hymns: the Hermetic Mysteries alone are the 'Mysteries of the Logos', thus eliciting a marked disgust towards the popular cult." [169]

Indeed, unless new documents should come to light, the problem of their existence will remain open to debate.

The Orthopraxy of Hermeticism

In addition to the dichotomy between "learned" and "popular" Hermeticism, Festugière has highlighted the presence of another two types in the books that gave life to Hermetic thought. A gnosis with optimistic connotations according to which matter is steeped in God, and consequently, as God is present in all things and contemplates and understands the entire Universe, man may assume the likeness of God. The other, featuring pessimistic characteristics, emphasises a gnosis which purveys a representation of evil in the material world and persuades man to avoid all contact with materials, thus choosing an ascetic life. This division likewise attracts both supporters and opposers.

However, the aspect of Hermeticism that I would like to underline here, as a source of inspiration for Freemasonry, is linked to its manifestation not as an *orthodox* religion, but rather as an *orthopraxis*, a "Method" by means of which Hermeticists, in the same way as Freemasons, were permitted to reach God in the Gnostic sense.

169 A D Nock, Prefazione al Corpus Hermeticum, Bompiani, Milano, 2004, pp 14-15

In this regard, Mariano Bianca, in a remarkable introduction to a book by Antoine Faivre, *I Volti di Ermete* writes:

"The hermetism of the Hermeticists, in the same way as all other forms of esotericism, is characterised by a knowledge that does not convey a theoretical gnoseological, ontological or metaphysical but rather conjugates the theoretical aspect with the 'practical' side, thus resulting in a gnosis which is at the same time a theoretical framework and the delineation of a method and a praxis which allow the user to be permeated with theoretic contents, in this way achieving a specific ontological condition (initiate) but also of being comprised in the ontological dimension to which this ontology is related, i.e. a dimension of the beyond, of intimacy and the divine. The hermetic pathway indicated by Hermes is thus a pathway devoted to the 'sacred' viewed as a dimension in which man realises himself through the understanding and use of the word, penetrates his essence as an integral part of the divine and, through the hermeneutic revelation of the signatura rerum and regeneration succeeds in placing himself in the dimension of the intellect and is thus rendered equal to god; only in this way shall he succeed in comprehending and in partaking in that which maintains the cosmos in a continuum of the creation." [170]

This *orthopraxis* therefore is aimed at achieving "deification", becoming God, a concept which is reiterated repeatedly in the *Corpus Hermeticum*:

"Thrice-greatest Hermes pronounces – Behold what power, what swiftness, thou dost have! And canst thou do all of these things, and God not? Then, in this way know God; as having all things in Himself as thoughts, the whole Cosmos itself. If, then, thou dost not make thyself like unto God, thou canst not know Him. For like is knowable unto like. Make thyself to grow to the same stature as the Greatness which transcends all measure; leap forth from every body; transcend all time; become Eternity, and shalt thou know God. Conceiving nothing is impossible unto thyself, think thyself deathless and able to know all — all arts, all sciences, the way of every life. Become more lofty than all height, and lower than all depth. Collect into thyself all senses of creatures — of fire, water, dry and moist. Think that thou art at the same time in every place — in earth, in sea, in sky; not yet begotten, in the womb, young, old, dead, in after-death conditions. And if thou knowest all these things at once - times, places, doings, qualities, and quantities; thou canst know God." [171]

This *identification* between man and God is masterfully defined by the German-Swiss scholar Titus Burkhardt:

"The perspective of Hermetism proceeds from the view that the universe (or macrocosm) and man (or the microcosm) correspond to one another as reflections; whatever there is in the one, must also in some manner be present in the other. This correspondence may best be understood by reducing it to the mutual relationship of subject and object of knower and

170 Mariano Bianca, *Introduction to* Antoine Faivre, *I volti di Ermete*, Atanòr, Rome, 2001, pages 9-10.

171 *Corpus Hermeticum*, Book XI, 20.

known. The world as object appears in the mirror of the human subject. Though these two poles may be distinguished theoretically, they nevertheless cannot be separated: each one can only be conceived in relation to the other first and foremost there is the Universal Intellect, whose object is not only the outward physical world, but also the inner world of the soul; nevertheless, in every knowledge, however much of it may be coloured by the individual or the species, there is something unconditional. Without the presence of intellect there would be no truth and unity as seen by so many and so widely varying individuals. All things considered, the hermetic doctrine of universal intellect coincides with the doctrine of Plato using a similar language: "The Intellect (nous) – teaches Hermes Trismegistus – derives from the Substance (ousia) of God, in so far as one may speak of God as having a substance, of what nature this substance is, God alone can know exactly. The Intellect is not a part of the Substance of God, but radiates from the latter as light shines forth from the sun. In human beings this Intellect is God... The image could not be clearer: as the light radiates from the sun at no detriment to the latter, intellect proceeds from the divine substance without causing the latter to lose its sovereignty and transcendental nature, and how the reality of the light and the sun is fully embodied in the sun, so that there is nothing but the sun. The Intellect in some way is God: Man himself, the most perfect cosmic reflection, is God." [172]

In Hermetic communities, the initiate undertook a pathway of inner *transformation* and *perfection* through the learning of "Mysteries", "Secrets", "Occult Truths" and "Nature" in a context of dynamic that underline the *unity* of all things.

Book VII of the *Corpus Hermeticum* refers to an allegory that closely resembles that of *freeing oneself* of the "metals", an action that is *imposed* on the initiate during the Ceremony of Initiation; this allegory should be construed, in both cases, as a rejection of contemptible material things, and particularly *conditioning* of this nature. The text underlines the concept with great clarity:

"Such is the hateful cloak thou wearest — that throttles thee and holds thee down to it, in order that thou may'st not gaze above, and having seen the Beauty of the Truth, and Good that dwells therein, detest the bad of it; having found out the plot that it hath schemed against thee, by making void of sense those seeming things which men think senses. For that it hath with mass of matter blocked them up and crammed them full of loathsome lust, so that thou may'st not hear about the things that thou should'st hear, nor see the things thou should'st see." [173]

It is moreover of interest to observe how Hermeticism assumes a decisive stance of condemnation of atheism, one of the *Landmarks* of Freemasonry. In Book XII, Hermes Trismegistus in addressing Tat says: *"The great ill of the soul is godlessness; then followeth*

172 Titus Burckhardt, *Alchimia,* Arché, Milan, 2005, pages 27-30.
173 *Corpus Hermeticum*, Book VII, 3.

fancy for all evil things and nothing," [174] and in Book IX entitled *On Thought and Sense* Thrice-greatest Hermes says to Asclepius: *"To understand is to believe, to not believe is not to understand. My word (logos) doth go before [thee] to the truth. But mighty is the mind, and when it hath been led by word up to a certain point, it hath the power to come before thee to the truth. And having thought o'er all these things, and found them consonant with those which have already been translated by the reason, it hath e'en now believed, and found its rest in that Fair Faith."* [175]

A further interesting similarity with Freemasonry can be observed in Book VI, traditionally referred to under the title of *In God Alone is Good and Elsewhere Nowhere*. This book compares a decidedly pessimistic gnosis, stating that Good is to be found in God alone, whilst the world represents Evil, explaining how the sole means of reaching God is through the *piety of knowledge*. The book recites: *"As, then, thou dost conceive of God, conceive the Beautiful and Good. For they cannot be joined with aught of other things that live, since they can never be divorced from God. One is the Path that leadeth unto It — Devotion joined with Gnosis."* [176] This link between gnosis and piety is present in Freemasonry, as uttered by the Most Worshipful Master to the Candidate during the Initiation Ceremony, in underlining how Freemasonry was established: *"...on the most pure principles of piety and virtue"*, where virtue is clearly to be intended as a Masonic gnosis.

I shall now examine the Books viewed as true initiatic "pathways", the *Poemandres*, Book XIII of the *Corpus Hermeticum*, the *Asclepius*, *Kore Kosmou*, the *Ogdoad* and the *Ennead*.

The Poemandres

This is the first of the fifteen books that make up the *Corpus Hermeticum*. In the book the *Nous-God* is represented as sharing the likeness of Poemandres who came to reveal the divine wisdom to Hermes. In the creation of the world that followed the apparition of Poemandres there are marked similarities with the *Book of Genesis*.

The appearance of Poemandres, the *Nous* or acting intellect, paralysed Trismegistus into a state of catatonic torpor. Trismegistus subsequently asked Poemandres to be able to gain knowledge of the nature of all things and of God, thus producing a mutation in Poemandres who, following the manifestation of a shining light turns to Trismegistus and says: *"That Light, He said, am I, thy God, Mind, prior to Moist Nature which appeared from Darkness; the Light-Word (Logos) [that appeared] from Mind is the Son of God."*

174 *Corpus Hermeticum*, Book XII, 3.
175 *Corpus Hermeticum*, Book IX, 10.
176 *Corpus Hermeticum*, Book VII, 5.

The *Demiurge-Nous* created by Poemandres following unification with the Word instructs the Seven Governors on how to manage the elementary lower world they are responsible for. Here, the *Logos* represents a *hypostasis* comparable to the *Word* referred to by John in the Prologue to his *Gospel*. The *Demiurge* is capable of creating by instilling the principle of life represented by breath and fire, as generated by God who is both One and Two, male and female, light and life. The theme of creation therefore is: the *Logos* of *Nous* contributes towards the task of creation; it is present in the created world as the divine Word of the world, but the *Demiurge* alone is the force and creative action. The *Logos* and the *Demiurge* have the same divine substance: both take part in the creation although remaining unfailingly more than this.

Poemandres subsequently explains to Trismegistus that as he is of the same nature as the Father, in order to understand Him he should first aim to understand all about himself. *"If then thou learnest that thou art thyself of Life and Light, and that thou [happenest] to be out of them, thou shalt return again to Life."* These words convey how for the Hermetic school of thought the immortal part of man continues to preserve his *divine* characteristics, determined chiefly by his intellect, although once again the fundamental concept of "Light", the fulcrum of all initiatic processes comes to the fore. Accordingly, Françoise Bonardel writes:

"In the Poemandres, revealing an infinite luminescence, the Nous-God who is the only 'light' and the only 'life' does not merely invite us to contemplate a sight: he generates the appearance of a vision of light and awakens man to awareness in himself of the luminescent nature of the Nous-God. The light is not content with illuminating the material but by being born thanks to a glimpse of a vision, it transfigures the same, reawakens a memory of its origin and a desire to return. This signifies how there was once a separation, a removal. This theme, common to the majority of Gnostic themes, dose not however in the Poemandres assume the dramatic connotations observed, for example, in the Pistis Sophia or Valentine. The second part of this Gnosis was the creation by the Nous-God of a Nous-Demiurge. The God of fire and breath, he in turn generated the Archons who enclose the sensitive world in circles; the government of the latter is known as Fate. In a parallel manner the Nous-God created Man in his image and entrusted Creation unto Him. However, seduced by the work of the demiurge, man too wished to create." [177]

Man, however, following creation in his image by the *Nous*, broke the outer circumference of the planetary circles and turned to Nature which in turn fell in love with the Human Being. Thus, man descended to earth triggering the irreversible mechanism of the "fall" which will result in his having two characteristics; a mortal bodily characteristic and an immortal one through his soul.

177 Françoise Bonardel, *La Via Ermetica*, Atanòr, Rome, 1998, page 41.

I have mentioned previously the similarities with the *Genesis*, and would like to emphasise how, although in the text of the Old Testament, on his first introduction to the world man is appointed co-creator with God, in the Poemandres, on the contrary, God turns his works over to man almost involuntarily.

The Book clearly contains features indicating an initiatic process, underlined terminologically at the time in which Trismegistus refers to the *Nous* and asks for clarification of the means by which to "ascend" to the Divine:

"Well hast thou taught me all, as I desired, O Mind. And now, pray, tell me further of the nature of the Way Above as now it is." [178]

Indeed, the term used is that of "ascent", a term present in the Masonic ritual during one of the culminanting stages, the ceremony of Installation of a Most Worshipful Master, the apex of the initiatic process.

The initiatic process and its conclusion in the "vision of God", or rather "deification", are excellently described towards the end of the book:

"And then, with all the energisings of the Harmony stript from him, clothed in his proper Power, he cometh to that Nature which belongs unto the Eighth, and there with those-that-are hymneth the Father. They who are there welcome his coming there with joy; and he, made like to them that sojourn there, doth further hear the Powers who are above the Nature that belongs unto the Eighth, singing their songs of praise to God in language of their own. And then they, in a band, go to the Father home; of their own selves they make surrender of themselves to Powers, and [thus] becoming Powers they are in God. This the good end for those who have gained Gnosis—to be made one with God." [179]

Book XIII

This book illustrates a true *esoteric-initiatic* dynamic, referring to the transmission of a "Mystery", seen not as a rite of cult, but rather as an actual *doctrinal secret* inaccessible to the profane.

Tat asks Trismegistus to be initiated into the doctrine of regeneration, as he has already been appropriately prepared and is now ready to receive the conclusive "Mysteries" and terminate his initiatic pathway. Tat says:

"Wherefore I got me ready and made the thought in me a stranger to the world of illusion. And now do thou fill up the things that fall short in me with what thou saidst would give me the tradition of Rebirth, setting it forth in speech or in the secret way.

178 *Corpus Hermeticum*, Book I, 24.
179 *Corpus Hermeticum*, Book I, 26.

I know not, O Thrice-greatest one, from out what matter and what womb Man comes to birth, or of what seed." [180]

On achieving knowledge of God, Trismegistus informs Tat of the other forms of knowledge that have been bestowed upon him: *"Now fourth, on Continence I call, the Power against Desire. This step, my son, is Righteousness' firm seat, Power sixth I call to us – that against Avarice, Sharing-with-all"*.[181]

The text lists three of the four *Cardinal Virtues*, the presence of which is requested of the Aspirant to Masonic Initiation in the Exhortation that follows Initiation, with the Most Worshipful Master informing the Initiate: *"As an individual, let me recommend the practice of every domestic as well as public virtue: let prudence direct you, Temperance chasten you, Fortitude support you, and Justice be the guide of all your actions."*

The Asclepius

This book, handed down in the Latin language, describes the rituals by means of which the Egyptians were able to transfer the creative power of the cosmos within the statues that represented their deities.

The *Asclepius* commences with a scene in which Hermes Trismegistus, Asclepius, Tat and Amon are inside a temple concentrated on performing a ritual to evoke the presence of God. Hermes starts to speak on behalf of the god who, having been evoked, appears and explains how all descends from the One who represents the Everything, underlining how man, *magnum miracolum*, through his *intellect*, is capable of achieving a divine nature in the same way as if he were a god.

Subsequently, turning to Asclepius, Trismegistus explains how man, in the same way as God, may succeed in instilling life into the statues of his deities, even performing prodigious acts, predicting the future, or punishing men by casting upon them illnesses or misfortunes or, conversely, by healing them or bestowing good fortune.

The sheer elitist nature of the initiatic process is clearly underlined:

"Some, then, though they be very few, endowed with the Pure Mind, have been entrusted with the sacred charge of contemplating Heaven. Whereas those men who, from the two-fold blending of their nature, have not as yet withdrawn their inner reason from their body's mass, these are appointed for the study of the elements, and all that is below them."[182] Further on, in the paragraph entitled "The Mightiness of man, provided with intellect", we read: *"But this can only be averred of a few men endowed with pious*

180 *Corpus Hermeticum*, Book XIII, 1.
181 *Corpus Hermeticum*, Book XIII, 9.
182 The *Asclepius*, 9.

minds. Still, of the rest, the visions, we ought to say no word, for fear a very sacred sermon should be spoiled by thinking of them." [183]

The book is frequently criticised, as highlighted by the scholar Claudio Moreschini, in view of its deficient logical structure and for a somewhat muddle sense of harmony. According to Moreschini: *"This is one of those compositions that make use of the literary fiction of a religious 'revelation' and thus assume an asystematic tone and trend. The author is aware he is creating a work to be used in imparting a mystery, and underlines this fact as frequently as he can. The Asclepius is the revelation of a mystery that the initiate learns in order to achieve gnosis."* [184] Subsequently, Moreschini emphasises how, at the end of the "ritual" teaching, the text provides an actual "agape", an "agape" which, similar to Freemasonry, as an integral part of the ceremony, it should rightly be termed "ritual". The scholar writes in this regard: *"The Master and the disciples, on terminating the lessons, prepare for a pura et sine animali bus caena, during a supper aimed not at conveying a pleasure of the senses, but which represents a choice of life."* [185]

Kore Kosmou

This remarkable and poetic book, featuring a particularly close association with Egyptian mythology, illustrates a sacred dialogue between Isis and Horus, his son. The dialogue is reported by an unknown narrator who acts as a backdrop to the theme of the "fall" and the punishment of the soul. Isis tells her son of the various phases of creation and of the divine intervention aimed at saving the world from the ignorance in which it is steeped. To achieve this aim, God sends Hermes Trismegistus, his *emanation*, to earth. Hermes has been entrusted with writing the sacred scriptures of revelation and concealing them; however, after having viewed the beauty of the Universe and prior to his ascent to heaven, he left Tat-Asclepius, his son, all his knowledge so that this could be transmitted to the chosen few. Subsequently, Tat hid the sacred symbols of the cosmic elements *"with the secret objects of Osiris"*.

Isis and her husband Osiris are represented as the decipherers of the ancient scriptures of Hermes and are sent as the second *emanation* of God to teach men of civilisation and to find the "secrets" that Hermes had concealed.

The story is lacking in order and is muddled. Indeed, after having sent Hermes to earth, God assigns the celestial vaults to the souls and bestows on the latter the ability to create according to the model of the zodiac. The souls therefore create the animals but, overcome

183 The *Asclepius*, 23.

184 Claudio Moreschini, *Storia dell'ermetismo cristiano*, Morcelliana, Brescia, 2000, page 115.

185 Ibid. page 16.

by pride, disobey God and wander from the celestial vaults to which they have been assigned and are thus punished by God who orders that Hermes create man. God however promises the penitent souls an "ascent" to heaven. This "incorporation" of the souls and the tension surrounding a return to the Divine is a singular Gnostic characteristic of the book.

Gnosis is accordingly represented as an essential element in the "deification", as emphasised by Françoise Bonardel:

"The revelation provided by the vision is not sufficient to ensure the originality of hermeticism, but does however allow us to deem it a gnosis. The notions of gnosis and revelation seem to become muddled here, as knowledge (Gnosis) is conferred on the disciple through a revelatory vision providing access to the invisible, turns him into an initiate and shows him the road to salvation. Hermeticism, in the same way as alchemy, certainly implies the revealing, transmission and interpretation of a discreet number of texts by a 'master' to a few disciples prepared appropriately. It should not moreover be overlooked how the revelation contained in the great books of the Corpus constitute a supreme gnosis, i.e. the esoteric science that guarantees salvation; the mere fact of having understood and assimilated the same corresponds in itself to initiation." [186]

Knowledge, that particular type of gnosis that the Hermetic texts aim to impart, however you wish to define it, is represented by the knowledge imparted by the *Nous,* and is therefore not presented merely as a knowledge taught and learnt, but rather as an awakening of awareness, a sudden illumination that from a state of ignorance provides the certainty that God exists and wishes to be known. In the Hermetic books this aspect is revealed first by Poemandres to Hermes, then by Hermes to Asclepius, and so on. It is to be intended as a true *maieutic process*, a cognitive process that brings to the light a truth which is already present within us.

The Ogdoad

A series of Coptic translations written on papyrus of the philosophical and theological Greek works bearing gnostic and hermetic connotations was discovered in 1945 in the vicinity of Nag Hammadi. Among the hermetic documents there is one of particular interest, the *Discourse on the Ogdoad and the Ennead*, the contents and style of which largely resemble those of Book XIII of the *Corpus Hermeticum*. Both the Coptic and the Greek texts highlight an evident pathway towards the *divinisation* and *elevation* of the man who passes through meditation, prayer and initiation in the Mysteries.

The *Ogdoad* is deemed a paradigmatic example of that which the renowned scholar of Hermeticism Garth Fowden defined a *"Hermetic text of initiation"*,[187] a pedagogic

186 Françoise Bonardel, op. cit.., page 38.
187 Garth Fowden, *The Egyptian Hermes*, Cambridge University Press, 1986, pages 97-99.

and philosophical initiatic pathway which, in the latter stages of the process, leads to awareness in the initiate of his true nature and his union with the Divine.

The *Ogdoad* and the *Ennead* indeed represent the final parts, the eighth and the ninth, of a spiritual development proceded, naturally, by seven other stages. The book does not describe all the stages, although it is implied that in order to attain the final two stages, the candidate should have lived a pure life and, above all, removed ignorance and replaced it with the knowledge imparted in the specific texts.

The entrance of the initiate into the *Ennead* represents a ritual in itself, and concludes with the *pronunciation* of the mysterious name of God in the form of invocations which are supervised by Hermes, acting as a "mystagogue".

The book opens with the disciple reminding Hermes of his promise to raise him to the *Ogdoad* and *Ennead*, and being given a positive reply by Hermes who deems the disciple as being "intellectually" ready, underlining moreover how the inner growth of the initiate is produced by the teachings imparted from the books. Following the prayers conducted under the exhortation of Hermes to perform these with "*the mind, heart and soul*", a verbal sequence commences followed by a request to see the image of truth. On having reached a state of *ecstasy*, Hermes is begged by the disciple to assist him in achieving this visible ecstasy, with Hermes then requesting that to achieve this aim he utters a silent prayer; finally the disciple achieves *ecstasy*: the vision of the *Ogdoad*, the *Ennead* and, lastly, of God himself.

In this *initiatic* process we may clearly observe the same dynamics present in Masonic Initiation, with the initiate undertaking the process in a condition of "obscurity" requesting access to the Mysteries, after having undergone an appropriate preparation (gnosis) and having obtained the Light, concluding his Initiation with a prayer.

In the Middle Ages other volumes of interest and of relevance to the purpose of the present study regarding hermetic connotations came to light, including a text dating back to the twelfth century, the *Liber XXIV philosophorum*, published by Clemens Baeumker, in which we may read the words: *"God is a sphere the centre of which is everywhere and the circumference of which is nowhere."* [188] In this book the symbology of the *Centre*, obviously representing God, resembles the symbol present in the Masonic rituals in which the *Centre*, the Divine symbol, is *"a point within a circle, from which every part of the circumference is equidistant."* [189]

188 *Liber XXIV philosophorum*, published by Clemens Baeumker, Das pseudo-hermetische 'Buch der XXIV Meister', "Beiträge zur Geschichte der Philosophie und Theologie des Mitteralters", fasc. XXV, Münster, 1928. The second proposition of this study describes God as a "sphaera infinita cuius centrum est ubique, circumferentia nusquam". Cfr. Koyré, op. cit., pp.18, 279 (note 19).

189 Emulation Ritual, page 32.

Chapter Three

The Neoplatonist Roots

Withdraw within yourself and examine yourself. If you do not therein discover beauty, do as the artist, who cuts off, polishes, purifies until he has adorned his statue with all the marks of beauty. Remove from your soul therefore all that is superfluous, straighten all that is crooked, purify and illuminate what is obscure, and do not cease perfecting your statue until the divine resplendence of virtue shines forth upon your sight. But if you try to fix on it an eye soiled by vice, an eye that is impure, or weak, so as not to be able to support the splendour of so brilliant an object, that eye will see nothing, not even if it were shown a sight easy to grasp. The organ of vision will have first to be rendered analogous and similar to the object it is to contemplate. Never would the eye have seen the sun unless first it had assumed its form; likewise, the soul could never see beauty, unless she herself first became beautiful.

Plotinus
Enneads, I, 6, verses 8 & 9

1. Neoplatonism versus Illuminism

In the context of historic and social studies the presence of a form of cultural isolation of Freemasonry is becoming increasingly evident. This is totally incomprehensible, it is important that we examine the reasons underlying this lack of consideration.

As observed in the previous chapters, the historic interpretations put forward have frequently manifested *conceptual* errors in the approaches taken in studying the origins, the initiatic nature and the ethical principles of Freemasonry.

These incorrect interpretations have contributed increasingly towards Freemasonry being deemed by western culture one of the mere "folklore" manifestations. A return therefore to the "sources" that guided those who, presumably in the mid-seventeenth century, created Freemasonry, should assist us in discrediting several blatant inaccuracies, and once again restore the historic ideals of Freemasonry to the place they deserve.

In the light of these premises, the diversity of opinions expressed over the last hundred years with regard to the *historico-philosophic* origins of Freemasonry is so vast that in addressing the issue one may well be overcome by a sense of profound confusion. Some of these opinions, as mentioned previously, are somewhat arbitrary and frequently groundless, whilst others may simply reflect the thoughts of their authors.

The latter comprises, as observed previously, the belief that as Freemasonry is an "Initiatic Society" aimed at achieving a *progressive* perfection of ethics and morals, and that this premise is extremely depreciative of the "Art" itself, in view of its rationalist and neoliberal nature, it is undoubtedly inspired by Illuminist philosophy.

However, as we are well aware, Empiricism and Illuminist rationalism take into account only that which can be *measured*, is real, whilst Freemasonry is transmitted by means of "allegories" and "symbols"; "symbols" and "allegories" represent the state of being something *beyond* the apparent. Indeed, the figure conceals a mysterious message which cannot be perceived through mere observation, but only through *intuition;* we are now in the field of *transcendent metaphysics*.

In this chapter I shall once again focus on the origins of Masonic thought, whilst attempting however to avoid unwarranted exhortations and striving to provide a substantially objective interpretation of the information available so as to contribute towards a better understanding of the complex phenomenon of Freemasonry.

In association with the *Traditional* "forms" that have inspired Freemasonry, including "Mystery societies", and Hermeticism, all discussedearlier, the rediscovery and revisitation of Neoplatonic thought have likewise played a key role. Thus, in view of the complexity of the issues to be discussed, I have opted to devote a separate chapter to this subject.

By embarking on a philosophical pathway with ethics, particularly Neoplatonist ethics, constituting the departure point based on a transcendent foundation, we will subsequently reach the origins of a *"system of morality veiled in allegory and illustrated by means of symbols"* that represents the Ethics of Freemasonry and characterises particularly the stage of its birth.

On referring to the "philosophy of Freemasonry" one wonders whether Masonic thought should be classified as philosophical or whether this should rather be identified simply with an ethical and moral code of conduct, an *orthopraxis* which is not based on any organic system of thought.

There is no doubt that Masonic thought bears witness to a series of *esoteric* and *philosophic* movements, both those from which it has stemmed and those which, over time, have inevitably left their mark. However, in spite of the above, Masonic thought cannot be viewed as either an ecletism or a form of syncretism. Indeed, in my opinion, it features the characteristics of an innovative project that attributes a new meaning to the ancient doctrines.

The essence of Masonic thought, its cutting-edge feature, is represented by the new significance conveyed to the constituents and, particularly, its originality which is not disclosed by the materials employed, but rather in its "design" as a whole.

If you dismantled the *esoteric-initiatic* system of Freemasonry you would discover in all its parts, even of the smallest dimensions, an element which although possibly not definable as a true "source", would include some sort of archetype, or model, or root strongly resembling a source. Indeed, throughout the centuries Freemasonry has developed its esoteric philosophy by relying extensively on the use of pre-existing elements; its originality however is represented by the new meaning that the final outcome has conveyed to the single features. Therefore, as commented by the Irish scholar Eric Dodds in referring to Neoplatonism, its true originality is not constituted by the materials used, but rather by the design itself.[190]

Therefore, I shall attempt to identify in the Neoplatonist doctrines the origin of the ideas that have animated the aspirations of mankind towards a better future through the awareness and independent thought that underlie the concept of *human dignity*. Accordingly, our journey will commence with a key player in Italian Humanism, Giovanni Pico della Mirandola, who developed one of the key thoughts of Neoplatonism: human nature encloses the essence of all other creatures and thus man is *likened* only to God who embraces the start of all things and substances.

As we will see, Renaissance Neoplatonism spread from Italy to other nations throughout Central and Western Europe. The general model adhered to appears to be a "readaptation" rather than a mere imitation, thus explaining why in several countries Neoplatonism has developed with a series of differences.

Which symbols or allegories best portray the *influence* of Neoplatonist philosophy on Masonic thought? The documents most suited to demonstrating the analogies between Neoplatonist and Masonic principles and symbols are undeniably the rituals themselves.

It is an acknowledged fact that in its Medieval form Freemasonry was a predominantly practical, or "operative" movement; there was no particular emphasis on *philosophical* and *esoteric* issues following its creation during the mid-seventeenth century, in what I would define as "accepted" Freemasonry. Indeed, it is only in the late eighteenth-century Masonic rituals that we start to observe the first traces of what may be defined as true Masonic *initiatic philosophy*, and the emergence of a "speculative" Freemasonry.

Therefore, although some degree of continuity is revealed between the Medieval catechisms (*Antient Charges*) and other manuscripts which marginally preceded the birth of the *Grand Lodge of England* in 1717, it is clear that it was only from the second half of the eighteenth century that a marked development of the ritualistic and ceremonial

190 Eric Dodds, *Neoplatonismo*, Il Melangolo, Genoa, 2007.

elements of Freemasonry was manifested, including a more significant presence of *esoteric* and *initiatic* components.

Between 1680 and 1730, and particularly from 1730 to 1760, a series of changes were gradually introduced into the ceremonies by the "Accepted", although the process of extension and evolution continued throughout the remainder of the eighteenth century.

The most significant change was the division of the esoteric doctrine, and consequently of the entire ritual, into *three parts*.

This evolution has suggested that the "speculative" form of Freemasonry should be viewed essentially as the evolution of the "Accepted" Freemasonry, in my opinion, inspired and permeated by the Neoplatonist thought of the *School of Cambridge*, and was accordingly viewed as an *independent* and separate entity with a specific character of high originality.

Briefly, we may conclude that towards the middle of the seventeenth century in England, a group of men, zealous upholders of Neoplatonism, Esotericism, Hermeticism and Rosicrucianism, decided to borrow the "symbols" adopted by Medieval stonemasons with the initial aim of diffusing a system of moral and ethical principles. They aimed in this way to create a singular conception of man and thus gave rise to Freemasonry as we know it today. Subsequently, thanks to the influences already mentioned previously (Mystery societies and Hermeticism) and Neoplatonism this would be transformed (or attempt to be transformed) into a full-blown "Initiatic Order".

Throughout the period which witnessed the establishment of first "accepted", and subsequently the "speculative" Freemasonry, the Neoplatonism of the *School of Cambridge* represented the line of philosophical thought that above all others best resembled the *ethical* and *moral* principles of Freemasonry. It should however be underlined that in view of their "antimodernist" approach the Cambridge Neoplatonists were at the time considered a niche group of philosophers, and to date, remarkably few scholars have studied this phenomenon. One of the latter however is the renowned German philosopher Ernst Cassirer, who writes:

"Faced with the modern form of knowledge of nature as established by Galileo and Kepler, the School of Cambridge remains indifferent and renounces all manner of in-depth understanding, not deeming the former to include other than the support and heralding of a 'mechanical' conception of nature that the school zealously opposes on ethical and religious grounds." [191]

It is indeed precisely this adherence to a *traditional* form of *ethics* and *morals*, almost perceiving future damage to be caused by an unstoppable progress and moral limitations,

191 Ernst Cassirer, *La rinascenza platonica in Inghilterra e la scuola di Cambridge*, La Nuova Italia Editrice, Florence, 1947, page 1.

that so likens the Cambridge Neoplatonists to Freemasonry, and emphasises their appropriateness in opposing the prevailing *technicality* that characterises modern day society.

We may therefore conclude that the aspect that divided the Illuminism school of thought from Neoplatonism, was that although both apparently tended towards an *emancipation* of the individual and a *furthering* of his knowledge, in Neoplatonism this outcome was achieved with the individual remaining a *Homo religiosus*, and thus maintaining an unseverable link with the "sacred", whilst Illuminism, on the contrary, displayed a marked detachment from the traditions of the positive religions, and from a "sacral" view of life and the universe.

2. Masonic Symbology and Neoplatonist Allegories

What are the elements that induce us to affirm the presence of a clear influence of Neoplatonist philosophy as underlying the Masonic school of thought? Which concept of Neoplatonism can be observed in Masonic "symbols" and "allegories"?

Undoubtedly many, ranging from the interpretation of God as *Architect of the Universe*, to the allegory of Light and the numerous myths and symbols used, including "Jacob's Ladder", as a representation of the Masonic pathway to perfection and Divine ascension. However, it is particularly the focus on the *transcendental*, the heart of Neoplatonist thought, that was of major interest to the founders of the esoteric philosophy of Freemasonry.

God the Architect and Surveyor of the Universe

Plutarch was first to attribute to Plato, who failed to maintain explicitly such a notion, the idea of a God who created the world by means of geometry.

Throughout the Middle Ages, God continued to be viewed during the act of creation using the very sciences applied by man to investigate nature: arithmetic, geometry and music. However, it was undeniably through Neoplatonism that additional emphasis was placed on the almost religious valence of geometry, with the added influence provided by Pythagorism and Hermeticism. Accordingly, geometry came to represent a true form of initiatic knowledge.

The founders of the Masonic school of thought maintained that a philosophically appropriate notion of God should necessarily imply the principle of His absolute *transcendence*. However, to assign Theist, Deist or Pantheist connotations to the *Great Architect of the Universe* would imply not only a lack of understanding of the *aims* of the Masonic initiatic pathway, but would likewise create a dangerous and embarrassing state of confusion.

The Light

For a Freemason the metaphor of Light, the constant search for the latter, represents an unfailing reference point on the pathway to perfection. As mentioned previously, the above metaphor is of Neoplatonist origin; God, the One, the Surveyor of the Universe, is a perennial and endless source of Light, and in the same way as light, gradually dims the further it gets from the source of the Light. Likewise, a series of steps descend from God – the further they are from the centre the more they descend towards imperfection.

This embodies the fundamental Neoplatonist concept of "emanation", the stemming of all things from a source. In this case the source giving rise to the *Nous* (spirit) is our very soul; we are absorbed in contemplation, we are no longer ourselves whilst we contemplate, although all this occurs within ourselves.

A Freemason is expected to travel this pathway in an upwards fashion, ascending the steps (Jacob's Ladder) which will lead him into the presence of the Truth. In this context it is clear that the human soul embodies two tendencies: one reaching upwards towards the Light in an attempt to contemplate the Spirit and the One, and the other reaching towards the material and corporeal world. Consequently, mankind comprises both a *material* being, in the negative sense of the word, and a *soul*, which affords a possibility to return to God once again.

This dynamic has been observed previously in *Pimandro*, the key text included in the *Corpus Hermeticum*, in which the infinite luminosity of *Nous-God*, the only Light and the only "Life" is manifested. *Nous-God* does not invite us merely to contemplate a view; he wishes to reawaken our conscience and lead us to the awareness within ourselves of the luminous nature of the Divine. The Light is not replete by merely illuminating matter, but by obtaining life from a visionary glance it *transfigures* the latter, reawakening memories of its origin and a desire to return to it.

The Transcendent

The most beautiful images handed down to us by Neoplatonism must surely include what we may define as an "opening onto contemplation". This term is perhaps most appropriately translated through the German word *aufgehen*, meaning "to disclose, to open". In line with Neoplatonist thought, this term implies a true *subsistence* with Nature, a model of the experience of being and a *metaphysical* archetype.

When, in the Ceremony of Passage the Worshipful Master faces the Candidate and affirms: "*... you are now allowed to further your research into the occult mysteries of Nature and Science*", he is indicating that the *opening of one's eyes*, should be approached with a spirit of *contemplation*. The candidate will then start to *see* what he was indeed already capable of seeing, thus emphasising how the faculties of observation in the Initiate are deemed to have been considerably strengthened.

This ritual act should be interpreted according to a dynamic that could even be defined *holistic* in its unity-totality. The subject implicated in the rite, of whatever nature, may be compared to the spectators in Greek theatre who never took a passive role but were rather seen as members of a cult in which to act as a spectator implied an all-embracing participation extending to the entire group of bystanders, as a true opening onto "contemplation". The same dynamics are produced in Masonic rituals in which there is no distinction between participant and observer, between initiator and initiate. We are, together with the protagonist (the initiate), absorbed by events and, leaving our anxieties to one side, we are "entranced" by the new present. For Freemasons, in the same way as for Neoplatonists, this all terminated in the One, the *Great Architect of the Universe*, in the transcendental. A veritable ascending pathway towards the inexpressible.

Learned Ignorance

"Knowing you know nothing" is one of the key concepts of Neoplatonism. In his essay on "Learned Ignorance" (1440) Nicholas of Cusa, reiterated the ancient saying introduced by Socrates to explain that when attempting to solve a problem far removed from one's knowledge, for example relating to the nature of God, man must be ready to confess his inability to comprehend. A learned ignorance therefore is born of the awareness of the limits of human knowledge; if truth may be likened to a circle, human intellect is similar to a polygon inscribed inside the circle, and however much we increase the number of sides, these will never coincide with the circumference. In the same way, however much knowledge may advance the human mind, it will never be in a position to fully comprehend the truth so precisely and in such a definitive manner. God is beyond human reason and may only be understood by means of conjectures, geometrical analogies that assist us in comprehending the differences between the finite and the infinite. As an example, straight lines and circles are different forms (finite), but if one extends a circle infinitely it becomes impossible to distinguish it from a straight line. Consequently, it may be affirmed that God, as an infinite being, is both one and the other, simultaneously straight line and circle. God therefore embraces an encounter of opposites, God is more and less, the centre and the circumference.

The Microcosm-Macrocosm and the Soul of the World

Allegory reminds us that every man is a Microcosm, a miniature world with a psychic and anatomical structure representing a reduced-scale repetition on the structure of the universe. Conversely, the cosmos, the stars, the plants, the Earth are all similar to man as they are provided with organs and, above all, a soul. This doctrine is of ancient origin and can still be observed in a wide range of cultures. Julian Rees, in referring to the Hermetic origins of this concept, writes:

"The philosophy of Hermes was that Man, representing the microcosm of the physical world, is a reflection of God, representing a macrocosm of eternity, and therefore the non-physical, or spiritual side of ourselves and our existence. This is expressed in the phrase 'as above so below' referring to the oneness of God and man. This philosophical truth is demonstrated many times in Freemasonry, most graphically in the form of the Temple itself which, being as broad as it is high and twice as long, forms a double cube, one said to represent the microcosm, the other the macrocosm. Man, by this principle, has an immediate connection with the Supreme Being, called by the name." [192]

The doctrine was heavily opposed in the Middle Ages in view of its features of animism and pantheism, only to return to favour during Renaissance Neoplatonism. In 1619, the great astronomer Kepler in his work *The Harmony of the World* depicted a splendid simile between the earth and the body of a whale, indicating the breath of the whale as the cause of the high and low tides of the sea.

The doctrine focusing on the *soul of the world*, further to that featuring the *microcosm-macrocosm*, teaches us that the physical Universe should be viewed as being similar to a living being with organs, capable of movement and, consequently, provided with a *soul*.

This notion had already been expressed in Oriental thought and was subsequently introduced to the West by Plato's *Timaeus* which represented it, as stated previously, as a logical consequence of the analogy between *microcosm* and *macrocosm*. Plato was of the opinion that if man and the Universe are structurally similar, it should also be taken into account that the Universe may feature characteristics typical of man, including life, thought and, above all, a soul.

Plato identified the Universe with the cosmic pneuma, a divine force immanent to Nature that governs and assures life throughout the Universe. Plotinus likened it to one of the *hypostases* of Being, the second intermediate emanation between the *One-God* and the material world it gives order to.

During the Renaissance this notion reached its height, representing in the thought of the Renaissance Neoplatonism the idea of *universal affection* that justified the practice of Alchemy. Everything is linked to everything else, as all things are but a mere part, an organ, of a unique, immense animal, the Universe. According to the Renaissance school of thought, the Earth was invariably identified as an animal, the phenomenon of plant fertility likened to animal fertility, mines and caves were depicted as a "womb" giving

192 Julian Rees, *So you want to be a Freemason?*, Lewis Masonic, Hersham, 2009, page 26.

birth to mineral crystals and gems. Accordingly, alchemists viewed the production of gold as a mere "speeding up" of the laws of nature.

The above concept was naturally mocked and attacked by modern science which saw in it a form of anthropomorphism. It was however subsequently revived by Schelling during the Romantic Era in the context of a philosophy whereby nature represented a form of continuity between the organic and inorganic worlds.

Today the concept has once again returned to the forefront with the modern psychology proposed by James Hillmann.

Mathesis-Gematria

The approach taken by Renaissance Neoplatonism towards mathematics comprised a speculative comment on geometric figures and numbers aimed at achieving deeper levels of knowledge. The geometric forms, the *platonic solids*, were viewed as archetypal figures, i.e. visible manifestations of the perfect Platonic ideas. The influence of Pythagoras, who purported that the latter were not necessary in developing scientific theories but rather represented symbolic images illustrating transcendental notions that were otherwise hard to convey, figures to be contemplated and interiorised in order to grasp their mystic meaning, is clearly evident. This view of mathematics was termed speculative *Mathesis*.

Other symbols, including Jacob's Ladder and the division of the path to perfection into *three stages*, or degrees, will be discussed in the section focusing on the ideas of Giovanni Pico della Mirandola.

3. Renaissance Neoplatonism

The firm establishment of Neoplatonism in Florence was represented by the reiterating and commenting of the philosophies of Plotinus and Plato; indeed, the Renaissance Neoplatonists believed in a sole Truth, manifested in different languages such as mathematics, physics and art. Marsilio Ficino and Pico della Mirandola were to become the key actors in this rediscovery of Platonism.

Marsilio Ficino

The Platonism adhered to during the Italian Renaissance, which culminated in the work of Marsilio Ficino, leader of the *Florentine Academy*, and his friend and pupil Giovanni Pico della Mirandola, was in many aspects the expression of a Humanist movement. Both Ficino and Pico had indeed received an extensive humanist education and were permeated by the stylistic and classicist standards of Humanists.

The passion displayed by Ficino in the translation and publication of the works of Plato and the ancient Neoplatonists was comparable to the work undertaken by Humanists on other classical authors. Ficino maintained that mankind is divided into two groups: the simple, i.e. the *vulgus malignus* and ignorant, of an inferior and solely instinctive-passionate nature, and the philosophers, those who perceive an additional sense beneath the surface. Thus arose the key concept of an *elitist* culture that almost felt the need to express itself in a cryptic manner, the Truth not being within reach of all men.

Ficino considered Plotinus as the basis for the Neoplatonist philosophy, reiterating the idea put forward by the philosopher who wrote the *Enneads* whereby everything leads to a single Unity, implying how one should not be wary of the world of physics, or of mathematical abstractions, or poetry, as these would all bear the sign of Truth.

It should not however be overlooked that the roots of Renaissance Platonism lay outside the tradition and interests of early Humanism, as highlighted by the Renaissance scholar Paul Oskar Kristeller: *"One of these roots was the Aristotelianism, or scholasticism, of the later Middle Ages, which continued to dominate the teaching of philosophy, at the universities and other schools."* [193]

Ficino neither condemns nor minimises the practical activities of life, but rather heavily underlines that the main purpose of human life is *contemplation*. By *contemplation*, Ficino maintains it is possible to comprehend the spiritual experience which begins with a detachment of the mind from the outside world, to then proceed, through various degrees of knowledge and desire, and finally culminate in the immediate vision and enjoyment of God. It should moreover be pointed out that for the Florentine Platonist, the concept of man and his dignity was not limited merely to a *solitary* experience and to the personal relationships of individuals, but led moreover to the conscious awareness of a *solidarity* of all men placing well-defined moral and intellectual obligations on the single individual.

Man as Described By Pico

In this section I shall attempt to identify in the context of the thoughts and works of Pico, references capable of demonstrating the link with the Masonic project of the "construction of man".

The answer will be provided through a careful analysis of Pico's concept of "Dignity". If for Pico the achieving of the dignity of man represents a journey, an itinerary that may lead man towards the transcendent, to God, or rather, to the *Great Architect of the Universe*, Freemasonry itself may also be interpreted as acting as a "code of conduct"

193 P.O. Kristeller, *Studies in Renaissance Thought and Letters*, Edizioni. di Storia e Letteratura, Rome, 1956, page 266.

featuring a transcendent aspect elicited by its striving towards identification, to its approach to an unrepresentable absolute: the *Great Architect of the Universe*.

According to Neoplatonist thought the human soul is directed both towards God and towards the body, or rather, towards the intelligible and the corporeal world. These ideas are embodied in Ficino's scheme of a universal hierarchy in which the human soul occupies a privileged, central, position: God, the Angelic Mind, the Rational Soul, Quality and Body.

The same idea is later developed by Pico in his renowned *Oratio*. Pico focuses mainly on the freedom of man and particularly on his freedom to choose how to live. As a consequence, man no longer occupies an established place in the universal hierarchy, not even a privileged place at the centre, but is completely detached from the hierarchy and constitutes a world unto himself:

"We have given to thee, Adam, no fixed seat, no form of thy very own, no gift peculiarly thine, that thou mayest feel as thine own, have as thine own, possess as thine own the seat, the form, the gifts which thou thyself shalt desire. A limited nature in other creatures is confined within the laws written down by us. In conformity with thy free judgment, in whose hands I have placed thee, thou art confined by no bounds; and thou wilt fix limits of nature for thyself. I have placed thee at the centre of the world, that from there thou mayest more conveniently look around and see whatsoever is in the world. Neither heavenly nor earthly, neither mortal nor immortal have we made thee. Thou, like a judge appointed for being honorable, art the molder and maker of thyself; thou mayest sculpt thyself into whatever shape thou dost prefer. Thou canst grow downward into the lower natures which are brutes. Thou canst again grow upward from thy soul's reason into the higher natures which are divine…" [194]

The originality of Pico's thought is represented by the outcome to his hermeneutic approach which is not to be observed in any other thinker of the period. Indeed, his interdisciplinarity constitutes a unique case in the history of Renaissance philosophy, with his attempts to "reconcile" Platonism and Aristotelianism, together with his religious syncretism present in the Christian Kabbalism he himself conceived.

A Common Root

Pico goes even further, and suggests that all religious and philosophical traditions concur towards a single, universal truth. Pagans, Hebrews and Christian theologians, as well as philosophers who purportedly maintain conflicting ideas, Plato and Aristotle, Avicenna and Averroes, Thomas and Scotus, all displayed an excellent *insight* into truth. On including propositions from all these authors among his *900 Theses*, it was

194 G. Pico della Mirandola, *De Hominis Dignitate*, E. Garin (ed), Florence, 1942, pages 104-106.

Pico's intention to illustrate this universality of truth that so justified his endeavours to incorporate and defend doctrines hailing from such a wide range of sources. This syncretism of Pico provided the true foundation for a broader conception of religious and philosophical tolerance.

Essentially, the three major concepts underlying the basis of Pico's thought are the following: 1) the principle of *docta ignorantia*, 2) the *coincidentia oppositorum* and, of particular concern to the present study, 3) the *knowledge* of and approach to God by means of "symbols".

Indeed the thinking in terms of "symbols" to render the methodology applied by Pico is similar to the singular philosophical approach to the Divine adhered to by Freemasonry, aspiring to perfection, and this ambition to strive to attain the divine perfection, in the image and likeness of God, is not innate but rather a project which man himself must undertake by embarking on a path made up of symbols and allegory.

It is thus evident that the concept of "creation" finds no application either in the philosophy put forward by Pico or in Masonic philosophy. Indeed, in creation the individual is presented as a being produced through the freely performed action of an entity which is alien to him. Conversely, in the conception of "free will" used by Pico, man slowly *acquires* his own identity, his own being, through the conduct he displays.

As Cassirer recalls, it is this singular feature that elevates man and singles him out from other beings placed higher up in the hierarchy:

"Upon the angels and the heavenly intelligences their nature and their perfection have been bestowed from the beginning of creation: man possesses his perfection only as he achieves it for himself independently and on the basis of a free decision." [195]

To attempt to create some degree of order in Pico's thought would, in my opinion, prove to be a difficult and dangerous operation. Difficult because the material available is vast but as yet incomplete, awaiting a reclassification that Pico, due to his early death, had been unable to undertake. Dangerous because to make Pico's thought revolve around one single key topic would be detrimental to the richness and multiplicity of his interests, the outcome of his original method of interpretation that might be termed as "interdisciplinary", a completely new approach for the times. Accordingly, as emphasised by the renowned scholar Eugenio Garin, Pico's endeavours: *"were addressed at demonstrating both the universal nature of the Truth as present in its extensive series of expressions, and the integrability of these endeavours towards the Truth, but also in illustrating the limitations of the various positions, and therefore the need to reach beyond the latter whilst gaining awareness of the conflicts of intellect - contradictoria in natura*

195 Ernst Cassirer, *Dall'Umanesimo all'Illuminismo*, La Nuova Italia Editrice, Florence, 1967, page 80.

intellectuali se compatiuntur".[196] Briefly, this was the meaning that the words "peace" and "concordance" subsequently assumed in the thought of Pico della Mirandola.

As mentioned previously, the activity undertaken by Pico was only brief, being developed over a decade from 1483 to 1494 when he was a young man aged in his twenties and thirties.

If we wish to find a *common thread* in the course of Pico's thought, I would refer to an attempt to *revive* Christianity, a project which would have involved the whole of mankind, comprising the philosophy of love, poetic theology, the concord of doctrines, the universal synthesis of knowledge and the dignity of man.

The Dignity of Man

The features of Pico's thought that can be observed in the context of the philosophical vision of Freemasonry are represented by the two themes focusing on the *dignity of man* and of *peace between the doctrines*, prominent figures in the programme for the spiritual reconstruction of mankind.

The three works, the *Oratio*, the *Conclusiones* and the *Apologia*, cannot be separated, and in numerous aspects represent a single work, although written in different periods (over approximately one year from the spring of 1486 to the same period in 1487).

The "Oration" was intended to be solemnly delivered during a convention in Rome that never took place, and was subsequently printed posthumously at the end of the century. Eugenio Garin comments:

"...only a few pages, but they mark an era, ancient and at the same time contemporary. They invoke the peace between doctrines, a concordance of beliefs, they tell of the continuity and the convergence of the efforts made by man to pursue the light; they convey the significance of man in the world, and of his singular, provocative vocation. The importance of man is in his responsibility, his freedom. Man is the only being who truly chooses his own fate; he alone can influence the outcome of history and release himself from the conditions of nature; it is he who dominates over nature. The conscious image of the characteristic man of the modern world stemmed from here: man is intimately bound to the act whereby he is made, he has the ability to set himself free. The latter concept is an act of condemnation for oppression, slavery, and all other forms of conditioning." [197]

As mentioned previously, it is this very *tension* in man towards the Truth, the Light, find that its place among the most important allegories of Masonic thought inspired by Neoplatonist philosophy.

196 Eugenio Garin, *Ritratti di Umanisti,* Sansoni, 1967, reprinted by Bompiani 2001, page 217.
197 Eugenio Garin, op. cit., pages 217-218.

The Three Stages of the Path to Perfection

Pico maintained that God did not create man in his image as the orthodox Catholic theologians would have us believe, but rather provided man with the possibility of creating his *own* image. This extolling of the creative virtues of man, of his freedom of choice, persuaded numerous scholars to identify man's "free will" as the feature that distinguishes him from other creations, the central nucleus of Pico's doctrine on man.

However, the aspect of major interest for the purpose of the present essay is the *ethical* thought expressed by Pico, and in this regard the "Oration" can undoubtedly be defined as the quintessence of Pico's *ethico-moral* speculation.

The important similarity between the three fundamental stages on man's path of *accession* to the *Supreme Good* of the "Oration" and the Three Degrees of the Masonic path leading to the moral perfection of an individual (Entered Apprentice, Fellow of the Craft and Master Mason), viewing the ritual as an "orthpraxy" rather than "orthodox", constitute the key aspects of our conviction of the influence of the *ethics* adhered to by Pico on the *ethics* of Freemasonry.

Indeed, if the first of the itineraries for Pico was the *"cleansing from vice with the help of ethics"*, for Freemasonry the first of its Three Degrees is characterised by the *"principles of morality and virtue"*, and can therefore be rightly defined as a Degree of Ethics. The second stage on Pico's journey is the *"perfecting of reason through dialect and natural philosophy"* which concurs with the Second Masonic Degree of Fellow Craft. Accordingly, during the Ceremony of Passage from the Degree of Entered Apprentice to that of Fellow Craft, the Worshipful Master turns to the Brother and says: *"as you learned the principles of moral Truth and Virtue in the previous degree, now you may extend your enquiries to the hidden mysteries of Nature and Science"*. Therefore in this Second Degree, the Freemason perfects his moral awareness, through *human reason* and the knowledge of Nature. Lastly, the third and final stage of Pico's ethical thought, contained in the "Oration", is the *"Knowledge of the Divine"*, which corresponds to the Third Degree of Freemasonry, that of Master Mason, which *ritually* concludes the initiatic path of Freemasonry. During the ritual the Worshipful Master says to the Brother: *"Advancing further, still guiding your progress, by the principles of moral truth, may you be steered into the second degree, to see the intellectual faculty of it, and track your development in it, through the paths of celestial science, unto the throne of God himself,"* an experience therefore which places us in a direct *man-God* relationship.

Therefore, in the ethical pathway devised by Pico, the first preparatory grade is represented by Ethics, the science of morals, called upon to free man from his passion for pleasure, as it is only through Ethics that, according to Pico, the wars between men and the States will cease and a lasting peace will inhabit the earth. The subsequent grade, the *Philosophia Moralis* makes way for thc *Philosophia Naturalis,* which conducts man on the road to knowledge of the world and reveals the secrets of Nature. The last step is that in which human reasoning, prepared and educated by philosophy, will lead to discovery of the most deeply concealed secrets of the Universe.

Jacob's Ladder

The nature of the progressive perfection of man, in his quest for the Supreme Good, is underlined in the allegorical example of Jacob's patriarchal ladder, which *"rises by many rungs to the height of heaven"* symbolising man's path throughout life. In his *Oratio*, Pico observes that by climbing this ladder we cleanse, almost as if immersed in a river, the most sensitive part of our soul which encloses bodily temptation. He continues by stating that *"exercising philosophy in line with the height of the rung, corresponding to nature"*, we shall be in a position to analyse and synthesise the meaning of all things, *"raising ourselves"* to the bosom of the Father, who reigns above the ladder, to rest in the "felicity of theological knowledge".

The allegory of Jacob's Ladder that so ably depicts the individual pathway to perfection encloses the Masonic ritual, and is undeniably one of the cornerstones of the *ethico-moral* ideals of Freemasonry.

We may thus conclude that, in the same way as Masonic thought, *ethics*, the *philosophy of nature*, and the *approach to the Divine*, likewise represent the principal degrees of Knowledge which man must aspire to when referring to the ethics adhered to by Pico.

Who better than Pico has represented by means of philosophy the fundamental Masonic allegory of the Unhewn Stone that is transformed by means of sheer hard work into a Smooth Stone? Indeed, in the "Oration" man is portrayed in an entirely arbitrary manner as his own educator: *"sui ipsius quasi arbitrarius honorariusque plastes et factor"*, a true *shaper* called upon to sculpt and create his own form.

To summarise, I would like to recall how Pico acted as a splendid forerunner of Lessing in his *Masonic Dialogues, (Ernst & Falk)*. For Pico della Mirandola man's happiness is not yielded by *knowledge* of the Truth, but solely by *seeking* the latter, the typical Platonic conception of Eros. It is thus of little importance to know the Truth, to achieve this state, but rather to undertake the *search* required to identify it: it is indeed through this extreme manifestation of "free will" that its full spiritual power is revealed. In the light of this, Pico states that all obligations in matters religious are to be totally shunned: it is essential to ensure a *Libertas credendi* as the true faith will be born only of freedom. According to Pico the sins of man do not represent an irremovable defect of his nature, as nature sees nothing but the correlative and opposite of that which is different and superior. It was necessary for man to be capable of sin in order to allow him to be capable of doing good. The fundamental concept is that , for better or for worse, man will never be a finished creation; he will never be capable of lying safely in the lap of the good and will likewise never be so overtaken by the bad as to be beyond redemption. The roads leading to the good and the bad are always open to him and the decision is entirely in his own hands.[198] Thus, Pico della Mirandola maintains that in man sin is not only a question of guilt but, on the contrary, is an expression of the force that enables him to do good. His freedom is unleashed to display its sheer force only once man is in a position to forge his own existence and pass through its mandatory stages.

4. The Cambridge Platonists

Philosophical Origins

It was in sixteenth century England that the Neoplatonist concept of a religion devoid of any form of dogma reached a peak with the publication of Thomas More's *Utopia,* the most important work relating to the Platonic and Plotinian doctrines governing *Eros* and *Beauty*, together with the works of Spenser *(The Faerie Queene* and *Hymns to Love and Heavenly Beautie)* and enabled Platonist ideas to achieve the height of poetic expression of the period.

It was however particularly through the School of Cambridge that Platonism was, in a different historic context and another spiritual environment, to carry out the same functions that had been undertaken two centuries previously during the Italian Renaissance, i.e. a reiteration of the issue of freedom from dogma, ethics and religion.

The position usually assigned to the *School of Cambridge* in the history of philosophic thought is, in the light of available studies and documents, undoubtedly modest standing. The small space devoted to this issue is undeniably due to its "antimodern" connotations and its role as an open adversary of Empiricism. By opposing the prevailing trend observed in the sixteenth century school of thought in England, Empiricism, the Cambridge Platonists came to be seen as a niche group of scholars, at times marginalised, although by no means of any less originality than their contemporaries. Indeed, even following their decline, they unexpectedly continued to exert an influence on British society. However, to remain within the scope of this chapter, it should be emphasised that, contrary to common belief that considered Masonic ideas the fulfilment of Illuminist and Rationalist philosophy, it was rather Cambridge Neoplatonism that featured several chracteristics likewise observed in the esoteric philosophy of Freemasonry and therefore influenced the latter.

198 Ernst Cassirer, op. cit., page 89.

But who were the Cambridge Platonists and what were the reasons underlying the establishment of the Neoplatonist School? They were initially a small group united by personal associations, common interests and similar persuasions. They had no acknowledged leader, although the fact that they owed much to Benjamin Whichcote is undeniable. They had points of view in common, although use of the term "school" would seem to be somewhat extreme, as it implies a more formal, established type of relationship which was not present to such an extent.[199] All members of the group were associated in some way with Cambridge University; the key figures, in addition to Whichcote (1609-1683), were Henry More (1614–1687) and Ralph Cudworth (1617–1689) both fellows of Christ's College. The group also included John Smith (1618–1652), Nathaniel Culverwell (1619–1651), Peter Sterry (1613–1672) as well as other lesser members.

Their optimistic view of human nature is clearly emphasised by the importance placed on free will, and their anti-determinism led them to put forward arguments aimed at underlining the *autonomy* of man.

They strongly supported a state of *cognitive innatism* in open conflict with their times, and in particular with the materialism of Hobbes and Gassendi. Innatism conceives the existence, both in the soul and the intellect of man, of well-defined ideas that originate *prior* to any form of experience, thereby asserting that knowledge does not derive from things but rather from God who places common and general notions in the minds of men, the same state that Jung in his studies on the collective unconsciousness was later to define an *archetype*.

Therefore, knowledge is not derived from things but rather precedes them; consequently, man does not rise from singular things towards the universal, but, on the contrary, as he hosts the *universal* within him, he descends to apply these to things, and singular moral principles are *innate* within him.

Thus, the Cambridge Platonists proposed a universal idea of religion founded on the innate evidence of the concept of God (a notion common to all men) and, placing this on an identical plane to Christianity, Neoplatonist tradition and Renaissance Hermeticism, as an expression of the sole true religion, being based on the concepts of good and divine common to all men, the Cambridge philosophers condemned the disputes of the time between Anglicans, Catholics and Puritans.

Rather than blindly reproducing the theories put forward by Plato, the Cambridge Platonists provided their own original interpretation, which at times differed considerably from the original. As Ernst Cassirer recalls: *"In these writers the teachings of Plato always appear, as it were, as though transformed through a diffracting lens."*[200]

199 Gerald R.Cragg, *The Cambridge Platonists*, Oxford University Press, New York, 1968, page 3.
200 Ernst Cassirer, op. cit., page 39.

It is above all from the *Florentine Academy*, and particularly Marsilio Ficino, that the Cambridge Neoplatonists drew in subsequently conceiving "their" version of the speculative Platonic world. Accordingly, in the same way as Marsilio Ficino and Pico della Mirandola, likewise for the Cambridge philosophers Plato was part of that unbroken chain of divine revelation which included, in addition to Plato, Moses, Zoroaster, Socrates, Hermes Trismegistus, Jesus Christ and Plotinus, the renowned *Prisca Theologia.*

One *Traditional* idea upheld that everything is explained as having originated from the providential control of God over the Universe. Henry More comments in this regard: *"The Antients, particularly Hermes Trismegistus, have defined Him as a Circle the Centre of which is everywhere and the Circumference is nowhere".*[201] With the figure of More we are facing a trend towards the *rational mysticism* manifested by the Cambridge Platonists. More was one of the first partisans of Cartesianesim in England, although he subsequently turned against it and attacked the movement, accusing it of promoting atheism. The breach between More and Descartes was caused largely by the firm belief of Descartes in the total separation of body and mind. In his fundamental work *From the Closed World to the Infinite Universe,* Alexandre Koyré states:

"For More it was difficult to understand or to admit the radical opposition established by Descartes between body and soul. How indeed can a purely spiritual soul, that is, something which has no extension whatever, be joined to purely material body, that is, to something which is only and solely extension? Is it not better to assume that the soul, though immaterial, is also extended; and that everything, even God, is extended? How could He otherwise be present in the world? His attitude towards Descartes consisted in a partial acceptance of Cartesian mechanism joined to a rejection of the radical dualism between spirit and matter which, for Descartes, constituted its metaphysical background and philosophical basis." [202]

To some extent, More complied more with the history of Hermeticism or Occultism rather than Philosophy, *spiritually* a contemporary of Marsilio Ficino, lost in the disenchanted world of the "new philosophy", against which he was fighting a losing battle. Yet again, despite his partially anachronistic starting point and his invincible tendency towards syncretism which led him to combine Plato, Aristotle, Democritus and the Kabbalah, Hermes Trismegistus and the Stoa, it was More who provided the new science with some of the more important elements of its metaphysical structure which heralded its future development.[203]

201 H. More, *Poems*, page 409.

202 A. Koyré, *From the Closed World to the Infinite Universe,* The John Hopkins Press, London, 1957, pages 111-125.

203 A.Koyré, Ibid. page 126.

On leaving More, another interesting allegory can be observed in Cudworth's *True intellectual system of the Universe*, in which the philosopher refutes *atheism* whilst at the same time affirming the presence of an "order" that permeates the Universe. This "order" was supported by the allegory depicted in the *Scale of Nature* which was so popular during the Middle Ages and the Renaissance. The Cambridge Platonists fully agreed with the theories whereby "all things are forever linked" and the many parts of the Universe are the "limbs of one entire body". Indeed, as Cudworth proposed, *"A Scale or Ladder of Perfection in Nature, one above the other, as of Living and Animate Things, above the Senseless and Inanimate*", a similar concept was conveyed in Whichcote's *Scale of the Creatures,* together with the idea expressed by More of dividing the order of all things into *"Three Distinct Stages"*.[204]

A "pious philosophy", a *sophia perennis* demonstrated the possibility of a perfect *cohabitation* between philosophy and Christianity, a philosophy that dated back to *before* the revelation of Christianity.

Their writings, a mixture of quotations from the Sacred Scriptures and constant references to Neo-Platonist metaphysics, emphasise how one of the most recurrent accusations of theological orthodoxy facing the *School of Cambridge* was indeed how to arbitrarily combine the "sacred" with the "profane".

However, to define this union of Platonic and Christian doctrines as a mere syncretism is somewhat depreciatory. To gain a better understanding of the origins of this approach between the "sacred" and the "profane", we should take a look at the description of the doctrine of the soul provided by Plotinus. According to him the soul occupies no predefined place in the cosmos as it is the conduct of the soul to determine where it should reside. The soul described by Plotinus therefore, albeit devoid of any initially defined form, evolves into whatever it chooses to determine, particularly on an *ethical* and *metaphysical* level. It is indeed the soul alone to leave the sensible and tend towards the intelligible, thus aspiring to Knowledge of the divine. It is not therefore through revelation that the soul may gaze upon the divine, but, as the divine is contained within ourselves, the soul can *generate* this internally in an attempt to resemble the divine. In the splendid excerpt taken from the *Enneads* quoted at the start of this chapter, it is impossible to overlook the wonderful similarities with the initiatic pathway and the aims of Freemasonry, particularly with the allegory of the Unhewn Stone which will be transformed into a Smooth Stone following the initiatic pathway, and the importance of the role played in this process by the *illumination* known by the term "Light".

204 C.A. Patrides, *The Cambridge Platonists*, Harvard University Press, Cambridge, Massachussets, 1970, page 35.

A New View on Religiousness

The seventeenth century was distinguished not only by a new wave of religious sentiment but also by a series of speculative influences; indeed, it is this double characteristic that conveys strength of meaning to the Cambridge philosophical movement. Not only did they advocate religious freedom but they likewise claimed ownership of and modelled to their own needs all the intellectual trends of the time. They debated major issues and principles, and attempted to combine philosophy with religion and to confirm the indestructible bases of reason and the essential elements of our highest humanity.[205]

Who were the theologians and what were the doctrines on which the Cambridge Platonists based their beliefs? With very few exceptions, they came from a puritan background, although they should certainly not be classed as Puritans. They maintained several of the better qualities of Puritanism, its high sense of morality for example, but they deviated markedly from its theology.

In particular, the "doctrine of predestination", one of the aspects of the Calvinist dogma that was so widely present in Puritan circles, was totally unacceptable to them, in addition to the Calvinistic *denigration* of man. This in spite of the fact that man had been created in the image of God and had been given the capacity to reason. Whichcote was fond of repeating, *"The spirit of man is the candle of the Lord, illuminated by God and providing light for God"*[206] and went on to state: *"Universal charity is a thing final in religion."* The touching aphorism of the *"candle of the Lord"* contributes towards clarifying the theological approach adopted by Whichcote and explaining why he was viewed as the main supporter of the concept of "tolerance" within the movement. Contrary to Calvinism and Hobbes, Whichcote holds man in high esteem and deems him a rational being (the reason is represented by the candle of the Lord) created in the image of God, *"Virtue"* – as he was wont to underline in his sermons – *"is connatural and conservative to the nature of man: vice is unnatural and destructive."*

The approach to religion therefore should inevitably be based on reason, and *"the moral law on which man's well-being, and ever being, depends is not hard to discover. Its essential principles are written within him. They are truths of first inscription, more ancient than the oldest Scriptures."* [207]and to define the ideals adhered to by the Cambridge Platonists a "theological rationalism" typical of the seventeenth century Deism in England would imply far likening their view of religious reason simply with the force of

205 John Tulloch, *Rational Theology and Christian Philosophy in England in the Seventeenth Century. Vol.II: The Cambridge Platonists*, William Blackwood and Sons, Edinburgh & London, 1874, page 14.

206 B. Whichcote, *Moral and Religious Aphorisms*, London, 1753.

207 Frederick J. Powicke, *The Cambridge Platonists: A Study*, Harvard University Press Cambridge Massachusetts, 1926, page 62.

thought, and this would be decidedly disparaging, if not downright misleading. Indeed, they not only combated theological dogmatism but also fought against "logical" views, attacking therefore both the ideas of faith and intellect which hindered an understanding of the Divine, deemed possible, as we have observed previously, only through a positive orientation of the human "will".

In this regard Ernst Cassirer underlined:

"In all the writings of the Cambridge thinkers, it is not so much a matter of extending the religious horizon as of penetrating into another dimension of religious experience. Differences of doctrinal opinion are not only tolerated, but welcomed... Yet the Cambridge Platonists are neither deists nor, as their adversaries constantly charged them with being, 'Arminians', 'Aryans', or 'Socinians': they are simply religious 'ethicists', the central point of whose faith lies in moral and religious conviction."

The Cambridge Platonists were convinced that reason alone might not suffice. The precise nature of their challenge may be better comprehended by evaluating the different versions provided for the abovementioned metaphor included in the Book of *Proverbs* (20:27), *"The spirit of man is the candle of the Lord."* The Protestants generally applied this metaphor to emphasise the inadequacy of natural knowledge, arguing that the Greek and Roman philosophers were steeped in darkness as they only possessed *"The dimme candlelight of Nature"*.

A modern scholar could be forgiven for thinking that the Cambridge Platonists had applied their sources somewhat liberally, but this degree of *eclecticism* certainly did not confuse their ideas. They indeed heralded Plato and Platonism as an inspiration due to the very fact that the Church had long considered Plato a precious ally in its mission of interpreting religion.[208]

It should however be mentioned that the acceptance by the Cambridge thinkers of Plato and his pupils under the guidance of Plotinus was accompanied by the firm rejection of the entire Western theological tradition, from Saint Augustine to the Medieval theologians up to the classic Protestantism of Calvin, Luther and their successors in the eighteenth century. The Cambridge Platonists inverted this process with an almost mathematical precision. They tended to ignore Tertullian completely, and invoked Augustine only when the latter was in agreement with the ideas they supported. Only two of the main Western theologians found favour with them: Saint Anselm, on whom their views of atonement were based and Saint Thomas Aquinas, who provided them with the most updated version of the Greco-Roman theory of the law of nature.[209]

208 Gerald R. Cragg, op. cit., page 15.
209 C.A.Patrides, op. cit., pages 4-5.

In my opinion, another interesting analogy is represented by the interpretation of the Neoplatonic concept of Nature. The metaphysical approach present in Masonic rituals is markedly emphasised by the words uttered in these rituals; indeed, during the Ceremony of Passage the Candidate is reminded that *"You are now permitted to extend your research into the hidden mysteries of nature"*. Likewise, the Cambridge thinkers adopted the same 'metaphysical' approach to the Mysteries of Nature, subsequently commented on with singular efficacy by Cassirer: *"The science of nature, in so far as it is carried on in the proper sense, is therefore only apparently concerned with the world of the senses. It pursues a purely "intelligible" goal and seeks to liberate the reason which is fettered to the material world from its bondage and obscurity and make it clear and visible to the inquiring spirit as being of its own kind."* [210]

Reason and religion

However, in my opinion the Cambridge Platonists reached their pinnacle in the extremely precarious field of the bond between reason and religion. For English Empiricism the field of science was quite distinct from that of faith, the latter being conferred with an absolute autonomy. According to Bacon, as science and faith belong to two different dimensions they are not able to converge, but neither to diverge, leaving the divine mysteries which cannot be acknowledged philosophically to be venerated in silence. It is however this very religion which is so completely dissociated from reason that the Cambridge philosophers refute, persuaded that there is no way of achieving a marked distinction between the "natural" and the "spiritual" as the spiritual is nothing more than the purest and highest form of the selfsame rational being.

For the Cambridge Platonists the search for reason came to represent a moral discipline. The association between thought and actions was by its very nature intimate: *"When the doctrine of the Gospel becomes the reason for our mind, it will be the start of our life"*.[211]

The Baconian demarcation which was to free the field of experimentation from the religious sphere was however viewed by them as a sort of escape, a desertion that would have ultimately severed the bond between God and man, thus denying the latter the possibility of gaining knowledge of and access to all things divine.

This however does not imply that they were opposed to scientific research, as proven by the fact that two of the key thinkers, Cudworth and More, were members of the

210 E.Cassirer, op. cit., page 51.

211 B. Whichcote, *Aphorism*, No.94.

Royal Society. What they advocated was a view of *experience* that was not *unilaterally* directed towards the "natural" world but was rather accompanied by a "spiritual" experience. Bacon's naturalistic induction was required to interact in synergy with ethical and religious experience. The soul and the spirit, to reiterate Plotinus, likewise needed to be acknowledged by means of experience in exactly the same way as the more perceptible issues.

The Idea of God

The turning point however brought about by Cambridge Platonist thought was undoubtedly the transformation of the idea of God and consequently of the concept of religiousness. Accordingly, the religious conception advanced by the Cambridge philosophers was not confined to Christianity alone. Whichcote commented that *"the good will of a pagan is closer to God than the rabid zeal of a Christian"*, thereby supporting their *ecumenical* idea of religion, which is indeed comparable to the tolerance and acceptance of all forms of religion professed by Freemasonry.

To summarise, I would like to point out that the choice of the Florentine Neoplatonism and its European extension represented by the Cambridge Platonists constitutes an attempt to identify the philosophical thought that most resembles the ideas of Freemasonry and that may have *influenced* the establishment of the same. It is moreover an attempt to propose a thought that is in no way *in contrast* with the various expressions of religion, particularly with Christianity (in the light of the secular disputes between the Church and Freemasonry). To associate thinkers such as Pico della Mirandola or Marsilio Ficino with other scholars including Giordano Bruno would, in my opinion, constitute an error of concept, particularly in the light of the Masonic principle of "tolerance for all religions".

The antithesis between the above authors is clearly evident in the concept of Eros, the cornerstone of Neoplatonist thought. The theory of Platonic Love that the Florence Academy had attempted to unite with Christianity was indeed largely overturned by Giordano Bruno, who saw in Eros proof of the colossal strength of man. Eros provided man with the "heroic fury" needed to obtain a vision of the infinite Universe and to break the fetters that bound him to religion. Thus, if Pico della Mirandola and Marsilio Ficino never sought to enter into conflict with Christian theology, attempting to establish a peaceful existence between Platonic ideals, Bruno, on the contrary, was to use the Platonic doctrine of Eros as a veritable weapon against Christian doctrines. The Italian Neoplatonists, in contrast to Bruno, established themselves as guardians of a *Tradition* that they had no desire to demolish, but indeed wished to preserve.

The Independence of Ethics from Politics and Religion

The theories put forward by the Cambridge Platonists were ultimately interpreted by Shaftesbury who, in the late seventeenth century, in an era permeated by the heated disputes focusing on Ethics, Morals and Religion, maintained the independence of Morals from Religion and Politics, acknowledging its origin in sentiment or a "sense of morality". This indeed leads us once again to what is viewed as the cornerstone of English Freemasonry, an exclusion from engaging in politics and religion. This prohibition is likely aimed at meeting the requirement forming the basis of all activities carried out in a Lodge, of not mixing ethics and morals with issues from which they should be kept rigorously separate.

For Shaftesbury it was from this "moral consciousness" that one should set out to reach that immediate and inner perception of good and evil, of right and wrong. Thus, the possibility of acting according to the categories of ethics is based upon an ethical and aesthetic sentiment, in line with the union of beauty and goodness underlying the Platonic tradition and, in my opinion, Freemasonry.

In conclusion, in the light of the theories proposed in this chapter, although one cannot refer to the existence of an overt "philosophy of Freemasonry" seen as an *organised* system of Masonic thought, one may, in my opinion, confirm the existence of a philosophical *influence* of Neoplatonist origin on the birth of modern-day Freemasonry.

The Cambridge Platonists whose theories were deemed by their contemporaries obsolete and unsuited to solving the new problems of the era enjoyed a sort of posthumous comeback as their ideals lived on in the principles of Freemasonry, assuming an ever greater relevance and becoming increasingly necessary in stemming the profusion of technicality and relativism in society today.

Chapter Four

Transmission Through Use of Symbols

Man is a Tool-using Animal; weak in himself, and of small stature, he stands on a basis, at most for the flattest-soled, of some half-square foot, insecurely enough; has to straddle out his legs, lest the very wind supplant him. Feeblest of bipeds! Three quintals are a crushing load to him; the steer of the meadow tosses him aloft, like a waste rag. Nevertheless he can use tools, can devise tools; with these the granite mountain melts into light dust before him; he kneads glowing iron, as if it were soft paste; seas are his smooth highway, winds and fire his unwearying steeds. Nowhere do you find him without tools; without tools he is nothing, with tools he is all.

Thomas Carlyle
Sartor Resartus

1. The Task of Symbols

In all traditional organisations symbolism represents the principal means of initiatic teaching, the actual *tool of knowledge* to be used in gaining insight into the deepest truths. Roland Martin Hanke in the Introduction to an essay by Irene Mainguy, *Symbolique des outils et glorification du métier* writes:

"The gestures and the carrying out of symbolic activities convey the art of life in a highly specific, singular manner focused on illustrating the habitus, i.e. a way of life. They are the tool by means of which a new member is initiated and integrated into the group (Brotherhoods). The acceptance and adopting of a habitus is a founding cultural process at the end of which a new cultural identity is established, in addition to the sense and the conviction of having been admitted to become part of something new. In the case in question we are dealing with a new identity assumed on becoming a Mason. The establishment of the habitus is undertaken in the venue in which the Masons operate. In line with the significance they convey to symbols they refer to the space in which they 'work' symbolically as a 'Temple'... For them the utensils employed therefore are much more than

a mere sieve, a chisel or a plumb line: they represent the substitute for an interiorised idea, an idea which they themselves represent."[212]

In achieving this outcome, the superiority of symbolism over discursive reason is evident; only symbolism provides an appropriate means for obtaining and imparting a higher religious and metaphysical Truth. Symbolism succeeds where Philosophy cannot even hope to prevail, writes Julius Evola: *"Philosophy is both subalternate to and the opposite of symbolism. Its form of expression is the language which is essentially analytical, whilst symbolism is synthetic. The language is discursive in the same way as human reasoning. On the contrary, symbolism is intuitive. For these characters it is incomparably better suited than language for use as a vehicle for super-rational intellectual intuition, and is the best means of expression for all forms of initiatic teachings. Symbolism is the support of transcendent intuition. Conversely, philosophy is a type of discursive thought, it is exclusively rational and constitutes an already quite singular use of reason, as proof of the existence of science."*[213] Evola moreover uses the example of the beautiful symbolism of the "stone" which gives rise to an unconditioned consciousness: *"The 'stone' used as the matrix is a symbol of the body. The body is the substrate of the cosmic yearning, and all that underlies the humid substance; under the 'waters' therefore lie a set of those stages and faculties of men- whether they are termed 'spiritual' or not – that in a bodily substrate find their condition or something essential they are associated with. To undergo initiation is to free oneself of the 'stone' and achieve a state of awareness no longer conditioned by a link to the bodily vehicle."*[214]

Symbolism, therefore, a tool rejected or overlooked by the modern spirit, is for the conveying of Truths that belong to the order or pure intellect. As human nature is not purely intellectual, it necessarily has to rely on a sensitive foundation in order to reach the higher levels, and in this symbolism represents the most appropriate means of satisfying man's intellectual needs. Where language is an analytical and discursive means, in the same way as reason for which it serves as a tool, symbolism, on the contrary, is substantially synthetic and, for this reason, intuitive. The properties of symbolism thus underline its appropriateness in acting as a base for *intellectual intuition*, as it possesses an ontological reality far beyond any form of mental construct. As underlined by Seyyed Hossein Nasr, *"man does not make symbols: he is transformed by them"*.[215]

In view of its synthetic nature, symbolism therefore affords the possibility of acceding to an unlimited wealth of conceptions, conversely to language, characterised by more strictly defined and rigid meanings that force the intellect to work within

212 Roland Martin Hanke, *Introduction to Simbolica degli Utensili* by Irene Mainguy, Mediterranee, Rome, 2008.

213 J. Evola, *La via della realizzazione di sé secondo i Misteri di Mithra, Ultra*, No. 3, 1926.

214 Ibid.

215 Seyyed Hossein Nasr, *Ideali e realtá dell'Islam*, Rusconi, Milan page 68.

restricted confines,[216] as highlighted by the great Spanish poet Fernando Pessoa: *"All symbols and rites are not directed at a rational, discursive intelligence but rather at an analogical intelligence. For this reason it is not absurd to state that even on wishing to reveal and clarify the occult, this would not prove possible as no words would be available to express it. Symbols are by their very nature the language of truth that transcends the intelligence of man, whilst words are by their very nature the language of truths over which the intelligence of man dominates, precisely because it exists for the purpose of domination."*[217]

The fundamental role of the symbol in an Initiatic Society is clearly illustrated by the dynamics of initiation, explained by the French anthropologist Gilbert Durant by stating that the main virtue of the symbol is to ensure the presence of *transcendence* within the personal mystery. Thus, symbolism represents a sort of gnosis, a process of mediation undertaken by means of a concrete, experimental knowledge.[218]

Consequently, it follows that in traditional societies symbols constitute a privileged tool of higher Knowledge that operates in the metaphysical and transcendent dimension of the "sacred". In this regard, the French scholar René Alleau describes the dynamics involved:

"A symbol does not signify; it evokes and focuses, assembles and concentrates, in an analogical versatile manner, a multiplicity of meanings that cannot be reduced to one or many single meanings. Even a musical note does not possess a prevailing determined sense, unless this occurs only casually: it is strictly linked to the mythical and ritual context with which it is associated. To penetrate the world of symbols is to try to perceive harmonic vibrations and, in a way, to divine a music of the universe."[219]

It should not however be overlooked that symbols do not in themselves have any sacred value, nor any magical powers, otherwise they would be transformed into totems to be worshipped, sacred objects; in the context of a true *esoteric* knowledge, symbols are conversely a *means* of reflection, of knowledge, intellect, i.e. of gnosis, devoid of any magical powers or univocal codified or dogmatised significance.

To comprehend fully the significance and motivations of the presence of symbols in Freemasonry, we should commence from what is deemed the accepted definition of the movement: *"A peculiar system of morality veiled by allegory and illustrated by symbols."* This is the definition we shall use in attempting to clarify, particularly from a terminological point of view, inside the depths of the universe of definitions in which *symbols, signs, emblems, allegories, parables* and so forth that are frequently garbled and confusing.

216 Eugenio Bonvicini, *Esoterismo nella Massoneria Antica*, Vol.1 *La simbologia celata nelle regole costruttive*, Atanòr, Rome, 1993, page 17.

217 Fernando Pessoa, *Pagine Esoteriche*, Adelphi, Milan, 1997, page 59.

218 Gilbert Durand, *L'Immaginazione Simbolica*, Red Edizioni, Como, 1999, page 39.

219 René Alleau, *La Scienza dei Simboli*, Sansoni, Florence, 1983, page.9.

On encountering symbols and in allegories, the main problem to be addressed is that of terminology, as highlighted by Alleau:

"From an epistemological point of view, there is no field of knowledge that is harder to delimit, as the process of symbolisation implicates numerous levels of experience, ranging from the complex mechanisms of man's perceptions to the highest degrees of elaboration and systemization of man's representations of the world." [220]

To gain an insight into a different form of terminology, let us observe the definitions provided by the French anthropologist Gilbert Durand, according to whom:

"The idea of justice will be depicted by a figure that absolves or punishes, and I will therefore obtain an allegory; this figure may be surrounded or make use of a series of objects: tables of testimony, sword, scales, and in this case we shall we dealing with emblems. To better focalise on this notion of Justice, we may choose to imagine the recounting of a scene of justice, either real or allegorical, and in this case we shall be faced with an apology. Allegory is the concrete translation of an idea that is difficult to grasp or to express simply. Allegorical signs unfailingly contain a concrete element or an example of the meaning." [221]

In the light of the statements made by Durand, it is clear how in the context of the symbolic Masonic representation numerous allegories can be observed on the Tracing Boards of the 1st, 2nd and 3rd Degrees, whilst in the Legend of Hiram, represented in the 3rd Degree, includes the representation of an *apology*, a short narration of an allegorical nature provided for moral purposes.

In differentiating between symbol and allegory it should be pointed out how the former has frequently been viewed as a *higher* form of representation, as the definitions for symbols are all grouped under a common denominator, that of collocating the symbol in the world of the non-sensitive, the metaphysical, the supernatural, of unconsciousness. Indeed, in view of the impossibility of representing transcendence, the symbolic image employed is that of the *transfiguration* of a concrete representation through use of an essentially abstract sense. A symbol is therefore a representation that makes a secret sense *appear*; it is the epiphany of a mystery.[222] Thus, its use is appropriate in traditional societies based on a "sacred" foundation.

The contrast between *a symbol and allegory* can be clearly observed in the definitions applied by P. Godet, who presents the latter as its opposite: *"Allegory commences from an (abstract) idea aimed at completing a figure, whilst symbols are first and foremost a figure, and as such, a source, among other things, of ideas,"* a definition subsequently confirmed by

220 René Alleau, Op. cit., page 7.

221 Gilbert Durand, op. cit., page 21.

222 Gilbert Durand, op. cit., page.22.

F. Creuzer, who states: *"The difference between a symbolic and an allegorical representation is to be found in the fact that the latter merely conveys a general notion or an idea of a different significance, whilst the former is the idea itself rendered more sensitive, made flesh."* [223]

The German philosopher Hegel in *Estetica I* defines allegory as a *"chilled symbol"* whilst Durand, in *Nouveau traité de Psychologie,* refers to *"semantics desiccated in semiology and featuring of mere signage and academic value".*

It should also be mentioned how historically symbolism has not always been considered as above. Indeed, Descartes provided the first clear depreciation, which subsequently culminated in the positivism of August Comte where the *three stages* of the progress of knowledge seemed to result in an overt abdication and abandonment of the spirit and its capacity towards symbolic representation.

To once more return to the "traditional" definition provided for Freemasonry, *"A peculiar system of morality veiled in allegory and illustrated by symbols"*, it is immediately evident, in the light of the considerations made, that there is some degree of confusion between the definition of the two terms, symbol and allegory. Indeed, in the light of the above premises, the symbol, thanks to its particular singularities, is not capable of "illustrating", but rather of "veiling", waiting for the individual who, on approaching the symbol and drawing close, will discover its hidden meaning; on the contrary, allegory is more explicit in its definition, and consequently capable of "illustrating" in a less cryptic manner.

This said, on perusing the definition of "allegory" provided by the Great UTET Dictionary of the Italian language our doubts are rekindled as we read that allegory is defined as:

"Stylistic process (rhetorical figure) that enhances the conveying of an ideal, moral or religious (metaphoric sense) concept, overshadowing and almost veiling the same through use of an image that conveys a different, independent reality," whilst the Great UTET Encyclopaedic Dictionary states that "Allegory is present every time that the material meaning (literal or historic-descriptive) of a conversation or a graphical representation overshadows another abstract, mystic or supernatural meaning."

This confusion, and at times similarity, between symbol and allegory may be observed as early as the eighteenth century, with an example being reported in the *Encyclopaedia Britannica* published in 1771 in Edinburgh, which defines symbol as *"a sign or representation of something moral, by the figures or properties of natural things. Hence symbols are of various kinds, as hieroglyphics, types, enigma, parables, fables, etc. Among Christians, the term symbol denotes the Apostles' creed."*

223 F. Creuzer, *Symbolik und Mythologie der alten Völker*, I, Leske, Leipzig and Darmstadt, 1810, page 70.

In this overwhelming sea of definitions, the explanation of a renowned linguist, the Swiss Saussure, might aid us in clarifying and better understanding the peculiarities of the symbol; according to Saussure:

"The word symbol is sometimes used to designate the linguistic sign, or more exactly that part of the linguistic sign which we are calling the signal. This use of the word symbol is awkward, for reasons connected with our first principle. For it is characteristic of symbols that they are never entirely arbitrary. They are not empty configurations. They show at least a vestige of natural connexion between the signal and its signification. For instance, our symbol of justice, the scales, could hardly be replaced by a chariot." [224]

In the light of the statements made by Saussure, on bearing in mind the symbols of Freemasonry it can be observed how among the *Tools of the Craft* of a Freemason the Level could signify no other than "Equality", and could not be substituted in this representation by any other tool or utensil; the same is indeed true for the Plumb Line, symbol of the "rectitude" of life. With regard to the Chisel that indicates education, things are slightly different, as there is no correspondence between the signifier and what is signified; accordingly, in this case the choice is purely *arbitrary*, and consequently the signifier could be replaced by any other tool.

It thus follows that on referring to the definition given by J. Piaget, whereby the symbol *"should be defined as an association of resemblance between the signifier and the significate, whilst the 'sign' is arbitrary and is necessarily based on a convention"* [225] in our case the Chisel, and the manner in which it is used in Masonic ritual, would be classified as a sign rather than a symbol.

René Alleau specifies what Saussure means on using the term "arbitrariness" not so much in the sense of "free choice" of the signifier by the "speaking subject", but rather to convey a sense of "unmotivated", of *"arbitrary with regard to the significance, with which it possesses no natural association in a real context,"* [226] underlining moreover how, in his opinion, symbols possess an undeniable "sacred" value. Alleau writes:

"A symbol does not signify to an individual a predetermined thing: it is contemporarily a fulcrum of accumulation and concentration of images and their affective and emotional 'charges', a vehicle for the analogical orientation of intuition, a magnetic field of anthropological, cosmological and theological similes... Symbols therefore do not belong unreservedly to the signs of the human universe, or to the categories of concept or the imaginary. The symbolic function is inseparable from the 'sacred orientation' of the same, or

224 F. de Saussure, *Cours de linguistique générale,* Payot, Paris, 1974, page 101.

225 J. Piaget, *La psychologie de l'intelligence*, Armand Colin, Paris, 1998, page 28.

226 René Alleau, op. cit., page 40.

from the hierophantic tension of the 'numinous' or 'non-human' forces which myths and rites link these to mankind, by 're-uniting' the anthropos and the cosmos with the force of the logos, which is not so much a language, as the verb and the word 'resuscitated', 'recreated', beyond the cultural and social identity of the 'tribal words'." [227].

In the words of the French philosopher and grammarian Du Marsais, allegories should be distinguished from metaphors as: *"Allegory is a speech that is first presented under separate vestiges, seeming to be something completely different from what is actually being conveyed, which however is used merely as a comparison for the purpose of rendering intelligible another sense that is expressed. Metaphors associate a figurative word with an actual term; the fire in your eyes; eyes is the actual term. Conversely, with allegory all words convey first and foremost a figurative meaning, all words in an allegorical sentence or speech constitute a literal meaning which is not the meaning one wishes to convey"* [228] and referring once more to metaphors, the Bulgarian philosopher Todorov maintains that in the latter, *"the word has one sense alone, this being a figurative sense; the change is indicated by the fact that, without it, the known sense of words surrounding it would be inadmissible. As the word eyes has only one sense (noun), fire also has one alone (figurative). Things otherwise are governed by allegory; in this case all words are treated in the same way and it would appear as though they form a first literal sense; subsequently however, we discover that we must seek a second allegorical sense. The opposition is between the univocal sense in the metaphor and the double sense in allegory."* [229]

The "punishments" present in the Masonic ritual, and which have frequently been stupidly interpreted in a literal sense by the opposers of Freemasonry, are merely allegories used to represent the concept of initiatic *silence*.

It was particularly during the Romantic period that an opposition to symbols and allegory developed. Goethe was undoubtedly the most illustrious representative, and delineated a clear dichotomy between the two terms: *"Objects shall be determined by a deep sentiment which, when it is pure and natural, will coincide with the highest and most noble objects and will take these to the limits of symbolism. In this way the objects represented shall seem to exist for themselves alone, and despite this shall be significant of the deepest part in view of the ideal that such a generality invariably produces. If the symbolic indicates other than a mere representation, it will always be indirectly ... Now, there are works of art that shine with regard to their reason, witticism, gallantry, and we likewise understand all the allegorical works. It is precisely these that we should expect less as they destroy equally any interest in the representation, and thus*

227 René Alleau, op. cit., pages 51-54.
228 C.C. Du Marsais, *Des Tropes*, Paris, 1730, page 179.
229 T. Todorov, *Teorie del Simbolo*, Garzanti, Milan, 1984, page 112.

reject, so to speak, the spirit, likewise subtracting from its view all that is truly representative. The allegorical is distinguished from the symbolic as it designs indirectly, whereas the other is direct."[230] It is clear therefore how for Goethe symbols refer consequently to perceptions (and their comprehension), whereas allegory is concerned with comprehension alone.

Up until 1790, the word symbol did not convey the meaning it came to assume during the Romantic period; it was merely seen either as a synonym of other more widely used terms (allegory, emblem, etc), or to indicate the sign in an arbitrary and abstract significance, as for example with mathematical symbols. Kant, in his *Critique of Judgement* was to invert these dynamics, with the word "symbol" taking on the meaning we give it today, an intuitive instrument to be used in perceiving the significance of things.[231] Consequently, Todorov highlights how the symbol differs from an allegory: *"The former elicits the fusion between signifier and significate, whilst the latter divides them."* [232] This view is shared by the German scholar Meyer, who states: *"Symbols have no relationship, but truly are what they represent: Jupiter, an image of great dignity in an unlimited power ... Venus, woman created for love, etc.; characters therefore of the highest species, or general concepts embodied in art; these representations are known as symbols, at variance with allegories... The representation by means of symbols applies the same general concept rendered sensitive; an allegorical representation signifies merely a general concept of a different meaning."*[233]

On once again analysing the symbol from a general point of view, I agree with Cassirer that: *"The sign is no mere accidental cloak of the idea, but its necessary and essential organ. It serves not merely to communicate a complete and given thought-content, but is an instrument by means of which this content develops and fully defines itself. The conceptual definition of content goes hand in hand with its stabilisation in some characteristic sign."*[234]

To conclude this lengthy overview on the strictly "terminological" aspects of the symbol and allegory, in the light of the numerous definitions encountered, frequently discordant and at times even contradictory, I am essentially in agreement with the opinion of Jean-Eduardo Cirlot:

"The elements of allegory are symbolic and can in no way be distinguished from symbols themselves. Their function is however inverted and altered, thus, instead of alluding to the metaphysical and spiritual principles, instead of creating an emotion, these have been designed artificially to convey to concrete realities a unique or dominant significance."[235]

230 J.W. Goethe, *Goethes Sämtliche Werke*, vol.33, Stuttgart and Berlin: J.G.Cotta, c. 1910-20, page 94.

231 T. Todorov, op. cit., page 255.

232 T. Todorov, op. cit., page 270.

233 H.H. Meyer, *J.J. Winckelmann's Werke*, Dresden, 1808-1820, page 684.

234 Ernst Cassirer, *Filosofia delle forme simboliche*, La Nuova Italia, Florence, 1996, page 20.

235 Jean-Eduardo Cirlot, *Dizionario dei Simboli*, Eco, Milan, 1996, page 37.

As mentioned, important allegories can be observed in the Masonic Tracing Boards, among which we may glimpse the previously cited Jacob's Ladder and the Exalpha.

In the Bible, Jacob dreamt of a ladder by means of which the angels ascended to and descended from above: *"And he dreamed, and behold, there was a ladder set up on the earth, and the top of it reached to heaven. And behold, the angels of God were ascending and descending on it."*[236] By means of the ladder, God not only shows Jacob the way to reach the celestial reign but also how this ladder will provide us with two ways of behaving, showing both angels who "ascend" towards God bearing with them the requests of mankind, and angels who "descend" to earth bearing His divine providence. This association between heaven and earth demonstrates how God and man are at "one", as man is the representation of God on earth, microcosm and macrocosm.

The ladder has long been seen as the symbol *par excellence* of the "ascension", a symbol representing the relationship between heaven and earth, connecting the two. In Egypt the Celestial Ladder led to the God Ra, with the rays of the sun acting as rungs. Buddha ascended to Mount Meru by means of a ladder, whilst the staff with seven or nine rungs is used by Siberian shamans. The rungs of the ladder, a footbridge towards spiritual heights, recall the seven colours of the rainbow, a bridge cast between the earth and the other world, the depicting of a primordial contact (and a contract) between heaven and earth. In numerous mythical representations of the North American Indians a ladder provides access to the rainbow, which is likewise frequently depicted as a series of steps. A gradual ascent marks the stages of knowledge, the subsequent stations of the soul in its pathway to the ascent.[237] Referring to Jacob's Ladder Guénon writes: *"The angels strictly speaking represent the higher states of the being; it is then to these states that the rungs correspond particularly, which is explained by the fact that the rungs must be considered as having their feet resting on the earth, which means that for us it is necessarily our world itself that is the 'support' from which the ascent must be made... This is why, especially when the ladder is used as an element of certain initiatic rites, its rungs are expressly considered as representing the different heavens, that is, the higher states of the being."*[238]

However, there is another ladder that symbolises the progress of a Freemason in the Craft; this is found in the 2nd Degree and is represented by a Spiral Staircase. On entering the porch, the Apprentice has started his Masonic life; the 1st Degree, however, similar to the Ancient Lesser Mysteries, is merely a representation of a preparation and purification for something of a higher level. On passing through the porch and through

236 *Genesis*, 28, 12.

237 Catherine Pont-Humbert, *Dizionario dei simboli dei riti e delle credenze*, Editori Riuniti, Rome, 1995, pages 203-204.

238 René Guénon, *Simboli della Scienza Sacra*, Adelphi, Milan, 1990, page 291.

the Columns of Force and Foundation, the Apprentice is directed towards the Halfway Chamber by means of the Spiral Staircase, a pathway symbolising the passage from childhood to adult life. In this Degree the Brother will develop his intellectual faculties through a moral, and particularly spiritual, elevation.

The allegory of the *Exalpha*, also known as Solomon's Seal or Six-pointed Star illustrates our *union* with God; it is indeed formed from two overlapping triangles, in such a way that one points to the sky and the other to earth, indicating the *one-ness* of God and man.

Another important allegory is represented by the blindfolding of the Candidate; we are of course aware that Freemasonry is a journey in which the aspirant should no longer focus on "external" things, but rather on his "inner" dimension, whilst however not overlooking his limitations, as pointed out by Julian Rees: *"...undertakes in a personal darkness, since he is blindfolded. This blindfold is an allegory of two things: that his attention might be focused inwards rather than outwards, and also to underline his spiritual poverty."*[239]

In the "search" for the Keepers of the "Lost Word" a significant allegorical meaning can be construed, as highlighted by Fernando Pessoa: *"Everything is to find something. Even to lose is to find that you have lost something. Nothing is lost: everything is found. At the bottom of this well, as in the fables, the Truth is to seek."*[240]

To proceed from allegories to symbols, in Masonic symbology the Temple is possibly the most well-known. The *spiritualisation* of Solomon's Temple indeed represents the first teachings of Freemasonry and probably, as emphasised by Mackey, if this symbolism were to be removed from the rituals the entire system would collapse. If the idea of using the Temple as a symbol of the body is not exclusive to Freemasonry, undoubtedly the manner of treating symbolism by referring to Solomon's Temple and to the "operative" craft used in its construction is uniqueto Masonic rituals.

Another well-known symbol, the All-seeing Eye, may be seen as a symbol of the omnipresence of God, purveyor of the human race alluded to by Solomon is his Book of *Proverbs* (15, 3) when he says: *"The eyes of Jehovah in every place behold the good and the evil."*

In the higher degrees of Freemasonry the Triangle is the most important symbol and goes under the name of *Delta*, in reference to the fourth letter of the Greek alphabet which has the same form. The *Delta*, or mystic triangle, is generally surrounded by a circle of rays known as "glory" which, when distinguished from the figure and surrounded by a circle is an emblem of the eternal glory of God. When these rays radiate from the centre of the triangle they symbolise the divine light.

239 Julian Rees, *The Stairway of Freemasonry*, Lewis Masonic, London, 2007, page 37.

240 Fernando Pessoa, op. cit., page 58.

However, symbols and allegories can also be found in interesting synergies. Among the actual symbols, the Set Square, a tool used in the 2nd Degree and symbol of the Most Worshipful Master, teaches how our lives need to be regulated, harmonising them with the progress of our moral conduct, whilst the Compass, a tool used in the 3rd Degree, teaches us to direct our conduct towards ourselves and others within the confines of two *bounds*. But on combining these two symbols we gain an important allegory, the allegory of the Set Square "intertwined" with the Compass, to teach us how the principles of *moral* progress and personal growth go hand in hand with a clearly defined *code of conduct*.

To return to symbolism, Mircea Eliade underlines the importance and the fundamental role that this has held in the life of all traditional societies. It is indeed in the *Traditional* context that the particular gnoseological value of the symbol and its importance as an "instrument of knowledge" is observed, as stated by Eliade:

"The overcoming of 'scientism' in philosophy, the rebirth of religious interest following the First World War, the numerous poetic experiences and particularly a search for surrealism (with the rediscovery of occultism, books on the occult, of the absurd, etc) have caught the attention of the public at different levels and with varying results, on the symbol intended as an independent means of knowledge. This new perspective is comprised in the reaction to rationalism, positivism and scientism of the 19th century, and is sufficient alone to characterise the following quarter of the 20th century. The conversion to a diverse symbolism however is not an unedited 'discovery' worthy of the modern world: by recovering the symbol in its function as a cognitive instrument it is confined to resuming an orientation that in Europe was generally accepted up until the 18th century and which is moreover correlated to other extra-European cultures, whether these be 'historical' (i.e. those of Asia or central America) or archaic and 'primitive'."[241] *He continues: "Symbolic thought is not the exclusive domain of children, poets and the maladjusted, it is connected to the human race: it precedes language and discursive reasoning. Symbols reveal specific aspects of reality – the deeper aspects that escape any other form of cognition. Images, symbols, myths are not irresponsible creations of the mind; they correspond to a need to address an important function: to bare the most secret methods of being. Consequently, the study of symbols results in an enhanced understanding of man, man as a whole, man who has not yet reached a compromise with historic conditions."*[242]

It should therefore be asked whether the choice of symbols used to portray Masonic ritual was quite casual. Is there any degree of *continuity* between the Medieval "Operative" Masons and the modern "Speculative" Freemasons? Personally I am do not

241 Mircea Eliade, *Immagini e Simboli*, Jaca Book, Milan, 1980, page 14.
242 Mircea Eliade, op. cit., page 16.

hold with the idea of a temporal *continuity*, although it is however undeniable that the "operative" Freemasonry to some extent *inspired* the choice of Masonic symbols. Indeed, *Tradition*, of which Freemasonry is a "form", was established following the inspiration of numerous other lesser traditions, as the intuition of a being needs to be provoked or assisted through human actions in so far that the crafts may be consecrated: thus, each utensil, each gesture of the craftsmen may be seen as the symbol of a step towards *the intuition of a perfect being*. Elémire Zolla writes: *"Work in the Medieval Confraternities was exploited for spiritual gain, with financial purposes being relegated to a second level in the intentions of the brethren. All human actions are in their optimum form a means of Tradition."*[243] For this reason, in the opinion of the Italian scholar Eugenio Bonvicini, as early as "operative" Freemasonry symbols possessed esoteric and initiatic connotations, stating that: *"accompanied by the idea of a spiritual elevation of man, they invariably held for Freemasons the function of exalting their inner toils and, for the artist, of extolling the 'creation of his work', his 'masterpiece', an expression of his spiritual quest. At variance with other corporate associations who made use of utensils, or the product of the same, as 'marks' or 'Emblems' of the corporation itself, for the Freemasons the tools, instruments and materials used by the stonemasons assumed a symbolic worth of an esoteric, correlated with other symbols referring to the notion of a spiritual elevation of man."*[244]

Another problem frequently encountered by the scholars and the members themselves of Initiatic Societies, is whether all members are fully *aware* of the profound significance that symbols intrinsically possess, to allow them to be handed down and transmitted. This debate has been widely addressed by Guénon, who maintained that the "lack" of awareness should not affect the initiatic transmission, a concept moreover shared by Mircea Eliade, who essentially confirms the same theory: *"The validity of the symbol as a form of knowledge however, does not depend on the degree of understanding by whomsoever. Illustrated texts and monuments widely prove how, for certain individuals of an archaic society at least, the symbolism of the 'centre' was clearly transparent in its totality; the rest of society merely 'took part' in the symbolism. It is indeed rather difficult to specify the limits of this participation: it varies in line with an undetermined number of factors. We may only say that the actualization of a symbol is not a mechanical concept: it is related to the tensions and the changes registered in the life of the society, and ultimately with cosmic rhythms."*[245]

243 E. Zolla, op. cit., page 100.

244 Eugenio Bonvicini, *Esoterismo nella Massoneria Antica*, Vol.2 *La simbologia celata nelle opere e nelle logge*, Atanòr, Rome, 1993, page 202.

245 Mircea Eliade, Op. cit.., page 26.

2. Symbolism in an Initiatic Order and in a Political Context

Myth and Ideology

The controversy between Myth and Democracy is often depicted as one of those acknowledged forms of apodicticity that do not need to be demonstrated. I have previously challenged this hypothesis in a comparison of two completely different contexts in which Myth, although under different guises, is present — Freemasonry and Fascism — by analysing the quite different and opposite mental approach applied in construing and experiencing the mythological component present therein.

Indeed, both Fascism and Freemasonry bear a clear presence of and relationship with Myth, strongly emphasised by the use of a symbolic-ritualistic apparatus exerting *evocative* powers which, in the case of Fascism was transformed into the *force of persuasion*, indispensable for the elite who wished to make an impression on society rather than being confined to the area of mere doctrinarism.

It should first be mentioned that the relationship between Fascism and Myths and the symbols linked to the latter was merely instrumental, ultimately leading the movement to conceive Myths as something entirely different from the originally intended model and to conclude by underlining an evident degeneration into what could be termed a "pseudo myth".

The renowned scholar of religions, Károly Kerényi, proposed a distinction between a "Genuine Mythology", implying the spontaneous and disinterested elaboration of content emerging from the psyche, and a "Technicalised Mythology", a forced evocation and elaboration of materials that serve a specific purpose.[246]

The distinction proposed by Kerényi, between genuine epiphanies of Myths and the technicalisation of those very Myths (pseudo-epiphanies), allows us to grasp the important difference between Fascism and Freemasonry. Indeed, in Fascism Kerényi identified the "technicalisation" of Myths and, claiming that mythology is no less, but also no more than a mere representation of human life, substantially denies the existence of an extra-human substance revealed in man and in history. Thus, he denies that the Myth put forward by traditional right-wing parties, of which Fascism was one, should be to all intents viewed as such, suggesting that it should perhaps be considered rather as an inevitable form of *degeneration*.

It is an acknowledged fact that Fascism elaborated its own idea of a political Myth for the main purpose of creating an image and a symbol capable of raising the interest of the masses, of arousing enthusiasm and a desire to take action and, in the

246 Furio Jesi, *Cultura di Destra*, Garzanti, Milan, 1993, page 80.

manipulations to which the Myth was accordingly subjected, the ideological qualities of the initiative are clearly evident.

As a result of this "instrumentalisation" of the Myth, the Fascist ideology has been defined as having rejected the supremacy of reason and rational culture, but did not forgo a rational use of the irrational. However, in ideology, as emphasised by Jean-Pierre Sironneau:

"the underlying symbolism and mythical traces are portrayed in a situation of decline: the energetic dynamism of Myths is harnessed, clenched in a rational sheath as tight as a corset, and is losing its intensity: the equivocalness, the depth of meaning, characteristic of all forms of symbolism and all mythical speeches, are giving way to a conceptualism that is veering towards uniqueness. Following this rationalisation and secularisation, the fictional ideology resembles rather an impoverished imagination which has, in my opinion, deteriorated." [247]

In the "technicalisation" of Myths, Kerényi envisaged a doctrinal basis for their social and political use of the same which was aimed at inhibiting and subduing man when faced with incumbent extra-human forces (i.e. when standing before his manipulators). In this way therefore, targeting – for a specific purpose – the exact opposite of a "widening of the conscience", an assumption which, as I shall demonstrate subsequently, is one of the main focuses of Masonic thought, in which, thanks to its *traditional* function of "custodian of authenticity", the typical connotations of the "genuine" Myth can be observed.

It may thus be concluded that once technicalised, Myth not only excludes any form of non-visionary widening of conscience, but likewise allows its manipulators effectively to act as clairvoyants.

Fascist and Masonic rituals

Having underlined the different approach to the issue of mythology applied by Fascism and Freemasonry, and by emphasising the dichotomy coined by Kerényi between a "technicalised" Myth and a "genuine" Myth, I will now attempt to shed light on the different methods used by Freemasonry and Fascism in conceiving and interpreting their rituals. To achieve this I shall resort to another dichotomy pertaining to "synthesis" and "syncretism", put forward by the renowned scholar and expert on traditions René Guénon. Guénon affirmed that syncretism consists in combining from the outside a varied range of elements that, from the point of view in question, can never aspire to being truly united. Substantially, we are dealing with a sort of eclecticism with all that is fragmentary and incoherent; thus, with something exquisitely external and superior, the elements of which, gathered hither and thither and combined in an essentially artificial

247 A. de Benoist, *L'impero interiore*, Ponte alle Grazie, Florence, 1995, page 22.

fashion, will unfailingly appear as patched together items, incapable of becoming effectively integrated in a secret Doctrine worthy of this name. Conversely, synthesis is, in substance, undertaken from the inside: by this I mean that it implies a consideration of things in view of the Unity of their very principle, through uniting the same, or rather gaining awareness of their effective union which, in view of the inner nature of the relationship, is inherent to the deepest realms of nature.[248]

A clear manifestation of symbolic syncretism can be observed in the Fascist phenomenon, underlying a tendency to use symbols belonging to different doctrines, all of which are the outcome of a lengthy search for a lay religion for the "new Italy" undertaken from the Renaissance up until the First World War. Originating from numerous movements, the Fascists created their rituals by "syncretically" unifying the already existing symbols to form a set of beliefs that would result in the establishing of a lay religion focusing on the "sacralisation" of the homeland.

Fascism was well aware of the *circular* relationship between myths, rituals and symbols, maintaining the latter to be a necessary condition with which to instil and perpetuate a collective faith, although Fascists were mainly concerned with the "political" importance of the undertaking. Indeed, the symbols and rituals used to imply a form of visualisation and dramatisation of Myth were fundamental in providing access to the myths of the "Fascist religions" through the sentiment of the masses and converting the people to the faith.

This exploitation of Myth by the Fascists for political purposes contributed towards the establishing of a State liturgy to be used not only by the party militants but likewise by all Italians implicated, willing or not, in the periodic celebration of the rituals of the Regime. In establishing this liturgy, Fascism followed a logic entirely of its own, clearly emphasising a "realistic awareness" of the function that rituals and symbols exercise in mass politics.

Symbols and rituals were used increasingly as propaganda and as instruments aimed at influencing public opinion by appealing to people's sentiments, emotions, imaginations and enthusiasm. Fascism invested symbols with a sacral worth, assigning a magic power, a mystical, ecstatic ability, thus transforming them into idols and totems to be worshipped.

For Mircea Eliade, the "Ritual" unfailingly consists in the repetition of an archetypal gesture, undertaken *in illo tempore* (at the beginning of time) by our ancestors and the gods. In repeating this gesture, the "profane" time is abolished and the action assumes a certain meaning only to the extent that it reiterates a transcendent model, an archetype. Thus, the purpose of this repetition is to achieve the normality of the gesture, to legitimise

248 René Guénon, *Considerazioni sulla via iniziatica,* Basaia, Rome, 1988.

the same by conferring it with an ontological status; indeed, if the gesture is made "real" this will only occur through repetition of an archetype.[249] As a consequence, the ritual is both a ceremony (that integrates man into the sacred area) and a real world intervention.

This interpretation of the ritual by Eliade that assumes the typical implications of the "synthesis" described by Guénon can also be observed in Freemasonry, particularly in the ceremony of Elevation to the 3rd Degree when, in referring to the previously mentioned Legend of Hiram, the same allegory has been faithfully reiterated throughout the centuries. Indeed, an *apology* narrating the violent death of the architect Hiram Abif, murdered before he could complete the construction of King Solomon's Temple is re-enacted. As in all rituals, here too, the time in which the event was commemorated or repeated has been actualised, "re-presented", "relived" as the occurrence, although undertaken at the present time, was first set in a mythical time. As underlined by Eliade:

"This contemporaneity with the great moments of myth is an indispensable condition for any form of magic-religious efficaciousness... By repeating an archetypal gesture, one is projected into an ahistoric sacred time, an event that can only take place if the profane time has been abolished." [250] This particular "ahistoric" relationship with time, this substitution of the "profane" time with a "sacred" time is missing from Fascist rituals which, in the manifest technicalisations of mythical images, clearly emphasise a fundamental "coldness", non-participation, and mere exploitation rather than devotion, characteristics that all denote a radical rejection or at least a radical ignorance of the secret *quid* implicated in the ritual.

In this regard, Furio Jesi states:

"The mythological language of Italian Fascism, at variance with other European right-wing areas, is almost exclusively 'exoteric': i.e. it is made up of 'gimmicks' rather than rituals in the true sense of the word. Although indeed, there is no lack of instances of esoteric ambition such as those displayed by Julius Evola or Massimo Scaligero, at times linked to a more consistent mystic view of death, frequently presented as mere elements of some form of heterodoxy when compared to the official orientation of the Regime. Only latterly, in conjunction with the advent of a sacred neo-fascism, will we see a move from the right-wing ideology of a non-esoteric sacrality towards a right-wing idea of sacred esotericism." [251] Indeed, throughout the first decades of the twentieth century the ideology of a profane right-wing had featured several "sacred" components that were however devoid of esoteric significance. This ideology entertained the notion of a relationship with the past

249 M. Eliade, *Trattato di storia delle religioni*, Bollati Boringhieri, Turin, 1996, page 41.

250 Ibid, page 44.

251 F. Jesi, op. cit., page 32.

that was in some way sacred, whilst at the same time conveying aspects of an exceedingly historic relevance to enable the past to flow into the "Great Time" of traditionalists, the same "Great Time" which, according to Kerényi, is the custodian of true Myth. If this "Great Time" is lacking then esotericism cannot be complete, and history represents its main enemy.

Conversely, in Freemasonry rituality is conceived as something irreplaceable for the individual who has opted for the Masonic way of perfection. Masonic rituals indeed, although making use of symbols for which the original meaning has been completely lost, are performed in such a way as to convey the characteristics of a living Myth to the ceremony through a process of intellectualisation and interiorisation of the general view held of Freemasonry, seen as the ideality of personal experiences. This "awareness", achieved through the practising of rituals and the use of symbols, is completely missing from the methods and procedures that the Fascists applied so slavishly and mechanically in organising their rituals.

Through their rituals both Fascists and Freemasons impart directives on how to behave in life situations. In this regard, therefore, rituals may indeed be viewed as a "key" leading to the comprehension of tasks to be undertaken. However, whilst thanks to these rituals, Freemasons will acquire an "awareness" that will assist them in deciding of their own accord which direction to take, Fascist rituals will infuse members with a full-blown *indoctrination* that will leave little space for freedom of choice and independence.

At first glance, Fascist rituals may appear to resemble a sort of *initiation* procedure, although they actually are in no way linked to the conception of initiation construed as a guarantee of the *regeneration* of the initiate, and the imparting of secrets of a metaphysical nature. Only an authentic initiation comprises a close association between theophany (in view of the fact that in the initiatic ritual the true nature and the true name of the divinity is revealed) and metaphysics (revelation surrounding the principle and the origin of the Universe, the origin of the human race, etc).[252]

The Fascist symbology

As illustrated in the previous section, symbols comprise a wide range of possible interpretations and underlie *a synthesis* of unification capable of projecting man towards the "archetypes" — ideas or inspirations. Symbols represent a means of reflection, of knowledge, intellect and intuition.

In Freemasonry, the fundamental concepts are expressed by means of a coherent system of symbols, all of which are closely interlinked and convey a profound sense of

252 Mircea Eliade, op. cit., page 64.

initiatic activity. In the same way as Myths, the utilitarian use of symbols applied by the Fascists, invariably focused on achieving the political aims established, underlines the extent to which they were inevitably rendered vulgar and debased.

Conversely, the Masonic conception of man and of the universe is developed throughout the process, within which the use of symbols is of fundamental importance. Indeed, as Freemasons view the cosmos as a hierophany and deem human life sacred, their work is enriched with a liturgical value that allows man to be introduced into the realm of the "sacred" through his work as a *homo faber*, as the author and manipulator of tools, naturally from an allegorical point of view. This leads us to the *origins* of Freemasonry, as highlighted by Eliade: *"When the global experience of the world was changed following the onset of technical and cultural innovation produced by the establishing of urban civilization, the primordial experiences associated with a sacralised Cosmos were subjected to a periodic revival elicited by means of initiations and trade rituals."* [253]

I would now like to examine briefly the symbols applied in Fascism and Freemasonry, with the aim of better emphasising the fundamental differences between the two.

As mentioned previously, right from the outset Fascism aired its views of a nation as the sacred focus underlying the party doctrine through an appropriate use of rituals and symbols. As immediately remarked on by Emilio Gentile: *"This use was by no means ignored by other political movements, from the Republicans to the Socialists, and from the Nationalists to the People's party. But no-one had yet applied a methodical approach to the political liturgy... at varia nce with other parties moreover, the Fascists assigned a predominant function to political symbols in their actions and organisation, thus attributing the same through their use of language and gestures, with an explicitly religious significance and relevance. Similar to their dealings with mythology, in elaborating their liturgy the Fascists behaved in the same way as a syncretic religion, assimilating the materials they deemed to be of use in developing a set of rituals and symbols which were casually incorporated with ritual traditions from other movements and integrated with their own. The Fascists held no concern for the originality of their rituals and symbols, tending rather towards ensuring the efficacy of the latter in their actions, to represent their myths and thus strengthen the sense of identity of the movement, as valid instruments to be used in the fight against the 'enemies of the nation'. The majority of the rituals and symbols used during the years of the Fascist paramilitary squads were devised spontaneously, at times by invention and at times by imitation."* [254]

253 M. Eliade, *Arti del metallo e alchimia*, Bollati Boringhieri, Turin, 1980, page 128.

254 E. Gentile, *Il culto del littorio*, Laterza, Bari, 1994, page 45.

Among the symbols used by the regime the "truncheon" and "fire" were the most widely exploited terrorist symbols implying the purifying violence of the squads. A sort of cult was devoted to the truncheon, seen as a singular talisman, whilst fire unfailingly ended all Fascist expeditions; the public burning of symbols and places of worship of their enemies, as was the case with the Masonic Lodges, sealed each victorious expedition.

A further element of significance in the symbols used by Fascism was undoubtedly represented by "pennants". These were exhibited during the ceremony of the taking of the oath, a ritual that had been used previously in Rijeka as described by D'Annunzio, and one of the first acts of the Fascist liturgy in which the pennant was handed over and previously blessed. This standard, the key symbol of the faith and the constraints of the communion of the squads, was increasingly worshipped during the years of the Fascist regime. Generally, the blessing of the pennant was performed by a clergyman, although at times the ritual was undertaken even in the absence of a member of the clergy, and the officiator was the head squad leader.

The Fascists invested the cult of the flag with particular importance, organising an even more solemn version of the festivities held to celebrate National Jubilees, and obliging municipal authorities to budget for the expenses required in celebrating lay events "with the required external manifestations". It moreover became mandatory for the government and municipal offices to fly the national flag. However, the cult of the flag was not confined merely to public offices, military ceremonies and public festivities. On January 23rd 1923 the Ministry for Education made it compulsory for schools to salute the national flag.

It is clear therefore that the Fascist strategy focused on a use of symbols that was intended to make the definitive and revolutionary significance heralded by the change of government undertaken through the "Fascist revolution" more perceptible. For this reason, once they had come to power, the regime embarked on the fascistisation of the State.

In 1922, the historian Emilio Gentile wrote:

"Throughout numerous Italian cities the scene had changed completely. The lengthy parades of red or white flags had been replaced, at the end of a victorious 'war of symbols' to obtain the exclusive monopoly, by a parade bearing the Italian flag or the black pennants of Fascism."[255] *This "war of symbols" was destined to be resumed shortly afterwards, this time not in an attempt to gain exclusive rights, but to preside over the conscience of the Italian people: although now the enemy to overcome was represented by Freemasonry.*

The *fasces lictoriae*, an expression of ancient Rome and of the new Italian State, depicting a bundle of sticks with a laterally placed axe and chosen by Mussolini himself,

255 E. Gentile, op. cit., page 57.

came to represent the symbol *par excellence*. The representation chosen was viewed as a faithful expression of Roman symbolism which had been distorted during the French Revolution, and subsequently passed on through the Renaissance, consisting in an axe or halberd surmounted by a Phrygian cap placed on top of the sticks. Subsequently, the symbol was applied to the seal used by the Foreign Ministry, a series of stamps bearing the symbol was issued, and it was then gradually introducéd into the iconography of the Italian State. Following its consecration in the Roman style, Mussolini issued a bulletin on December 1st 1925 dictating that the symbol should be displayed on all Ministerial buildings. A decree issued on December 12th 1926 appointed the symbol as emblem of State and on March 27th 1927 it was decreed that the emblem depicted on the armband should be placed to the left of the emblem of State represented by the coat of arms of the House of Savoy, in use since 1890.

To summarise, as established by the "evolutionist" school of thought, Myths should not be confined to the initial stages of human development but should rather be viewed as a *permanent structure* of the human spirit. According to Van der Leeuw, Myths and Magic constitute the deepest layer of human spirituality, and the author makes a parallelism between the dreamlike dimension and the magical-mythical domain: *"The magical-mythical domination represents the same part that the dream life maintains compared to the waking conscience. The recent psychologist has taught us that one is no less real than the other. The study of dreams, to be able to penetrate the secret of life, does not follow the by no means more uncertain route of research into the state of consciousness."*[256]

These words give rise to an interesting and complex cultural scenario that lead to another intriguing area in the field of analytical psychology that we will examine in a subsequent chapter.

256 , Bollati Boringhieri, Turin, 1992, page 430.

Chapter Five

For an Initiatic Coalescence

Heaven is the work of the best and kindest men and women. Hell is the work of prigs, pedants and professional truth-tellers. The world is an attempt to make the best of both.

Samuel Butler

Notebooks

1. The Integralist Esotericists

As mentioned in a previous chapter, the interpretations of Freemasonry, with regard to both its origins and its principles, are frequently discordant. These differences often lead to confusion among Freemasons themselves, who find, even within the same Lodge, that they are required to share their initiatic experience with Brothers who, at a first glance, may have a completely different opinion of Freemasonry.

These differences of interpretation have essentially resulted in two different types of representation; one viewing Freemasonry as a society of mutual assistance with *ethico-moral* connotations, and the other interpreting Freemasonry as a true Initiatic Society. Are these two views reconcilable? Can people continue to be "Brothers" in the same Temple whilst having different ideas with regard to the interpretation of the ritual and symbols contained therein? I am personally convinced this is possible; the interpretation of rituals *may* differ, as long as they remain within the confines of Freemasonry, in respect of the ancient *Landmarks*. It would moreover be dangerous to exclude one interpretation in favour of another and might lead, as we will see, to two different forms of "integralism" and, as we are all aware, Freemasonry abhors such a thought.

I shall mention a few examples with reference to the above dichotomy and we can attempt to understand the consequences.

I would like to commence from the "category" of those I would tend to define as esoteric "integralists", among whom the more aggressive were undoubtedly the followers of the theories of Guénon, frequently interpreted as zealous imitators of their creator. Several opinions reported by Guénon himself leave us somewhat puzzled, as reiterated by Mariano Bizzarri: *"deafness, dumbness, stuttering, limping, blindness, the presence of deformities to the chest or spine, alterations to the structure of the foot or mutilation to the limbs are all de facto conditions that impeded the conferring of Initiation to their bearers... Physical defects and infirmities not only represent an obstacle to the ritual work, but at the same time are seen as 'the external signs of certain imperfections of a psychic nature', revealing the presence of a 'disharmony and imbalance in the constitution of the individual', which would prejudice their admission to an initiatic organisation,"*[257] assertions that, as stated previously, resemble those written by Guénon.

René Guénon, a renowned representative of *Traditional* thought displays an approach to "initiatic qualifications" that I would undoubtedly define as "integralist". Moreover, as we shall see subsequently, his theories on the qualification for initiation, and here I refer to Masonic initiation, largely debatable and difficult to ratify, are often based on convictions that lack any vestige of historic proof.

According to Guénon, starting from a viewpoint that acknowledges *authentic* Freemasonry as the Medieval "operative" form:

"If the initiatic ritual takes the craft as a 'support' in such a way that it is so to speak derived from it by an appropriate transposition (though in the beginning things were no doubt envisaged in reverse, for from the traditional point of view the craft is really only a contingent application of the principles to which the initiation directly relates), then in order to be really and fully valid, the accomplishment of this ritual requires conditions that include those required by the practice of the craft itself for the same transposition applies equally here in virtue of the correspondences that exist between different modalities of the being."[258] Guénon however, hurries on to specify that the inadequacy produced by physical defects is not correlated solely to a "practical" point of view, but particularly regards a "spiritual" demeanour: *"Thus, if Masonic initiation excludes women in particular (which, as we have said, does not mean that they are unqualified for every initiation), as well as men with certain infirmities, this is not merely because those who are admitted used to have to carry burdens or climb scaffolds, as some assure us with a disconcerting naiveté; rather, the Masonic initiation itself could not be valid for such people and could have no effect because of their lack of qualification. The first thing that can be said here is that even if the link with the craft has been broken with respect to outward practice, it nonetheless continues in a more essential way insofar as it remains necessarily inscribed in the very form of this initiation; for if this connection were eliminated, the initiation would no longer be Masonic but something completely different."*[259]

Indeed, Guénon's explanation is decidedly vague, although he confuses it even further by including additions such as "stuttering" which have nothing to do with the "Craft", and even mentioning the ancient *Landmarks* in an attempt to ratify his theory: *"There is still more: if we*

257 Mariano Bizzarri, *La via iniziatica*, Atanòr, Rome, 2002, page 86.
258 René Guénon, *Considerazioni sulla via iniziatica*, Basaia, Rome, 1988, page 141.
259 René Guénon, op. cit., page 141.

closely examine the list of bodily defects considered to be impediments to initiation, it will be noted how some do not seem outwardly very serious and, in any case, would not prevent a man from practising the craft of the builder. And so this, too, is only a partial explanation, although exact in the measure to which it applies, for, besides the conditions required by the craft, the initiation requires others having nothing to do with these but relating solely to the modalities of the ritual work considered not only in its 'materiality', so to speak, but above all as having to produce effective results for the one who accomplishes them. This will appear all the more clearly when, from among the diverse formulations of the landmarks (for although in principle not written down, they have nevertheless often been the object of more or less detailed enumerations), we go back to the most ancient ones, that is, to an epoch when the things in question were still known." [260]

The idea that the ancient Masonic *Landmarks* may provide any sort of reference relating to *impediments* to initiation, and particularly to physical defects, should certainly be clarified. It is not my intention to address such a complex issue as that of the *Landmarks* here, and I will therefore merely provide a few simple considerations. The first thing that should be underlined is how Guénon contradicts himself on this subject; having written that the requisites for initiation could be assumed from the ancient *Landmarks*, in another document he maintains that the same *Landmarks "...cannot in any way be assimilated to a set of written regulations that express at the most an indirect and far removed mention."* [261] Referring to the literature published on the subject, and, as on previous occasions, to studies undertaken by the *Quatuor Coronati* Lodge in London, among the most reliable, I will quote three essays obtained from the eminent journal *Ars Quatuor Coronatorum,* that publishes the writings produced by the Lodge.

It is an acknowledged fact that no official definition or number of *Landmarks* has been provided, although some authors, for example Albert Mackey, have inappropriately proposed and described twenty-five of them; unfortunately, the previously mentioned physical impediments are also listed.

With regard to the historical *inaccuracy* and initiatic *unacceptability* of these lists, I wish to cite the historian W.B. Hextall who, in the essay *The Old Landmarks of the Craft* published in 1912, writes in relation to the list compiled by Mackey: *"Many of Mackey's twenty-five certainly are not Landmarks properly of Freemasonry,"* [262] whilst Axel J. A. Poignant, in an article dated 1911, specifies with regard to another list defining, in his opinion, the *Landmarks*: *"The prevalent opinion seems to be that it is now impossible*

260 René Guénon, op. cit., pages 142-143.

261 René Guénon, *Études sur la Franc-Maçonnerie et le Compagnonnage,* Vol.II, Paris, Editions Traditionelles, 1965, page 301.

262 W.B. Hextall, *The Old Landmarks of the Craft,* AQC, Vol.XXV, 1912.

to ascertain what exactly the founders of modern Freemasonry meant to include under the heading, and authorities greatly vary in their enumeration of the 'landmarks'." [263]Poignant, in referring to the *traditional* definition of Freemasonry as *"A system of morals veiled by allegories and illustrated by symbols"* clarifies that, in his opinion, neither symbols nor allegories, important as they may be, are included in the category of *Landmarks*, although the significance of their teachings may be listed: *"... no allegory or symbol, however important, is in itself a Landmark, though what it teaches may be one"*. And, he continues, in the light of the definition of Freemasonry, it is impossible that the *Landmarks* would have been written down, as this would not justify *"A peculiar system of morality veiled in allegory and illustrated by symbols"*. John R. Rylands, in more recent times, and again with reference to the *Landmarks*, states how the concept should be interpreted metaphorically, referring to the Masonic "tradition" of the *United Grand Lodge of England* and to the principles upheld, whilst taking into account the importance in relation to the context in which they belong:

"It follows that the preservation of the original purity of any Masonic system must depend on the retention, unchanged, of its basic dogmas, whatever these may be, and it is this retention as a whole which may metaphorically be described as 'preserving the Ancient Landmarks'. To argue whether this concept or that is or is not a Landmark of Freemasonry is thus besides the point. A Landmark per se is not immovable, neither has it an absolute value. Landmarks are relative to the particular Masonic system to which they belong... To preserve the old Landmarks, therefore, is simply to retain the character and principles of our freemasonry basically unchanged. But within this limitation there is a great freedom, the liberty of the individual mason to interpret personally, as he wishes, the allegory and the symbolisms which are the vehicles whereby we teach our principles." [264]

Particularly, however, in the three studies cited, no reference is ever made to the presence of "physical defects" as one of the potential impediments to initiation as one of the *Landmarks*.

Once again returning to the issue of "qualification", in a parallelism with religious rites, Guénon specifies further that, whilst in Catholic ritual it is the priest alone who actively performs the rites, and in lay functions a merely "receptive" role is played, in a rite comprised as part of an initiatic method there should, conversely, be an "active" rather than a "receptive" form of involvement requiring, in addition to an "intellectual" qualification, that termed by Guénon as "secondary" qualifications that vary in accordance with the rites and initiatic "forms". Among these "secondary" qualifications Guénon lists: *"The absence of certain bodily defects always plays an important role, whether*

263 Axel J.A. Poignant, *The Landmarks*, AQC, Vol.XXIV, 1911.

264 John R. Rylands, *The Ancient Landmarks*, AQC, Miscellanea Latomorum, Vol.LXXII, 1959.

these defects be a direct impediment to the accomplishment of the rites or the outward sign of corresponding defects in the subtle elements of the being."[265]

The debate, however, already sufficiently unlikely and artificial, is further complicated when Guénon adds to the list of the above mentioned "infirmities" which "occurred" after birth, those caused by accidents:

"If we are to consider infirmities or merely bodily defects as outward signs of certain psychic imperfections, it will be fitting to make a distinction between defects that the being exhibits from birth or that develop naturally over the course of its existence as a consequence of a certain predisposition, and those that are merely the result of some accident. It is evident that the first reveal something that more strictly inheres in the very nature of the being, and that consequently is more serious from our present point of view, although, since nothing can happen to a being that does not really correspond to some more or less essential element of its nature, even apparently accidental infirmities cannot be considered entirely indifferent in this respect... Some may be astonished that accidental infirmities thus correspond to something in the very nature of the being affected by them; but this is after all only a direct consequence of the real relationships the being has with the environment in which it manifests itself: all the relationships among beings manifested in one and the same world, or what comes to the same thing, all their reciprocal actions, can only be real if they are the expression of something that belongs to the nature of each of them. In other words, everything a being undergoes, as well as all that it does, constitutes a 'modification' of that being, and must necessarily correspond to one of the possibilities in its nature, so that there can be nothing that is purely accidental if this word be understood in the sense of 'extrinsic' as it commonly is."[266]

Accordingly, I would like to underline the importance of correspondence between Guénon and Julius Evola relating to the incident in which Evola lost the use of his lower limbs in Vienna in 1945. From the three letters written by Guénon (we regrettably do not possess Evola's letters) between 1948 and 1949, it is clear that Evola, in referring to the "incident" suggested that this could have been the outcome of Masonic "operations" on several "operative" Masonic rituals (in the sense conveyed by the Evolian alchemy) which was undergoing a "revival" at the time. He moreover asked for an opinion from Guénon, knowing of his theories on the subject, as to whether his infirmity could have been caused by the *onset* of problems of an 'inner' nature.

In the first letter dated June 24th 1948 written in Cairo, following several considerations pertaining to comments made by Evola on his book *The Reign of Quantity and the Signs of the Times*, as well as other editorial matters, Guénon refers to the Vienna incident:

265 René Guénon, op. cit., page 144.

266 René Guénon, op. cit., pages 145-146.

"I have no idea whether the story of the rituals that you mention could be in any way associated with the fate that befell you; indeed there have been instances in which similar reactions have been manifested unsolicited, although I have no knowledge of Freemasonry being implicated; as a general rule, this is the demonstration that it is never wise to be associated with certain things (although it may be with the best intentions) when this occurs in the lack of a regular transmission..." Guénon's letter reveals how he did not exclude the "possibility" that the incident that had befallen Evola may have been caused by an initiatic "deficit" committed by Evola himself, due to the lack of a "regular initiation", on the subject of "initiatic transmission" which has invariably come between the two due traditionalist thinkers.[267] Many years later Evola, probably realising the absurdity of this theory, in his biography *The Path of Cinnabar* even denied the event (despite the letters written by Guénon), providing a somewhat more credible version (the infirmity was caused by an air raid).

2. Against Esotericism

From the "integralist" esotericists I should like now to mention the proponents of an "integralist" associationism; those who see in Freemasonry little more than one of the numerous forms of charitable and recreational, if not political, *associationism*, and view the initiatic component merely as one of the pieces of the "game".

For this purpose, I have opted to examine the *transformation* of several Masonic rituals, underlining their *degeneration* from an *initiatic-esoteric* into an *associationistic-political* form. At the same time I have attempted to highlight how the distorted view of several historians who, lacking all forms of distinction, have arbitrarily depicted all Masonic Obediences as merely associationistic, if not overtly political, thereby contributing towards creating in the public mind a false, unfounded view of Freemasonry.

In the first part of this paper I have compared the Masonic Rituals adopted in the Consecration of a Temple and of a Lodge, originating from two different Masonic contexts: British (England and Scotland) and French (*Grand Orient of France*). The confrontation will underline substantial differences in the initiatic and esoteric content of the rituals examined, differences that, as will soon become evident, are one of the causes underlying the progressive degeneration that has led Freemasonry increasingly towards profane, associative forms.

In the second part I will analyse the text written by T.O. Haunch, *The Constitution and Consecration of Lodges* in which the author, whilst providing an unexceptionable historic

267 Fabio Venzi, *Julius Evola e la Libera Muratoria: Una verità scomoda*, Settimo Sigillo, Rome, 2010, page 15.

reconstruction of the Ritual for Consecration of a Lodge, at the same time conveys a sense of constant *underestimation* of the *esoteric-initiatic* significance of the ceremony. This criticism of the work of Haunch, an author of important essays and one of the most knowledgeable in the field of Masonic studies, should not be construed as criticism of the author, but is intended to shed light on a vision of Freemasonry, common to numerous other authors of the period (referring to the 1960s) that held the issue of Masonic esotericism in such low regard. Today, however, clear signs of change are being heralded.

In the third and last part I will briefly illustrate the origins of the rituals used in the Consecration of a "sacred space", referring specifically to the archaic rites of foundation. Thus, the fundamental importance given to orientation of the Temple and to spatial collocation, an operation corresponding in ancient society to a "cosmisation" of the area occupied, progressing from a state of "chaos" to one of "order", a concept constantly present in Masonic rituals, will be underlined.

Consecration: An Esoteric or Profane Ritual? Inauguration of a Temple and Installation of a Lodge

No substantial differences are present between the ceremonies adopted in the English ritual for the Consecration of a Lodge and the Scottish ritual of Consecration of a Temple. Both ceremonies are indeed characterised by an Opening Prayer, although in view of the diverse nature of the ceremonies the prayers differ, by a Hymn of Consecration in the Scottish rite alone and by the reading of *Psalm 133* in both rites. The Scriptures subsequently adopted are of a diverse nature and are greater in number during the ritual for Consecration of a Lodge. Both rituals involve circumambulations during which the Temple is sprinkled with incense; in the ritual performed to Consecrate a Lodge wheat, wine, oil and salt are scattered, whilst in the Temple dedication ritual wheat, wine and oil are strewn, but not salt.

None of these features are present in the rituals performed by the *Grand Orient of France*, an essentially "atheist" Masonic Grand Lodge which in 1877 removed all references to the GAOTU (Grand Architect of the Universe) from its rituals. On analysing the French ritual it is immediately evident how the term "Consecration" has been abandoned and replaced by the profane term "Inauguration" when referring to a Temple and "Installation" when referring to a Lodge. Although the premises state in a contradictory manner how *"one should adopt an esoteric approach to the inner decorations of the Temple of Solomon"* (*on se rapproche ésotériquemente au décor interieur du Temple de Salomon*), no elements conveying esoteric connotations are present in the ritual, although it is subsequently underlined that *"Inauguration thus evolves into an exceptional and moving ceremony that 'sacralises' these singularly symbolic premises"*(L'inauguration est alors toujours une cérémonie exceptionelle et émouvante qui 'sacralise' ce lieu particulièrement symbolique).

Indeed, the ritual is *devoid* of any esoteric or symbolic reference to the *metaphysical* nature of the ceremony, the *transformation* of a profane site into a "sacred" space. On the contrary, during the ceremony a marked influence produced by the Enlightenment and progressive movements typical of eighteenth-century French Freemasonry is clearly evident. The ritual recites that the *"flame is the symbol of Reason (capital letter)"* and *"that the Blazing Star will lead us towards progress"*; Reason and Progress were the acknowledged key issues of the eighteenth-century Enlightenment. Of all the theories that have harmed and proved particularly damaging to a correct understanding of Freemasonry, one of the most commonly acknowledged maintains that the origins of Freemasonry derive from the Enlightenment movement. This theory is hard to eradicate, and the damage caused by this situation within the confines of studies analysing Freemasonry has been considerable.

Undeniably, during the eighteenth century "several" Masonic bodies in Europe introduced the principles of enlightenment into their rituals, thus distorting their esoteric and initiatic origins. In these Obediences the ritual has gradually been *deprived* of its true symbolic significance and replaced by commentaries and exegeses characterised by a desolating banality and a dull moralism reminiscent of the *"century of the Enlightened"*. This "progressivist" degeneration of the principles of Freemasonry has consequently led to a misconceived interpretation of the concept of Fellowship, increasingly construed as an independent "individual subject" invested with a real power within the context of socio-political confines, or levelling out into a form of essentially moral and material solidarism.

The sentimental aspect, largely crystallised in the moral element, is particularly typical of religious forms and, as is well known, Freemasonry is not a religion. Consequently, we have witnessed from time to time the *transformation* of an initiatic society in which Brotherhood is a feature shared by all individuals undertaking a "personal" journey of research and knowledge, into a generic associative phenomenon based on morals springing from an initiatic-religious syncretism.

However, through "intuitive knowledge" the Masonic process is delineated as a method enhancing the implementation of an active process of inner transformation leading to the development of an actual change in status in an "individual" and "personal" rather than a "social" context.

To return to the ceremony of the Inauguration of a Temple, the entire French ritual is seasoned with the triptych *Liberty, Equality, Fraternity*. There is a complete lack of Prayers, Beseechments, Bible readings, circumambulations and esoteric formulas, all widely present in the British Masonic ceremonies.

The Installation, or creation of a new Lodge, is in rituals employed by the *Grand Orient of France*, likewise substantially *devoid* of esoteric elements, underlining the enlightenment implications contained in the ceremony for inauguration of a Temple.

Indeed, the premise recites: *"Freemasonry, being an institution essentially philanthropic, philosophic and progressive... has for its object the search for the intellectual and social perfection of Humanity and its motto is Liberty, Equality and Fraternity."* The entire Ceremony of Installation in the *Grand Orient of France* is ritually confined to the transportation of the Star of the Lodge, which is then added to the emblem of the Obedience. Accordingly, in this vision, philanthropy, philosophy and politics constitute the tools, and intellectual and social progress the aim of Freemasonry.

Conversely, an Initiatic Order focuses solely on an *individual* journey of progressive self-discovery, tracing back an age-old uninterrupted learned *Tradition* defined as esoteric as it addresses a single follower within a specific context and ignores and rises above the worldly presence of politics or philanthropy.

The Esoteric Component in the Ritual of Consecration
Evolution of the Ritual

In Anderson's *Constitutions* published in 1723 a paragraph on "The Manner of Constituting a New Lodge" states how the ceremony for the foundation of a Lodge was comprised in the ceremony of Installation of the Venerable Master of the Lodge itself, being reduced to little more than a mere formal undertaking performed by the Grand Master or his Deputy. The *Constitutions* recite:

"Does not appear to involve any ceremonial rite of Constitution at all but merely the formal pronouncement by the Grand Master 'I constitute and form these good Brethren into a Lodge' followed, it is suggested, by something like an oration on the nature and principles of the institution."

Thus, it would seem that the changes applied, following which the ritual assumed its current *esoteric-initiatic* semblance took place between 1723 and 1815, the year in which the consecration ritual used today was probably established.

Subsequent modifications to the ceremony for the Consecration of a Lodge were based on the first edition of the *Illustrations of Masonry* by William Preston (1772), although further important changes and additions were included in his eighth edition. In his third lecture, in mentioning the Ceremony of Consecration, he provides considerable cues for discussion.

Preston naturally does not describe the actual ritual but rather provides a wealth of elements enabling its reconstruction. Up until 1880, the year in which the ritual formula *The Lecture of the Three Degrees in Craft Masonry with the ceremony of Installation and Consecration* was published by A. Lewis of London, the only reference available was contained in the work by Preston. It can therefore be concluded that the ceremony used today is an *evolution* of the Prestonian model, although no form of documentation is available to reveal how the evolution took place.

Indeed, the documents available seem to denote a marked evolution in the Ceremony of Consecration that was to lead from an initial absence of ritual to development of the same following fundamental additions of an esoteric nature.

Constitution, Consecration and Dedication

T.O. Haunch, historian of Freemasonry and specifically of the London Lodge No. 2076 *Quatuor Coronati*, in his important study of the evolution of the rite of consecration of a Lodge, reported in *Volume 83* of *Ars Quatuor Coronatorum,* defines the differences between Constitution, Consecration and Dedication. I, however, agree only partially with the definitions put forward by Haunch for the following reasons.

Haunch refers to Constitution as: *"the formal act which brings a new Lodge into being, gives effect in Masonic law to the terms of the warrant, and empowers the members of the lodge to carry out the function specified in the warrant"*, and here I of course concur with the statements made. On proceeding, Haunch maintains that Consecration is: *"the Masonic rite, religious in form, by which it is regularly constituted, i.e. the practice of Freemasonry"* and goes on to conclude that Dedication is: *"the religious and Masonic rite by which a building or room is allowed and sanctified for the practice of Freemasonry, in distinction to 'Consecration' which performs the same action towards the corporate body of Masons forming a new Lodge"*.[268]

In particular, important considerations should be made with regard to the definitions provided for Consecration and Dedication. Indeed, Haunch differentiates between the Consecration of a Lodge and the Dedication of a Temple, two rites that although both performed for the same reason and being *religious in form,* are addressed to two different entities, the first to the corporate body of Masons (The Lodge) and the second to a building (The Temple). I personally do not agree with this differentiation and maintain that the two rites feature an identical *esoteric* and *initiatic* vocation: the first the establishment of a "sacred space" and the second to creating an "initiatic body" to perform inside the former. Consequently, the term "Consecration" may correctly be applied to both ceremonies.

Considerable importance should be placed on the presence of an *"unbroken initiatic chain"*, with the *Anderson Constitutions* stating that consecration of a Lodge should be undertaken *"agreeably to the ancient usages and customs of the Fraternity"*. The Consecration of this initiatic body, the Lodge, *"agreeably to the... customs"*, therefore implies that the initiatic chain together with the esoteric *Tradition* from which the latter originates, should not be *broken* and, should such an occurrence take place, the Lodge would be viewed as an irregular Lodge from an *initiatic* point of view.

268 T.O. Haunch, *The Constitution and Consecration of Lodges under the Grand Lodge of England,* AQC Vol.83, 1970 page 1.

To address once again the Rituals of Consecration, the *Grand Lodge of Scotland* refers to the two ceremonies, the Foundation of a new Temple or the creation of a new Lodge, using the term "Consecration". Accordingly, the document *Ceremonial for the guidance of Grand Office-Bearers, Provincial and District Grand Office-Bearers and Office-Bearers of Daughter Lodges* published by the Grand Secretary under the authority of the Grand Committee, refers to the ceremony of the foundation of a new Temple as "Consecration", officially including the latter in the chapter "Consecration of a Temple or Lodge Room set apart for the purpose of Freemasonry".

Further confirmation of the profoundly esoteric and sacred component of the Ceremony for the Consecration of a Temple or other premises to be used for esoteric ceremonies is provided by the interesting addition whereby the Consecration ceremony should be performed even for the ritual use of a single room in which, *albeit only occasionally*, Masonic work is carried out. The latter implies that in the absence of an esoteric ritual conveying to premises "other" features previously lacking and rendering it suitable for use in initiatic tasks, these premises are not appropriate for use in Masonic issues.

On returning once more to the term "Dedication", it can be stated that this term is probably of ecclesiastic origin. The term is indeed found in the *Ceremonial of Bishops* adopted by the Catholic Church for the occasion of "dedicating" a Church to one Saint or another.[269] Could this be the reason why Haunch defined it as a religious Masonic ritual?

The "dedication" of a church may be undertaken at the time of its foundation, for the purpose of "dedicating" the church to the Lord by means of a solemn rite according to the ancient tradition of the Church. The Bishop appointed to attend to a given church will be responsible for dedicating to God all new churches erected in his diocese.[270] With the exception of the sprinkling of incense, the rite of Dedication has nothing in common with the Masonic rite of Consecration of a Temple. A ceremony known as Rededication is included in the Ceremonial of the Grand Lodge of Scotland, but is referred to as the *"Ceremony observed when a Daughter Lodge is celebrating an occasion such as a centenary, bi-centenary, etc."*, as is clearly evident, a ceremony devoid of any esoteric or initiatic components.

269 The *Ceremonial of Bishops* used to date was first published by Pope Clement VIII in the year 1600. However, this edition was merely a revised version obtained in accordance with the principles of the Tridentine reform of a previously approved text. Indeed, the *Ceremonial of Bishops* had taken the place of the *Ordines Romani* which, at the end of the seventh century passed down directives for papal liturgies performed by the Roman Popes.

More recently, in 1886, Leo XIII (reigned 1878–1903) ordered the publication of a new typical edition of the *Ceremonial of Bishops* that maintained unaltered the third book, although no longer of any importance following the abolishing of the Ecclesiastical State and confining to the Vatican City. Finally, the Second Ecumenical Council of the Vatican decreed the reform of all sacred rites and texts, thus leading to the complete revision and publishing of a new edition of the *Ceremonial of Bishops*.

270 The *Ceremonial of Bishops*, pages 140-141.

To summarise, the use of the term "Dedication" would appear to be not only inexact, but even misleading when addressing the ritual discussed herein.

More or Less Esoteric

Largely speaking, the historian Haunch, based on the writings of Anderson, doubts the presence of a ceremony of Consecration throughout the first decades of the eighteenth century, supported by the fact that to date no documents have been found to attest the existence of such a ritual: *"The description given by Anderson of 'The Manner of Constituting a New Lodge' in the Postscript to the 1723 Constitution is the earliest official account we have of a Masonic ceremony… It is, in essence, an initial installation ceremony preceded by a formal act of constitution by the Grand Master… In Anderson's account of the 'Manner' does not appear to involve any ceremonial rite of Constitution at all but merely the formal pronouncement by the Grand Master."* [271] The ceremonial is seemingly therefore dedicated entirely to the Installation of the Worshipful Master, and Anderson refers to the rituals employed using the words *"by certain significant Ceremonies and ancient Usages"*.

It is however Haunch himself who remarks on how in the *Constitutions* published by *UGLE* in 1815, the paragraph "Of Constituting a New Lodge" states:

"The lodge is then consecrated according to ceremonies proper and usual on those occasion, but not proper to be written, and the grand master constitutes the lodge in antient form." [272] Therefore, it could feasibly be concluded that the written ritual was merely part of a more extensive ritual handed down only *verbally* at the time. Furthermore, Haunch himself provides confirmation of this when, citing the renowned *Ahiman Rezon* by Laurence Dermott, the Constitutions of the Ancients, he states that he was referring to *"some Ceremonies and Expression that cannot be written"*, whilst adding that *"the act of constitution might indicate a consecratory rite in embryo."* [273]

However, why Haunch should have deemed the ritual to be *"in embryo"* is hard to understand, as the part that could not be written down may actually have rendered the ritual considerably more complex than Haunch maintains.

The most disconcerting aspect is that on referring to the ceremony as reported in the *Manner of Constituting* written by Anderson in 1723, Haunch comments, *"This may imply some procedure of a more or less esoteric nature."* It should first be stated that if similar "practices" observed within the confines of Freemasonry convey, according to Haunch, some degree of esoteric significance, these rites therefore are not "procedures", but rather

271 T.O. Haunch, op. cit., page 4.
272 T.O. Haunch, op. cit., page 6.
273 T.O.Haunch, op. cit., page 9.

"rituals" and Masonic rituals are undeniably wholly esoteric as they address and are performed by initiates in a *consecrated*, enclosed space. Moreover, to define a ritual as *"more or less esoteric"* conveys a confused, distorted, and questionable view of Freemasonry. In the same way that an individual cannot be more or less initiated, likewise a ritual cannot be performed in a more or less esoteric manner, otherwise, as mentioned by Guénon, we would end up by merely "playing at rituals", fulfilling initiatic rites whilst ignoring their full sense and failing to further understanding of them.[274]

Haunch, in explaining the significance of the ritual of Consecration and Dedication, defines both as being *"religious in form"*, thereby creating considerable confusion. Indeed, the rituals used by Freemasonry can in no way be defined as being of a "religious" nature in view of the substantial differences between an "initiatic" or *esoteric* rite and "religious" or *exoteric* rites.

Initiatic rites are by their very nature confined to the *elect* few in possession of specific requisites, the so-called "qualification", whilst religious rites are addressed indiscriminately to all members of a given faith for the purpose of deliverance and salvation. To define a Masonic ritual as "religious" would be confusing and risk transforming Freemasonry into an incoherent syncretism, a mere overlapping of elements from various sources.

Freemasonry is neither a religion nor a surrogate for religion, being rather an *initiatic philosophy* capable of providing cognitive and methodological tools to aid individuals to embark on a journey towards personal improvement and spiritual perfection. Indeed, Prayers and Beseechments are both present in Masonic rituals, but, in my opinion, these are the expression of spirituality viewed as the *possibility* of an experience of acquaintance with the Divine, heralding, in Freemasons, a true ontological metamorphosis.

3. The Sacred Space in Ancient Societies

The Consecration and construction of a sacred space was invariably performed in compliance with ancient rules, traditional standards, based particularly on a primeval revelation that "in the beginning" provided the archetype for the sacred space. This archetype would subsequently be perpetuated in the erecting of all new Temples, even underlying the establishing of Masonic rituals.

The consecration of a space using a ritual of orientation corresponds to a "cosmisation" of the area, the cosmos being viewed as a divine creation with a prevailing sacred structure. "Cosmisation" indicates a transition from chaos to order (the ceremony

274 René Guénon, op. cit., page 152.

for exaltation into the Royal Arch recites *"Almighty and Eternal Father of the Universe, at whose command the world burst from chaos, and all created matter had its birth"*). Thus, the Consecration of a Temple or a Lodge represents the imitation of a cosmognomic gesture, the reiteration of the "first gesture" (the ritual) implying a reiteration of the divine action of the exemplary construction of Creation.

The first gesture is constituted by consecration of the ground, by transformation into a *Centre*, a space diverse from the previously "profane" extension. Subsequently the "subject" is created, the Lodge, likewise consecrated to render the space suitable for use at a sacred time, as demonstrated by the date of the *Foundation Charter* (4,000 years ago), portraying the *metahistoric* and *atemporal* dimension in which all rituals are performed.

Delimitation and Secrecy

The "sacred" space is thus first and foremost a ritually defined delimited space at variance with the remaining "profane" space. The act of delimitation, present in ancient Vedic rituals, represents an attempt to establish *order*, to create a foundation in the midst of the instability and impermanence of things. On the one hand it is a power to be exercised, resulting in a need to dominate and control the space by delimiting it; on the other a marked sensation of the precariousness of the Earth.

The act of delimitation represents the performing and manifestation of a divine power capable of producing a *hierophany*, or rather a *kratophany*, capable of delimiting the space and subtracting it from the flow of all things, transforming it into a "sacred" abode.

As emphasised by Mircea Eliade, *"The hierophany therefore does not merely sanctify a given segment of undifferentiated profane space; it goes so far as to ensure that sacredness will continue there. There, in that place, the hierophany repeats itself. In this way the place becomes an inexhaustible source of power and sacredness and enables man, simply by entering into it, to have a share in the power, to hold communion with the sacredness."*[275] The latter assists us in understanding why a Masonic Temple should not be used for the purpose of performing activities other than *initiatic* rites.

The foundation of a Temple is thus a ceremony denoting marked esoteric features in view of the Temple being deemed the most sacred of places; therefore, the distinctive rite performed for this purpose is known as Consecration. Since the dawn of time the Temple has had a celestial prototype, as revealed repeatedly in the Old Testament, dating back to the moment on Mount Sinai when Jehovah showed Moses

275 Mircea Eliade, *Traité d'histoire des religions*, Payot, Paris, page 333.

the exact style to be used in constructing a sanctuary in his name: *"This Tabernacle and all its furnishings you shall make exactly according to the pattern that I will now show you...See that you make them according to the pattern shown you on the mountain."* [276]

The requirement of delimiting the "sacred" space wherein the ritual will be performed consequently implies an additional characteristic of Freemasonry and all initiatic societies: *secrecy*. The latter term however does not indicate actions conducted in the shadows, but rather a need to remain "segregated" from the rest of the world, to confine oneself to a "sacred" space in which to seek contact with a higher dimension, removed from the rest of the world lingering in a state of chaos and instability. It is solely by means of detachment from the cacophony of everyday life that the vertical pathway can be approached. *"The secret does not constitute a means of hiding something that would otherwise have been clear to all. The secret denotes access to an area in which all, from the significance onwards, is enclosed. The secret is the area delimited by the enclosure, in the same way as a frame surrounds a picture."* [277]

Cosmogony is the model underlying all types of constructions; each Temple imitates and, in a certain sense perpetuates, the *Creation* of the Universe. Indeed, each Temple is situated at the "centre of the universe" and accordingly can only be built once the "profane" spaces and times have been eliminated and a "sacred" space, a *transcendental* place, created. I should therefore mention that the tradition of "orienting" a Temple is in itself an action deemed to be "sacred". The orientation of the Temple actually recalls the notion held by primitive civilisations of orientation in space, or rather the separation of space into four horizons corresponding to the foundation of the world. This foundation of the world is aimed at transforming "chaos" into "order", in placing the Temple at the "centre of the world". Access to this *centre*, symbolising the rite of passage from the profane to the sacred, from the ephemeral and illusory to reality and eternity, from death to life, from man to divinity, corresponding to a consecration, an initiation.[278] The symbolism of the centre is fundamental in the rites of foundation and, through symbols used by the constructors of cathedrals, has survived in the Western world to the present day. The ancient conception of the temple as an *imago mundi,* the idea that it reproduced the essence of the universe, has indeed been passed on to the sacred Christian architecture in Europe, from the basilicas built in the first centuries A.D., to the medieval cathedrals, to the Masonic Temple, all of which symbolically reproduce the celestial Jerusalem.

276 *Exodus*, 25, 40.

277 Roberto Calasso, *L'Ardore*, Adelphi, Milan, 2010, pages 288-289.

278 Mircea Eliade, *The Myth of the Eternal Return*, Gallimard, Paris, 1949, page 35.

Opening onto the Cosmos

Ancient man lived in constant contact with the cosmos; the dwellings he inhabited featured openings above aimed at facilitating permanent communication with the world "above". The symbolic Ladder illustrated on the 1st Degree Tracing Board is metaphorically linked to the celestial vault which likewise represents the open roof of the Lodge. Indeed, Jacob's Ladder represents the symbolic evolution of the "sacred staff" used by ancient populations to exert a cosmological function and facilitate permanent communications with the world of the divine, allowing orientation and control of chaos. Of all the symbols used, the Ladder undoubtedly best represents the link with the upper world, denoting a breach in a level enabling the passage from one dimension to another, from the earth to the sky. In archaic rituals the Ladder generally rises from a *centre,* thus enabling communications between the various levels of being; likewise the Tracing Board rests on the Volume of the Sacred Law, the sacred *centre* of Freemasonry.

It may thus be concluded that the desacralisation and demythicisation of the modern world have markedly affected Freemasonry which, although continuing to undertake its ancient rituals, has evidently not been capable of removing itself from the chaos of time and maintaining intact its heritage of initiatic and esoteric knowledge. The loss of significance of its gestures, symbols and rituals can only precede an impoverishment of the very sense of Freemasonry that is currently wandering in search of its identity through the things of the profane world. However, its widely proclaimed purpose of hewing the raw stone to fashion the keystone to the immense building of Mankind, must not be overlooked.

The Esoteric Component

When attempting to convey the meaning of esotericism according to the true meaning of the term (deriving from the Greek *eso*, "within" as opposed to *exo* "without") we are obliged to reach the inner, spiritual dimension of reality. Esotericism is based on experience gained by the inner man (in Greek: *anthropos*).

The main scope of esotericism is therefore revealed in the notion whereby all religions, including spiritual and initiatic traditions, share a common root, whilst the primordial spiritual substance gives rise to the deeper reason underlying an overt *esoteric tradition.* Naturally, this idea is closely linked to the complementary conception according to which the handing down throughout the centuries of this tradition, with its related initiatic teachings, was not only possible but moreover represented a fundamental part of the *raison d'être* of esotericism. The second inherent purpose associated with the notion of esotericism is highlighted in the fervent conviction whereby all things featuring an actual link with the esoteric world are closely connected to a particular, meaningful inner experience of the "sacred". Accordingly, as underlined by Schuon, the reality of esotericism is intimately associated with the by no means less complex and ancient context of initiation:

"Esotericism, by its interpretations, its revelations and its interiorising and essentialising operations, tends to realise pure and direct objectivity; this is the reason for its existence. Objectivity takes account of both immanence and transcendence; it is both extinction and reintegration. It is none other than the Truth, in which subject and object coincide, and in which the essential takes precedence over the accidental – or in which the principle takes precedence over its manifestation – either by extinguishing it, or by reintegrating it, depending on the various aspects of relativity itself." [279]

I should therefore like to summarise by affirming that the desacralisation and demythicisation of the modern world have led to a loss of the esoteric significance of Freemasonry and of its initiatic element. Freemasonry has gradually lost the true and deep-rooted sense of its *esoteric-initiatic* component, in some case transforming the rituals into something completely different to what they represented originally. This is clearly illustrated in the loss of meaning observed in the ceremonies performed to consecrate a Temple. Should the esoteric significance of Masonic rituals not be recovered, this situation will result in a mere parody of Freemasonry, a simple association devoid of any intrinsic worth. Only by ignoring the initiatic aspect of Freemasonry can it be overlooked that the principal object of Freemasonry is to perfect the individual through performing of the Rite, or, to use the language of Masons, to hew the *raw stone* and chisel it into a *cubic stone* according to the rules of the Craft.

If no corrective measures are implemented, the consequence could be that the remaining initiatic and ritual vestiges based on metaphysical and esoteric doctrines dating back thousands of years will be transformed even further into a squalid syncretism of a pseudo-initiatic nature.

4. Towards Coalescence and Tolerance: Interpretation of the Ritual in an Allegorical-Moralistic or Anagogic Direction

As illustrated in a previous chapter, Freemasonry was not established immediately as an Initiatic Society. The important Hermetic and Neoplatonist components and the esotericism that characterises its current rituals (the allegorisation of the *Tools of the Craft* in particular), would only appear decades after its origin, when the movement was presented mainly as a form of association, although certainly featuring several *initiatic* phenomena.

279 Frithjof Schuon, *L'esoterismo come principio e come via*, Mediterranee, Rome, 1997, page 15.

In the light of these premises, therefore, we should interpret Freemasonry as a phenomenon that *evolves* but at the same time stays faithful to its origins; this fact has created problems that I will endeavour to address here.

I would like to make an attempt to form coalescence between different approaches and persuasions in Freemasonry, a delicate and thorny issue that other authors have frequently approached in *a politically incorrect* manner. I should like to mention here how the previously cited traditional thinker Frithjof Schuon addresses the issue:

"Although esoterism is reserved, by definition and because of its very nature, for an intellectual elite necessarily restricted in numbers, one cannot help observing that initiatory organisations have at all times included in their ranks a relatively large number of members... The explanation of this more or less popular participation in what is most inward and hence most subtle in a religion, is that esoterism, in order to exist in a given world, must be integrated with a particular modality of that world, and this will necessarily involve relatively numerous elements of society; this leads to a distinction within the Fellowships, between inner and outer circles, the members of the latter being scarcely aware of the real nature of the organisation to which they belong in a certain degree, and which they regard simply as a form of the outward tradition, which alone is accessible to them." [280] This form of approach is, in my humble opinion, hardly constructive, and would imply unpleasant discrimination within Lodges, in which we would see the "true" initiates on one side and, on the other, the "second-class" initiates. As I see it, we should, on the contrary, share together and harmoniously the Masonic initiatic pathway, albeit undertaken by means of different approaches.

In order to succeed in reaching a coalescence between its varying "natures", we could start by defining Freemasonry as an Initiatic School attended by different students who are taught according to different methods to better suit their characteristics.

The differences observed in the various approaches examined, the *esoteric* and the *ethico-moral* method of a non-political nature, is determined, in my opinion, by the different methods of "interpretation" of the ritual.

This indeed may be approached either in an *allegorical-moralistic* or *anagogic* direction, the latter permitting a deeper quest for significance. Both approaches may, or rather *must*, form a coalescence. I am convinced that the ritual, depending on the choices made, may provide us with a series of entrance doors leading to the ultimate aim, towards which the roads may lead, as mentioned above, in an *allegorical*, or *moral*, and *anagogic* direction.

I therefore attempted to identify a new epistemological code capable of closing the gap in interpretation by proposing the construction of a renewed Masonic identity, with the aim of controlling the hostilities between the proponents of the two forms of interpretation.

280 Frithjof Schuon, *Unità trascendente delle religioni*, Mediterranee, Rome, 1980, pages 49-50.

In these two different levels of interpretation, the two stages of the hermeneutic process are interdependent and recognise each other "through" each. We should always bear in mind that irrespective of the roads chosen, the Three Degrees of Freemasonry will invariably represent "states of awareness" rather than "intellectual stages".

As observed in the previous chapter on symbols, allegory, the vehicle of *allegorical-moral* significance, although quite distinct from the symbol itself, the vehicle for anagogic significance, is closely linked to the former as the literal sense of the term is to the allegorical sense. The Truth indeed would not be expressible in the absence of the veil of signs and types; only through use of *anaphora*, i.e. an "ascending" movement from the apparent towards the concealed, will man be able to raise himself to spiritual interpretation, from the *allegorical* to the *anagogic,* and the main means of achieving this is through use of the symbol.

Thus, the interpretation of the ritual would imply three distinct hermeneutic "levels" that would each be elevated by means of a strictly symbolic upward movement. For Alleau, *"only in the third degree does initiation to the 'Greater Mysteries' of the symbol commence and these are neither cosmological nor anthropological nor theological, but rather theogonic. They do not belong to either the language of nature or to culture, and not even to the science of religion and its diverse branches and doctrines, but their mystery is hidden in the depths of the Mysterious."* [281]

If interpreted in an *anagogic* manner, we will recognise in the ritual the numerous influences affected by other traditional forms by which it has been inspired, contaminations of a mystic, Hermetic, Neoplatonist and Rosicrucian nature.

To give a few examples: How do we know that the "Three Principles" on which Freemasonry is based are Brotherly Love, Relief and Truth? By applying an *anagogic* interpretation, we could construe Truth as a quest for the Truth, a return to *God,* an itinerary that man may start to undertake only through a return to himself. However, it is also possible to interpret Truth in a "moralistic" sense, as highlighted by the historian John Hamill in *The Craft*:

"The candidate for initiation learns very early in his Masonic career that the basic principles of Freemasonry are Brotherly Love, Relief and Truth … Truth in the sense of striving for high moral standards and in conducting one's life, in all its aspects, in as honest a manner as possible." [282]

Another example of *anagogic* interpretation or, alternatively, *moral* interpretation may be observed during the ritual for the Ceremony of Initiation during which we are asked to "divest ourselves of metals". By applying an *anagogic* interpretation this formula

281 René Alleau, *La Scienza dei Simboli*, Sansoni, Florence, 1983, pages 115-116.
282 John Hamill, *The Craft*, Crucible, London, 1986, page 12.

conveys a liberation from all *conditionings,* from the social and cultural superstructures acquired up to that time, as only by "divesting oneself of all things" will man's soul be able to be reunited with the *One.* To free oneself of all things does not imply becoming *impoverished* or annihilating one's self; on the contrary, it is by removing all that is not essential to discover the essential and allow the *soul* to return to itself. If we interpret the same sentence using an *allegorical-moralistic* approach, the term "metals" would imply a mere *attachment* to "material things", to profanity, from which the Candidate is requested to step back and become detached.

A further example of this possible hermeneutic approach to the ritual may be observed with reference to the moment in which the blindfold is removed from the candidate to Initiation; the Most Worshipful Master refers to the previous state of darkness of the Aspirant. Although in an *allegorical* sense this may refer to his cognitive "ignorance", from an *anagogic* point of view darkness is used to convey a sense of obscurity of his *spiritual life* up until that time, as explained by Julian Rees:

"Our approach to any Masonic work, in whichever degree, might therefore require such preparation as to 'put us in the right frame of mind', to help us relax, yet to be altered to the demands of the Masonic work we are about to undertake. As an example, after the entered Apprentice has made his vow, the Master asks him, 'Having been kept for a considerable time in a state of darkness, what in your present situation is the predominant wish of pure heart?'

Consider for a moment that the Master may not be referring simply to the period of time that the aspirant has been blindfolded, but rather that he may have been, spiritually, in a state of darkness for a greater part of his life. This aspirant may have spent a considerable time preparing himself for this moment." [283]

It is clear that taking the road of *allegorical-moralistic* interpretation of the ritual with its singular dynamics, instead of choosing the *anagogic-esoteric* road represents a strictly personal choice dictated by the customs and the predispositions of the individual.

As stated above, an *anagogic* interpretation based more on symbols than allegories will allow us to correlate the literal significance of the text to a higher significance on a level with the supernatural domains encoded by symbols; in this way the *anagogic* meaning leads us towards the divine and may only be analysed in an exegetic form by the Freemason who chooses to apply this method. Indeed, also *moralistic* interpretation will allow a value to be gained to act as an *incentive* and in *support* of a spiritual ascent, the ultimate aim of the initiatic process, as the *allegorical* or *moralistic* means of interpretation is capable, although from a different perspective, of linking the concept of reality with the corresponding sensitive world.

283 Julian Rees, *The Stairway of Freemasonry*, Lewis Masonic, Hersham, 2007, page 16.

Chapter Six

Freemasonry and Alchemy

The intuitive mind is a sacred gift and the rational mind a faithful servant. We have created a society that honours the servant and has forgotten the gift

Albert Einstein

1. Freemasonry and Science: The Illuministic Mystification

The association of several eminent personalities from the scientific world with Freemasonry during the eighteenth and early nineteenth centuries, essentially therefore during its transformation from the "accepted" to the "speculative" form of the movement, has contributed towards creating the false myth of a parallelism between Freemasonry, science and Illuminism.

It should first be underlined how the above association failed to produce a significant influence, and indeed, Masonic rituals, with their *esoteric-metaphysical* connotations, passed through the climate of Illuminism practically intact in both essence and conception.

Indeed, despite the initiation of numerous scientists into Freemasonry, I am of the opinion that no intrinsic relationship or ideological influence or link, other than the fact that both are inspired by a spirit of search and knowledge, has ever existed between modern science and Freemasonry.

The purported ideological proximity between Freemasonry and Illuminism—and the modern science it gave rise to—should not be taken for granted. Indeed, as I hve previously written,[284] I do not believe that Freemasonry developed as an expression of Illuministic thought and philosophy, but rather that it sprang from Neo-platonist thought and is therefore far removed from eighteenth-century empiricism and rationalism, which are clearly incompatible with the transcendent and metaphysical beliefs of Freemasonry.

Nonetheless, the question remains as to whether the irrelevance of Freemasonry to Illuminism and its methods of studying reality likewise implies its *removal* from science in

284 Fabio Venzi, *The Influence of Neoplatonic Thought on Freemasonry*, Book Guild Publishing, Brighton, 2007.

general, or whether there may be a common ground on which to integrate and harmonise the principles of traditional science derived from eighteenth-century thought, and the philosophical principles of Freemasonry inspired by Neoplatonism, in a new vision: a vision that transcends the contrast between reason and enlightenment and the dualism between spirit and matter.

In my opinion, there is however an undeniable ideological link between Freemasonry and the so-called pre-science of Alchemy. Indeed, following centuries of domination by Illuministic reasoning, the link might be re-established by means of the New Science, or post-modern science, which increasingly attempts to extend the limitations and oppose the contradictions posed by the previous approach of experimental scientific evaluation through the use of specialist knowledge and strictly rational and *logical-deductive* cognitive processes.

How therefore can a link be identified between the Masonic school of thought and the principles of Alchemy? As always, it is the ritual, the main *instrument* involved in our "Method", to provide the answers. In the Emulation ritual during the ceremony of Passing from the 2nd to the 3rd Degree the Worshipful Master expresses the hope that the Fellow Craft will undertake future studies in the area of *Liberal Arts and Sciences.*[285] Subsequently, in the Exhortation of the 3rd Degree the Fellow Craft is reminded that by *"... still guiding your progress by the principles of moral truth, you were led in the Second Degree to contemplate the intellectual faculty and to trace it from development, through the paths of heavenly science, even to the throne of God Himself."*[286]

On initial analysis the two latter references would each seem to contradict the other; but this is not quite the case.

Indeed, in my opinion, the Science to which the ritual refers is not science as we know it today—a rational and empirical science founded on the method of experimentation. This science, springing from Illuministic thought, considered all *Esoteric doctrines* applied to metaphysical studies, and consequently the initiatic societies associated with the latter, ridiculous manifestations of times long gone by.

The Science referred to in the ritual is rather what is known today as "metascience", the "Alchemy" which was flourishing in Europe when Masonic rituals first came into being, albeit in a manner that differed somewhat from its original form. As we will observe subsequently, numerous eminent figures of the eighteenth-century scientific revolution were collocated in the midst of Alchemy and Modern Science, halfway between the figure of the magician and that of the modern scientist.

285 Emulation Ritual, page 137.
286 Ibid, page 175.

Alchemy thus represented a border, a *grey area* between a *magical-metaphysical* and a *scientific-rationalist-empirical* method of evaluation. In spite of the lack of any degree of compatibility between Illuminist-based modern experimental scientific methods and Freemasonry, conversely, numerous analogies are present between alchemical methods and Freemasonry.

2. Freemasonry and Alchemy

On the establishment of Freemasonry in England at the end of the seventeenth century, the principles of modern science and the *empirical-rationalist* method had not yet spread throughout society of the period. An ongoing situation of coexistence and contrast between the preceding *magical-alchemical* opinion and the new *scientific* interpretation was manifest.

As mentioned previously, I am firmly persuaded that Masonic rituals on referring to the *"hidden mysteries of nature and science"* indicate a *metaphysical* knowledge which by *dividing* us from material things shall accompany us to the *"throne of God"*. This journey will be undertaken in the context of a symbiotic relationship with Nature, viewed as the focus of contemplation and *source of knowledge*, an approach better befitting the conception of an alchemist rather than that of a modern scientist.

Alchemy may be defined as a "form of knowledge" that tends towards the psychological and spiritual *transformation* of the individual through domination of the spiritual and creative energies which pervade nature and the human mind. The *lapis* or philosopher's stone, is a metaphor for the achieving of knowledge and understanding of the Hermetic tradition by the initiate.

Thus, in the same way as Freemasonry, Alchemy proposes a pathway of *spiritual elevation*, a "system", a "method of perfection" comprising a "practical" part, in which a deep-rooted knowledge of matter and its elements is required, and an initiatory path, *metaphorically* expressed in the myth of the transmutation of base metals into gold. As stated by the great traditionalist Titus Burckhardt, the purpose of Alchemy is to *"make the body into spirit and the spirit into body"*; this motto summarises in a few words the ultimate aim of Alchemy. Gold, which represents the outer casing of the task, is presented as an opaque body that has gained its gleam, or as solidified light. Transposed into the human and spiritual order, gold is the conscience of the body transmuted into spirit, or the spirit tethered to the body. The raw metal that represents the starting point for the creation is merely the conscience linked to the body and deep within the same. The latter is the "metallic body" from which the "soul" and the "spirit", i.e. the mercury and the sulphur, are extracted. If the "body" were not an inner reality, it could not be used as a material in the spiritual creation."[287]

Both Alchemy and Freemasonry however impart knowledge on how to *transmute* consciousness by accelerating evolution of the same, both being based on principles of hermetic thought, with its metaphysical aim culminating in union of the individual with the universal. Naturally the aim is purely metaphysical, the journey of the alchemist and the Freemason is a return of the individual to the Divine Principle, a *reintegration* of the individual Self into the divine Self. This arduous pathway is certainly not for all men. It is accessible solely to a mind devoid of superstructures, opinions; an uncorrupted and unconditioned mind.

As mentioned previously, while Masonic symbolism consists in giving form to a rough ashlar, Alchemy is based on the conception of achieving from an imperfect and impure material, a perfect matter capable of transferring the same perfection to other substances. Both the work of Alchemy and accomplishment of the Masonic ritual (which, it should once again be underlined, does not consist in committing a ritual *to memory)* take place in the presence of the transcendent. Indeed, alchemical and Masonic pathways to knowledge are not the result of theoretic or experimental knowledge, but rather the outcome of a task, the *opus,* in which the spirit consciously returns to its *material* source to animate and transmute the same.

Ultimately, the Mysteries present in both the Masonic ritual and in alchemical practices are aimed in particular at achieving the *transmutation* of the individual who, through the experience of death and resurrection present in the initiation, *mutates* his ontological status by progressing from a "profane being" into an "initiate".

Before beginning their work both the alchemist and the Freemason should be absolutely pure and spiritually elevated, as the revelation of the mysteries of Alchemy and Freemasonry descends from on high and may only be perceived by the spiritually elevated. The affinities manifested in the esoteric approach of both Alchemy and Freemasonry, the pathway towards perfection they propose and the similarities displayed in their specific symbolism, remind us that both are fully representative of the *Traditional* school of thought. Accordingly, Mircea Eliade, an eminent scholar of the history of religions, in his work *The Forge and the Crucible: The Origins and Structures of Alchemy* states:

"Being the Universe a hierophany and human life sacralised, work involved a liturgical value which still obscurely survives among rural population of present-day Europe. It is however above all our intention to underline the chance offered by archaic societies to man: the chance to become part of the Sacred by his own work as a homo faber, an author and manipulator

287 Titus Burckhardt, *Simboli*, Edizioni all'insegna del Veltro, Parma, 1979, page 53.

of tools. Those primeval experiences were preserved and transferred through numerous generations thanks to the 'secrets of the trade'; when global experience of the world was modified as a consequence of technical and cultural innovations following the establishment of urban civilisation [i.e. following civilization itself, etymologically speaking] and what we agreed to call History in the strong sense of this word, primeval experiences related to a sacralised universe were periodically revived through initiations and trade rituals." [288]

The number of analogies between the symbolism used in alchemy and Freemasonry is indeed considerable. The contrast between the Light and the shadows, the gradual passage from the darkness of night into the light of the sun, bearer of invigorating *energy* for Alchemy and *knowledge* for Freemasonry, heralds the liberation from the impurities of the body and mind. Likewise, the metaphor of the "journey" is one of the fundamental elements in both the alchemical and Masonic pathways. In an alchemical context it is repeatedly represented by the search for the philosopher's stone, a journey of the soul throughout the planetary spheres. In Masonic rituals, however, it portrays the journey undertaken by the wardens in search of the "hidden mysteries" following the murder of the architect Hiram Abif, and, to conclude, in the context of Templar Freemasonry, it is illustrated in the search for the Holy Grail.

However, it is the allegory of the Ladder that is encountered with a considerable frequency in alchemical documents, in Masonic symbolism, and in the Renaissance Neoplatonism. In the alchemical system the Ladder represents the gradual conquest of philosophical, mystical and esoteric elevation and acts as a link between the various levels of the "real" and as a metaphor for the "Great Work". This theme of Gnostic and Neoplatonist origin corresponds to the "ascent" of the soul through the planetary spheres, an initiatory journey aimed at purifying the divine part hidden within man from all contact with matter.[289] The ultimate end is to be reunited with the One, to contemplate the same, as underlined by Ramon Llull in his *Treatise on the Fifth Essence* in which he maintains that the main task of Alchemy is to lead man towards the *contemplation* of God. After centuries of derision, Alchemy today continues to be considered a sort of "proto-chemistry", taking its place in the history, or rather *prehistory*, of science. However, Alchemy is all this and much more besides. At variance with modern science, which is not concerned with spiritual matters, Alchemy focuses on the investigation of both the material and spiritual worlds. The alchemical "Method", in the same way as the Masonic approach converges on the search for a symbolic language capable of expressing this integration between the *spiritual* and the *material*, an *esoteric* language

288 Mircea Eliade, *Forgerons et Alchimistes*, Flammarion, Paris, 1977, page 128.
289 Matilde Battistini, *Astrologia, magia, alchimia*, Electa, Milan, 2004, page 368.

understandably dif[illegible]m philosophical and scientific language as it is conveyed by means of images aim[illegible] raising awareness in an *intuitive* rather than a *rational* manner.

Alchemy is the expression of a communion between mind and Nature, subject and object, without which no efficacious knowledge can be achieved, where Nature is construed not merely as the external reality perceived by our senses or as the focus of specialist studies undertaken following the traditional approach of mechanical physics. On the contrary, Nature is viewed by the alchemist as the custodian of a divine spirit that animates and governs the elements, the structuring force of all reality, although invisible to the senses, at times however, proving achievable through "work".

This same vision can be observed in the Masonic ritual in which, in the 3rd Degree Exhortation, the Master Mason – to whom the secrets of Nature and the principle of intellectual truth have been revealed – is invited to contemplate Nature.[290] This evidently does not refer to the *mechanical* concept of Nature typical of modern science, but rather a vision that hosts the discerning universal spirit revealed to man through inspiration, intuition and enlightenment.

It is interesting to note how in the same way as Freemasonry, Alchemy proposes a distinction between the "operative" and the "speculative". It has moreover been debated whether one form descended directly from the other. Roger Bacon was the first scholar to report such a distinction, writing in 1859: *"Alchemy is like a two-sided coin: speculative, or rather which concerns the generation of inanimate things from the elements and all other inanimate things. But there is another alchemy, operative and practical, which teaches how to make the noble metals and colours and many other things."*[291]

Although renowned authors in the field of esoteric studies such as René Guénon maintained that alchemy was concerned solely with the *inner* part of matter, others (including Fulcanelli, Eugène Canseliet and Mary Anne Atwood) advocated how the *transformation of matter* is fundamental to the alchemical process. Indeed, other authors, such as Herbert Silberer, a student of Sigmund Freud and a Freemason, developed the theory of the *spiritual* or speculative nature of alchemical perfection, identifying the raw material of the *opus* with the conscience, thus providing a highly suggestive *psychoanalytical* interpretation.

Who therefore actually inspired the inclusion of numerous references to the principles of Alchemy in the Masonic ritual? Certainly not the *empirical* scientists who, with their mechanical vision of the world and their experimental methodology, could hardly have produced a ritual infused with esoteric symbols and allusions to Alchemy.

290 Emulation Ritual, page 175.

291 Roger Bacon, *Opus tertium*, in *Opera quaedam hactenus inedita*, London, 1859, page 40.

More likely it was scientists who operated between the two worlds of alchemy and science. I shall now briefly mention a few.

Michael Maier, a Rosicrucian born in Germany in 1566, defined himself as a physician-philosopher. He was an academic and, for many years, physician to the Emperor Rudolf II. He believed that alchemists, through their symbolic images, aspired to "reach the spirit through the senses", using the singular capability of man to grasp "essential" things at an *intuitive* level, overlooking the faculty of dialectics. His work *Atalanta Fugiens*, published in 1618, contains a magnificent collection of alchemical emblems and symbols. Indeed, symbols are viewed as the vehicles of knowledge, not by means of a *logical-analytical* process typical of modern science but rather in line with a process of analogy and synthesis, intuition and imagination detached from rational thinking, in which meaning is not objective and unchangeable but is dependent on a process of interpretation of the subject.

Atalanta Fugiens also included an esoteric text on the combination of Alchemy, rationality and religion that provided an important ethical model for the *Royal Society*.

Similar to *Atalanta fugiens*, the Tracing Board in Masonic ritual is used with the same intent and for the same purposes as those mentioned by Maier, containing a *symbolic synthesis* of the Degree in which the Freemason works which, through the use of symbolic images, conveys knowledge by means of *intuition* and suggestive imagination.

Robert Fludd, physician and esotericist, shared the theories of his friend and colleague Maier. Fludd produced a monumental work in several volumes entitled *Utriusque Cosmi* in which the author – a follower of Paracelsus – undertook a study of man and his relations with the *macrocosm*, debating at length on the practice of medicine of the time which conveyed a magical interpretation to ill health, seeing it as the work of devils, with angels providing the cure. Fludd was both a scientist and esotericist, capable of dealing with scientific problems and finding their solution through systematic experimentation, but likewise an alchemist, with his *magical-religious* vision of the world.

Another figure of fundamental importance is that of the alchemist, writer and Freemason Elias Ashmole. He attempted to distinguish between a "serious" Alchemy, frequently represented by academics whose interest was not economic but rather truly philosophical interest, and the Alchemy of "charlatans". In his *Theatrum Chemicum Britannicum* he wrote:

"It is not less absurd and strange to see that some men…cannot help but count authentic magicians in with conjurors, necromancers and witches..., who with arrogance violate the principles of magic, in the manner of pigs which burst into a lovely garden and, after making a pact with the devil, take advantage of his help in their works, to counterfeit and corrupt

the admirable knowledge of magicians, with whom there is a difference as large as that as between angels and demons." [292]

However, the true watershed between the two visions was undoubtedly represented by Isaac Newton who, together with the scientist Robert Boyle (both members of the *Royal Society*), was struck by the appeal of Alchemy just as Illuminism was about to enter the stage. Newton studied Alchemy not only from a theoretical point of view but also operationally, with an aim to achieve a better understanding of the "ways of divine action in the world". He was seeking an original Truth to integrate into the theories of the new physics in an attempt to avoid the risk, feared by the Cambridge Platonists, of an atheistic degradation in mechanism. In his numerous works devoted to Alchemy, he wrote more on the above subject than on issues relating to physics, convinced that he was once again shedding light on knowledge originally in possession of the Ancient Egyptians having been revealed by God Himself in ancient times, which was now being rediscovered — a typically Hermetic vision.

A conference held by John Maynard Keynes in 1942 at the *Royal Society* after having studied Newton's secret papers for years was an historic event. Keynes presented a remarkably different image of Newton from that habitually proffered by scholars of the sciences for three centuries. Keynes asserted:

"Newton was not the first of the age of reason. He was the last of the magicians, the last of the Babylonians and Sumerians, the last great mind which looked out on the visible and intellectual world with the same eyes as those who began to build our intellectual inheritance rather less than 10,000 years ago." [293] Thus, one of the greatest scientists of all humanity walked the line between rational thought and creative intuition, between logic and imagination. Indeed, in doing so and in line with the vision referred to herein he acted as a forerunner of the New Science.

Elias Ashmole, Robert Boyle and Isaac Newton were all *scientists,* members of the *Royal Society* who continued to practise Alchemy side by side with the experimental methods applied by modern science.

It should moreover be emphasised how the fact that the *Royal Society* had admitted members who undeniably supported the Illuminist school of thought, necessarily implies how the Society represented an important *workshop* for that particular philosophy. In this regard, to disprove such a belief, it should be borne in mind that in addition to the abovementioned members, Cudworth and More, two of the most

292 Elias Ashmole, *Theatrum Chemicum Britannicum*, London, 1652, page 443.

293 J.M. Keynes, *Newton the Man*, in Royal Society, Newton Tercentenary Celebration, Cambridge University Press, 1947, pages 27-34.

important representatives of the Neoplatonists of Cambridge were likewise members of the *Royal Society*, as proof of how pure empiricism was not the sole key issue addressed. It was Henry More himself who emphasised the distinction between experimental and mechanical philosophy, explaining that a failure to distinguish between the two was a sign of ignorance, particularly in view of the fact that experimental philosophy, professed by the *Royal Society*, yielded results that were *"useful not only in everyday life, but also in the discovery of more sublime and truly metaphysical philosophies."*

As seen in aprevious chapter, Cudworth and More, concerned by the possible materialistic and atheistic consequences of science, were opposed to the prevailing mechanical philosophy in blatant contrast with the *spirit of Nature*, an immaterial substance that *"pervades the entire material universe, exercising a creative power, a vital principle responsible for the movement and cohesion of matter."*

Taking into account the considerable distance between modern science and the philosophy of Nature of the Renaissance, it cannot be denied that the plastic concept of nature created by Ralph Cudworth in the second half of the seventeenth century represents the continuing expression of a philosophy of nature based on pre-modern *theological-metaphysical* suppositions in contrast with the mechanical rationalism of Cartesian physics and Hobbesian materialism. By this I am referring to a "Philosophy of a plastic nature" with its organistic and vitalistic connotations *subordinated* to a spiritualistic theology linked to the interpretation of nature elaborated by Renaissance thinkers, and in particular by the religiously inspired philosophies such as Neoplatonism.

In the light of the above, and referring once again to the ceremony of Passing to the 2nd Degree of the Emulation ritual which states: *"As in the previous Degree you made yourself acquainted with the principles of Moral Truth and Virtue, you are now permitted to extend your researches into the hidden mysteries of Nature and science"*, we can rightly confirm that those responsible for compiling our magnificent ritual were not indeed referring to the science that had stemmed from the *experimental* method, modern science, but rather to the "Method" adopted by the alchemist's *mystical chemistry* which enhances a comprehension of the *unity* of the material principle of the world. That material principle encloses the vital spirit which works as a divine emanation. Indeed, it is not the material substances that perform wonders in *alchemy*, but rather the alchemist's ability to manipulate Nature in its most intimate essence using those substances; implying the ability of man to grasp and *understand* the spirit through an accurate study of material.

The Exhortation of the 3rd Degree affirms that the development of the intellectual faculty in the 2nd Degree takes place *"through the paths of heavenly science even to the throne of God Himself"*. Consequently, this science that focuses on the study of matter *ultimately* tends towards the discovery of the God who resides therein and arranges the matter into geometric perfection. In the process of discovery, matter and spirit are viewed as complementary and indissoluble.

The unitarian vision of knowledge that has unfailingly inspired alchemists and Freemasons is based on the need to overcome all forms of contrast and dichotomy. This dualism is symbolised in the Masonic Lodge by the Black and White Chequered Floor and in Alchemy by the formula *solve et coagula* used to identify the philosopher's stone, where the division of the elements must necessarily be followed by their harmonic union.

This feeling of *comprehensive understanding* seems to be at the base of what could be defined a post-modern New Science which, after pushing against the limitations of modern science and its fragmentary, analytical knowledge, attempts to emerge based on a new foundation, which, as will be illustrated subsequently, is unexpectedly close to the *alchemical-esoteric* form of pre- or proto-science.

3. The Modern Science

The modern scientific paradigm, the offspring of Illuminism, is developed through the application of *instrumental-empirical* methods, in a context of intellectual speculation in which all that surrounds us becomes a mere projection of the human intellect rather than a process in itself. The outside world, and Nature in particular, becomes the substrate for the creation of all inventions of reason, thus losing its natural connotation and its role as a vehicle of knowledge bestowed on man for the harmonic and empathetic understanding of life.

Nowadays there is an increasingly pressing need to overcome the Illuminist rationalism and scientism generated by the Cartesian view whereby Nature is a machine devoid of life, inert, that is explained beyond the context of man, devoid of any divine or spiritual significance, of vitality, intrinsic harmony. From this de-divination of the world, this counter-positioning between spirit and matter, the cult of modern science is said to have stemmed from the belief that technical progress would unerringly correspond to an inner evolution of man. Max Weber demonstrated how scientific rationalisation had produced an irreversible "disenchantment" (*Entzauberung*), secularising the ancient vision of the world of *mythological-religious* origin and replacing it with an "objective" vision.

As stated previously, in contrast to the philosophy advanced by Illuminism, Neoplatonism – and in particular the Cambridge Platonists – neither desires nor attempts to dominate Nature, but tries to understand it from within in an empathetic manner. As emphasised by Ernst Cassirer in relation to Nature, Neoplatonist thought:

"Does not divide nature into individual elements or specific 'forms' to be studied separately. In the place of this analytical method, is a search and a need for universal synthesis... Their philosophy of nature returns to the dynamic Pantheism of the Renaissance. It proposes a creative rather than a mechanic observation of Nature." [294]

Moreover, More and Cudworth, two of the major representatives of the Cambridge Platonists, maintained that the *macrocosm* reflected the *microcosm* and accordingly elaborated a cosmological theory taking into account the primacy of man over the world with a view to freedom. In Cudworth's *The True Intellectual System of the Universe* the fundamental concept of the "freedom of mankind" first expressed by Pico della Mirandola in his *Oration on the Dignity of Man* is manifested. Man is not the victim of a foreign divorced mechanism but is the master and commander of his own destiny. Thus, the world is the mirror of mankind, reflected in a higher spiritual reality, not, as alleged by Hobbes, a blind mechanism.

As illustrated previously, Masonic ritual affirms that the *"occult mysteries"* of Nature and Science are ascertained in the 2nd Degree. Subsequently, in the 3rd Degree, the Venerable Master exhorts the Candidate to *"Continue to listen to the voice of Nature, which bears witness that even in this perishable frame resides a vital and immortal principle."* [295] Through the contemplation of Nature and the Divine principle revealed therein, after having acquired the *"Moral Truth* and *Virtue"* (as counselled in the 1st Degree) and *"Intellectual Knowledge"* through the study of the *Liberal Arts* (in the 2nd Degree), a Freemason is ready to face an *Initiatic Death*. Intellect is conceived as a prodromic instrument of knowledge and thus on a lower level than true knowledge, which can be achieved only by means of *intuition*. Naturally, the *"hidden mysteries"* to which the ritual refers reveal the Mason's belief in something that exists beyond the field of the appreciable — the object of scientific investigation. I am in full agreement with Elémire Zolla regarding the fact that whoever enters into an initiatory society is already aware of the impossibility of achieving an explanation and understanding of everything through mere logic; he knows of the existence of a mystery and believes it can be grasped through intuitive knowledge, which – in its greatest form of expression – is enlightenment.

The Science of which the ritual speaks is therefore a science related to noetic, intuitive intelligence, an intelligence that allows man to understand the dimension of the sacred through Nature and thus reach the spirit through matter. This is the Spinozan vision of the existence of a sole essence that permeates all things, the Divine Spirit

294 Ernst Cassirer, *Die Platonische Renaissance in England und die Schule von Cambridge*, "Studien der Bibliothek Warburg" XXIV Leipzig-Berlin, Teubner, 1932, page 54.
295 Emulation Ritual, page 183.

which is immanent in Nature and constitutes its geometric-structural order. There is no understanding to be had through mere reasoning, viewed as the ability to grasp the connection between objects and ideas, but only by means of intuitive knowledge.

However, as conveyed by the rituals used, Masonic thought goes far beyond Spinoza's vision of a God immanent in Nature and the Pantheist vision. It acknowledges the existence of the Transcendent, of a Divine Principle that pervades Nature whilst reaching beyond the same to exceed the terrestrial dimension, beyond man and human concerns which constitute the beginning and end of the search. Contemplation of Nature, reflection of the Divine, as referred to in the 2nd Degree, is merely a means of reaching the Truth that resides "elsewhere", in the transcendent dimension reached only through comprehension of the demise of all things terrestrial and pertaining to one's own humanity, as imparted in the Raising to the 3rd Degree.

4. The New Science

When attempting to define in modern terms the Neoplatonist and Spinozan vision of the relationship between man and Nature, and to describe the search for a unified knowledge, a principle that permeates Masonic thought, we could refer to a *holistic vision* of reality. According to this holistic view, man and Nature are seen as part of the same harmonic, living and sentient organism, an expression of the spirit, rather than separate and independent parts of the same.

The traditional science of Cartesian and Illuministic derivation, the limits of which are increasingly evident, is becoming widely criticised. The undeniable merit of Illuminism was to free the researcher from the chains of theology and religious dogma dominant at the time, although throughout the centuries it has degraded into a dry materialism, insufficient both in methodology and results to explain many aspects of our existence. Today there is a new frontier of science represented by scientists and scholars from all over the world, at times collocated beyond the confines of the orthodox scientific community (the same community that condemned Galileo and Copernicus) which supports a new, no longer fragmented but unified knowledge — a knowledge frequently substantiated by scientific discoveries that challenge the certainties of orthodox scholars.

In the field of *cognitive psychology* for example, numerous experiments seem to confirm a correspondence with an ancient shared wisdom: reasoning or a rational process is a by-product of *intuition* which is a form of innate knowledge. In the field of medicine, there is no longer any doubt as to the interdependence of the mind and the body and the influence of the former in the development of illness, even serious illnesses such as tumours, rather than in the area of psychosomatic disorders. The human organism is increasingly seen as an inseparable unit of mind-body-conscience, capable of definitively overcoming the Cartesian division into *res cogitans* and *rex extensa*.

The hermetic principle of "as above so below" reproduced in Masonic Lodges by two globes representing the heavens and the earth is today exemplified in the so-called "principle of isomorphism" on the basis of which similarities between the *microcosm* and the *macrocosm* are sought. The application of the same conceptual models and corresponding abstractions is therefore deemed feasible today. Man is therefore seen as a holographic unit enclosing the matrix of total information pertaining to the system of which he is part and with which there is a continuous exchange of information and energy. The same relationship seems to exist between organs, cells and atoms. Thus, each and every part of creation seems to contain information on the whole, recalling the Platonic form of innate knowledge awaiting only to be returned to the light.

This revolution was probably commenced by Albert Einstein who confirmed that *"the cosmic religious sentiment is the strongest and noblest motivation of scientific research."* He was the first to attempt to propose, unsuccessfully, throughout his entire life, a Theory of Everything — a theory unifying all the laws of Nature.

The indivisibility of science and conscience is indeed nowadays supported by contemporary scientists. In this regard the Nobel Prize winner Eugene Wigner states that *"Consciousness is the primary reality... In the future physics will explain not only the phenomena observed, but also the process of observation,"* whilst another Nobel Prize winner, Francis Crick, who discovered DNA, affirms that *"Consciousness is the legitimate field of science."*

The matter observed and the conscience of the scientist who observes reality are thus united and are subsequently investigated in a single context. The subject is therefore seemingly closely linked to the object.

In all Initiatic Traditions, of which Freemasonry is one, unity resides in the consciousness that constitutes the essence of the Divine.

The question posed increasingly by scientists, only seemingly of a philosophical nature, is whether the Universe would continue to exist if there were no one there to observe it. A negative answer would seem to be mandatory.

The main reason for this is following the discovery of quantum physics and laboratory findings achieved in the early 1980s, it was first hypothesised that the existence of the Universe requires the presence of a conscious sentient being with a marked sense of awareness. Lacking an observer only the power of the Universe would exist; it would therefore seem that consciousness creates matter. The act of observation creates an interaction with the object being observed and modifies the same. This relevance of the subjectivity of the observer was anticipated by alchemists who saw in natural phenomena a continual exchange between the internal and the external. Such a discovery necessarily heralded a change to the scientific paradigm: from the materialistic in which all is matter, implied as elementary particles which interact according to a cause and effect relationship to which man is completely extraneous, to a more *idealistic* paradigm in which awareness is the foundation of existence and matter responds to spirit.

In Alchemy, the mercurial feminine principle explains the proteo-morphism of natural phenomena, their fluid mutations. Today, science affirms, on the basis of the so-called "Bohr's Principle of Complementarity" that the elementary particles of matter, the quantum, can be viewed both as particles and waves according to the way in which the phenomenon is observed. The Universe might not be the materialistic Newtonian cosmos made up of specific objects, visible and in motion along a defined trajectory, substantially static, but a dynamic universe constituted by "waves of possibility" or mere potentiality which becomes actuality and therefore material according to the awareness of the observer.

In this vision of particular interest to the world of science, man represents the centre and the sense of the Universe, exactly as hypothesised by Pico della Mirandola.

Another important experiment resulting in the establishing of the so-called "Principle of Nonlocality" put forward by the Nobel Prize winning physicist Wolfgang Pauli, revealed that the elementary particles contained in an atom are in constant, instantaneous contact with each other, enabling each to ascertain its own position in relation to that of the others and in the Universe without exchanging any form of signal whatsoever. In the view of scientists, the latter would tend to demonstrate how each particle is connected to the entire system and, therefore, how each part of the Universe is interconnected by electromagnetic fields as though they were linked by a single intelligent form of energy. For the first time, science has been forced to hypothesise the existence of a dimension that *transcends* the dimension we inhabit, and is today obliged to resort to the *transcendent* to explain the phenomena it observes. This is largely due to the fact that the transcendent dimension, previously excluded from scientific research, would appear to influence the behaviour of matter.

The connection between the heavens and the earth, between the immanent and the transcendent, seen as a continuum, constitutes one of the key issues underlying Masonic ideas and principles. Indeed, the symbol of the Triangle represents the totality of the manifestation: it is heaven and earth, essence and substance. The Starry Vault forms the ceiling to the Masonic Lodge and the spiritual Ladder joins earth to the heavens.

The abovementioned underlines the need for a definitive transcending of the materialistic separatism of Illuminist-based traditional science which, in an attempt to provide a better understanding of the world, can no longer exclude human consciousness and the transcendent dimension of an intelligent energy, or the mind of God, from which the sensitive world seemingly stems and is governed.

The New Science retrieves an ancient tradition of knowledge applied by the ancient Greek philosophers, the Neoplatonists, in *mystic-religious* tradition, and in initiatic societies. The All-seeing Eye inscribed within the luminous Delta in the form of a triangle is a frontal eye, neither right nor left; it is the third eye, the eye of the heart, of spontaneous, innate knowledge: the divine consciousness. This frontal eye sees all and discerns the unity in its multiplicity. This is the eye of the *Great Architect of the Universe*, but as illustrated by quantum physics, it could equally well represent the eye of the conscious observer who by observing attentively creates the world. And if the observer is a creator of worlds who, in the observation of his creation continuously re-creates it, he is therefore God. The Freemason who at the end of his initiatic path learns to die, learns to rise above his own humanity, and, finally elevates himself to contemplate the principles and divine force, reflecting himself in them.

The Freemason does not seek externally a demonstrable and universal truth, but pursues knowledge of himself through a unique and personal path towards the truth that resides in the Divine Principle.

However, no conflict is manifested as in the past, but rather a possible integration into the vision of a New Science focusing not on the reign of matter, but rather on that of consciousness, therefore evolving from an Illuminist towards a neo-humanistic form of science.

The dichotomy and contrast between spirit and material, subject and object, between Self and All, Man and God that has characterised modern scientific research must be transcended. The great antitheses represent an *elementary* stage of the learning process in which differences are fundamental in defining and understanding the sensitive world. But, as illustrated previously, research can no longer be undertaken merely in the sphere of the material dimension using strict rationalism alone as a tool, as if the spirit, creativity, imagination and intuition were not present to an equal degree in human experience.

The fall from Eden was determined by the discovery of good and evil, implying an achievement of distinction, separation, duality in the unitarian consciousness of the spirit.

Thus, the *coincidentia oppositorum* is a Divine requisite, and buried in the ancient knowledge of initiatic societies is the truth awaiting to be revealed by the New Science as an original, innate attribute of the human soul.

Chapter Seven

A Glance at the Jungian Psychoanalytic Approach: Self

Mythos breaks with no tradition, because no tradition precedes it, and it adheres to no tradition, because logically and temporally all tradition begins within it; whatever paths of development tradition might have established however diverse may have been the branches that grew out of it or continue to grow from it, no matter whether they tend toward the irrational or the rational, artistic or scientific attitudes and modes of knowledge – all these paths together are fundamentally indistinguishable as one single unity embedded in the mythical germ cell.

Hermann Broch
Hugo von Hofmannsthal and His Time

1. Myth

During the moral crisis that pervaded Europe at the start of the twentieth century, a revaluation of Theosophy and the Oriental religions, together with a marked expansion of Freemasonry throughout Europe and the United States, heralded a revival of Myth, of archetypes and of the collective unconscious.

The Myth is a highly complex cultural reality that can be analysed and interpreted from several complementary viewpoints.

The dilemma facing those who approach Myth for the first time is whether it is preferable to study mythological documents in the knowledge that study will, in ultimate analysis, promote the acceptance of mythology, by *"drinking from the source"* (to quote the words of Károly Kerényi), or knowing that the study should be undertaken with a view to "explaining" the reasons why mythological material has been forged into specific forms.

The second, more rationalist, approach to Myth is ironically subject to criticism by the advocates of another school of thought who claim that *"the breaking down of myths to understand their function, in an attempt to explain their nature, is to reduce oneself to less than the mere simpleton who dismantles a radio to discover which piece produces the sound".*

It is my opinion that the two approaches need not necessarily exclude the other, as both the "acceptance" and "explanation" of Myth may assist us in understanding its nature and significance.

Before attempting to analyse Myth in its multi-faceted aspects, I shall provide a definition to be used as a sort of guiding thread to lead us through the process, by quoting the definition afforded by Mircea Eliade in his *History of Religions*: *"Any myth, of any nature, enounces an event that occurred illo tempore, and sets an exemplary precedent for all the actions and 'situations' that replicate the event from thence forwards. Any ritual, or any meaningful action performed by man is the repetition of a mythical archetype... the consequence of repetition is the abolition of profane time and the projection of man into a magic-religious time that has nothing to do with duration in the strict sense of the word, but which is the 'eternal present' of mythical time".*[296]

In his studies C.G. Jung does not attempt to "explain" Myth as a more or less pathological feature of the psyche, but rather illustrates how Myths, in the manifold expressions assumed in different societies, merely represent a concrete and substantially uniform expression — notwithstanding the numerous differences and variations observed — of the timeless structure of the human unconscious. According to Jung: *"The collective unconscious appears to consist of mythological motifs or primordial images, for which reasons the myths of all nations are its real exponents. In fact, the whole of mythology could be taken as a sort of projection of the collective unconscious."* [297] Thus, essentially, unlike the Freudian school that claims Myths are deeply enrooted within a complex of the personal unconscious, for Jung, the timeless origin of Myths lies within a formal structure of the collective unconscious. Although Freud never acknowledged the congenital autonomy of the psyche, the unconscious, on the contrary, Jung revealed the existence in the latter of an *innate collective dimension* with an energy independent of Self.

2. The Archetype of Self

The archetypes of a collective unconscious tend, in the course of their phylogenetic and ontogenetic development, to assume a conscious semblance, becoming thus acknowledged and integrated by the conscious into a new and wider totality. These archetypes feature a compensatory dynamism with respect to the conscious; they may affect the latter, either in a routine manner or through pathological exasperations, with

296 M. Eliade, *Trattato di storia delle religioni*, Bollati Boringhieri, Turin, 1986, page 446.
297 C.G. Jung, *The Archetypes of the Collective Unconscious*, Bollati Boringhieri, Turin, 1977, page 11.

the aim of promoting a finished, complete personality, at conscious and unconscious levels and, in particular, the dynamism of the archetypes of the psyche is regulated, activated and conditioned by a central archetype.

Jung defined this central archetype as an "archetype of Self", or archetype of totality as, by rallying the unconscious to the conscious, it leads to the establishment of a more complete personality.

I believe that the same peculiarity may also be observed in Freemasonry which, although not a religion, is undeniably related to the "sacred". In Freemasons, there is a return to the conscious of the archetype of Self, thus satisfying man's pursuit of transcendence in order to consciously accomplish his own totality. Freemasons, through an initiatic pathway to perfection, search for expressions of this archetype within themselves so as to integrate these into their conscience and convey an individual solution to each by identifying in Self the divine component of personality which in Gnosticism and the Kabbalah was the spark of light demanding transformation into consciousness.

In the words of the art historian, Luc Benoist, the purpose of initiation is to strive towards actively reaching a higher state, defined as a "communion with Self", access to a state of deep harmony of existence, of a balanced equilibrium of all elements that make up an individual. In this regard, the Three Degrees of Freemasonry are representative of *states of conscience* rather than *states of intellect*. The tool through which it operates, "intellectual intuition", represents neither reason nor conversational thought, but rather the organ underlying immediate knowledge, "pure intelligence" that transcends reason. The backwards pathway undertaken by Freemasons constitutes an inner enrichment or a return of one's finite Self towards the Divine Principle, a reintegration of individual Self with the Divine Self, as highlighted by Mariano Bianca: *"For the initiate self is never achieved all at the same time: precisely because he is undertaking a pathway and can know no rest, he maintains that today is different from yesterday, and tomorrow will certainly be different from today. His self is undergoing continual change and every day he discovers new aspects and new expectations that will lead him to places he has yet to experience. The initiate is projected towards the horizon he has glimpsed, he pauses there and after experiencing it, uses the same as the outset for a new pathway: he is subjected to a continual dynamic, as only in such a way can he succeed in reaching increasingly distant and profound destinations. His self is not concealed, but is limited by the things he has seen or experienced, it is however open, ready to change and to project itself towards something it as yet has no knowledge of. For the Self of the initiate there is always something beyond that comprises all that he will become on removing himself from his present situation, and everything that he is not but could have been. His beyond, the beyond of his Self cannot be reached even through use of the imagination, and for this reason it is once again the unknown that he strives to achieve, and that he in some way discovers by overturning his inner world."*[298]

The archetype of Self, projected towards the skies, thus returns to the unconscious from which it originated. Only following a subsequent reintegration into consciousness can it restore faith in the transcendence that modern-day man so urgently requires.[299]

In Freemasonry, the acknowledgement of the unconscious is the modern transposition of Gnosticism, the Kabbalah, Alchemy, Hermeticism and Neoplatonism. This conscious self-accomplishment of personal totality represents the underlying theme of the Masonic project, in the context of the different historical contingencies in which the project has been undertaken, and which will continue to be proposed both in the present and in the future.

I previously mentioned the presence of a guiding thread that links the traditional "forms". The presence in Alchemy of a strong need for self-accomplishment of one's individual totality unconsciously projected into matter has been underlined. What indeed was the philosopher's stone if not an integrated personality, an accomplishment of Self? In turn, Freemasonry pursues this need for self-accomplishment no longer through a mirage of alchemical gold but by means of a philosophical project in which the alchemical tradition has clearly left its mark.

Based on these premises therefore, Myth may be defined as an external manifestation of the elaboration of a profound psychic activity, termed by Jung the "collective unconscious", or rather an association of essential innate life experiences conceived, in this dimension, from an impersonal perspective that applies to each individual at any time. These experiences are reproduced in mythological and "sacred" allegories and symbols representing the fundamental knowledge of life, but likewise the *a priori* of knowledge itself, the archetypes defined by Jung as the fundamental contents of a collective unconscious. The presence of specific archetypes illustrates the differences observed between various civilisations, the singularities manifested in each culture and in the individuals comprising the group.

Myth as the development of one archetypical image or another tells a story that self-represents the constitution of a civilisation and its energetic and spiritual foundation.

Each personal experience is the interpretation in the contingent language of the time of eternal archetypical images; the Myth has become part of history through personal interpretation. It is for this reason that no rigid or absolute interpretation of Masonic symbols and allegories of the Myth used in Masonic rituals, should be

298 Mariano Bianca, *L'Oltre e l'Invisibile*, Atanòr, Rome, 2002, page 35.
299 G. Tedeschi, *L'Ebraismo e la Psicologia Analitica*, Giuntina, Rome, 2000, page 16.

attempted, but should rather be adapted to the context. Indeed, if the pursuit of ethical aims is comprised in a project characterised by singular anthropological features, a Masonic anthropology, the applications that ensue will undeniably differ throughout the various historical periods of mankind.

It is here that the relationship between ideal and philosophical levels (focusing mainly on the conception of man), and the concrete, historical levels (featuring multiple applications) can be observed. An authentic comprehension of Freemasonry will be acquired if, and only if, both philosophical and historical levels, as well as reciprocal association, are fully expressed.[300]

Although under normal conditions the unconscious archetypal images are projected externally in the form of myths and religion, in the event of a collective crisis they return to their original unconscious state, thus causing a situation of disorder and spiritual confusion. As mentioned previously, Jung underlined the archetype of Self, perceived as the centre of both the conscious and unconscious personality, as being opposed to the Ego, the centre of the conscious. This archetype seeks acceptance of the unconscious by the conscious, promoting a synthesis between the conscious and the unconscious with the aim of achieving a more complete personality.

In the presence of a spiritual crisis, when the external values of the established creed fail, the archetype returns to its original psyche, while man is left to regenerate his sense of the sacred through a concerted effort of characterisation.

If the aim of a Freemason is the pursuit of perfection through an innate transcendental commitment, the displacement of the psychic centre of the Ego, the centre of conscience, to Self, the centre of the conscious and unconscious personality, then the *sine qua non* for achieving this aim is the subordination of Ego to Self according to a transcendental project.

Thus, the metaphysical process embarked on in Freemasonry comprises what Jung defines as an "individualisation process", or rather the conscious accomplishment of the yearning for completeness and, therein, of individual singularity, of a tangible difference. The activation of Self invariably generates a religious (or sacred) experience, through this synergy of both conscious and unconscious aspects leading to a broadening of personality.

I firmly maintain that the importance of Jung lies in this equivalence between the striving towards conscious self-accomplishment of personality and religiousness (or the quest for sacredness). The path leading to the accomplishment of individuality is but part of a much wider transcendental project.

300 G. Di Bernardo, *Filosofia della massoneria*, Marsilio, Venice, 1987, page 7.

Jung defines the collective unconscious as *"a part of the psyche which can be negatively distinguished from personal unconscious by the fact that it does not, like the latter, owe its existence to personal experience and consequently is not a personal acquisition. While the personal unconscious is made up essentially of contents which have at one time been conscious but which have disappeared from consciousness through having been forgotten or repressed, the contents of the collective unconscious have never been in consciousness, and therefore have never been individually acquired but owe their existence exclusively to heredity. Whereas the personal unconscious consists for the most part of complexes, the content of the collective unconscious is made up essentially of archetypes".*[301] The figure of the "archetype" therefore would seem to indicate the unfailing presence throughout the entire psyche of specific forms, or rather "pre-existing forms". Jung clarifies this concept by stating: *"In addition to our immediate consciousness, which is of a thoroughly personal nature and which we believe to be the only empirical psyche (even if we tack on the personal unconscious as an appendix), there exists a second psychic system of a collective, universal, and impersonal nature which is identical in all individuals. This collective unconscious does not develop individually but is inherited. It consists of pre-existent forms, the archetypes, which can only become conscious secondarily and which give definite form to certain psychic contents."*[302]

Myths and symbols therefore represent the fundamental components of archetypes, considered by the Jungian school as fundamental and exemplary categories that existed prior to the history of mankind, yet are impressed in the unfathomable depth of the human mind, destined to emerge in the conscious of a select number of individuals, taking on form and substance only in the minds of the "conscious" man.

I wish here to emphasise how, historically, during this phase of increased awareness it was frequently the elite, the politicians and the religious figures, who took advantage of their propensity to create a relationship with Myths and with the symbols that were associated to the latter.

Mircea Eliade was likewise of the opinion that the elite tend to have privileged access to Myth, maintaining: *"In archaic societies the reciting of mythological traditions was the prerogative of the few. In specific societies those called upon to recite were the shamans or medicine-men, or again members of secret confraternities... accordingly, the role played by creative minds must have been greater than one is led to believe... briefly, when privileged religious experiences are conveyed by means of a scenario of overwhelming imagination, they are capable of imposing specific models or sources of inspiration onto the entire community."*[303]

301 C.G. Jung, op. cit., page 69.
302 C.G. Jung, op. cit., page 70.
303 M. Eliade, *Myth & Reality*, Borla, Rome, 1988, pages 179-180.

Myths and symbols therefore belong to the generality of individuals, although few alone are capable of achieving full awareness.

Having discussed the definitions provided by Eliade and Jung, I will now proceed to expound the interpretation of Myth according to Bronislaw Malinowski in his anthropological version, within the context of the so-called "living mythology".

To quote Malinowski: *"Myth in a primitive society, i.e., in its original living form, is not a mere tale told but a reality lived. Not in the nature of an invention such as we read in novels today, but a living reality, believed to have occurred in primordial times and to exert a continuing influence on the universe and the destiny of mankind.... These stories are not kept alive by mere vain curiosity, or as invented or true-life tales. On the contrary, for the natives they are the assertion of an original, greater, more important reality currently governing the life, fate, and work of mankind, moreover providing the latter with a motivation for ritual and moral activities, and instructions on how to best implement these."* [304]

In Freemasonry, the presence of Myth is underlined in the Legend of Hiram, the characteristics of which are reminiscent of those afforded by Malinowski on referring to the "living" Myth.

Hiram was the builder of King Solomon's Temple, treacherously murdered by three of his companions in an attempt to steal the secret of the builder's craft, who then concealed his body. Masons admitted to the 3rd Degree ceremony are likened to Hiram who dies and rises again; thanks to his resurrection, he rises to the dignity of the rank of Master Mason. In the rebirth ritual, the repetition of Hiram's death is "authentically" experienced by the Mason aspiring to the rank of Master Mason.

A truly traditional society such as Freemasonry can be identified by means of its mythical structure perpetually ritualised through its rites and mysteries; this loyalty of Freemasons to the extra-temporal word is guaranteed by the central Myth: Hiram's "Word" that is reborn in each new Master.

In the conception of Myth as proposed by Malinowski, rituals represent the "narrative resurrection" of a primordial reality, thus alone capable of ensuring a true moral and spiritual regeneration. However, Malinowski utters a denial of the essentially symbolic nature of Myth (symbolising something other than their true vocation), maintaining in this regard: *"For the beholder 'Myth' primarily and directly expresses the tale it narrates: an event dating back to primordial times."*

304 K. Kerényi, *Prolegomeni allo studio scientifico della mitologia*, Bollati Boringhieri, Turin, 1994, page 19.

3. Genuine Myth and Technicalised Myth

Kerényi does not concur with the view provided by Malinowski and accordingly objects: *"Malinowski does not even consider the possibility that in turn this fact may still express something specific: something of an increasingly universal nature, something from the real world, a reality manifested under mythological semblance."* [305]

Kerényi's work as a mythologist consisted in the search for an approach to this "something more universal", and was to lead him to what is viewed as the most organic interpretation of Myth.He however goes even further, adding how a distinction should be made between "Genuine Mythology", meaning the spontaneous and disinterested elaboration of contents that rise spontaneously from the psyche, and a "Technicalised Mythology", the evocation and elaboration for personal aims of material serving a specific purpose.[306]

The distinction proposed by Kerényi between the genuine epiphanies of Myth and its technicalisation (pseudo-epiphanies) allows us to grasp the more important distinction between these two manifestations.

As an example, during the Fascist period Kerényi identified an evident technicalisation of Myth, thereby denying the existence of an extra-human substance revealed within man and in a historic context, maintaining how mythology was a mere representation of human life. In the technicalisation of Myth therefore, Kerényi perceives a doctrinal prerequisite for a social and political use of Myth aimed at inhibiting and subjugating man faced with impending extra-human forces (or rather when dealing with manipulators), thus, for predefined purposes, driving towards the exact opposite of "a broadening of consciousness", a fundamental assumption of Freemasonry. Indeed, the Masonic approach to Myth is located in a substantially different spatial and temporal context featuring diametrically opposed assumptions and purposes. Space is seen as "sacred", thus necessarily entailing the abolition of profane time. As recounted by Eliade: *"The desire to find oneself perpetually and spontaneously in a sacred space is equivalent to a desire to live endlessly thanks to the repetition of archetypal gestures, throughout eternity. The repetition of archetypes manifests a paradoxical desire to accomplish an ideal form (the archetype) within the boundaries of human existence, to remain for the duration without having to bear the burden, thus without being subjected to its reversibility."* [307]

Other authoritative scholars have also addressed the issue of Myth. Among these, Ernst Cassirer occupies an interesting position and on this subject affirms: *"In the period*

305 K. Kerényi,op. cit., pages 19-20.

306 F. Jesi, *Mito*, Mondadori, Milan, 1989, page 80.

307 M. Eliade, *Trattato di storia delle religioni*, Bollati Boringhieri, Turin, 1996, page 422.

between the First and the Second World Wars, a radical change in the forms of political thought took place. Perhaps the most alarming and important feature in the development of modern political thought was the creation of a new power: The Mythical Power." Conversely, Walter Otto, a renowned historian of religions and philologist, affirms: *"Myths are neither a way of thinking nor a representation, indeed not even the product of a brilliant and profound imagination, but rather the true revelation of being; thus, a Myth can affirm man in his completeness and forge his attitude in life."* [308]

To conceive Myth as a mere way of thinking would indeed signify that we have strayed from it to such an extent that we are no longer capable of contemplation should it be offered up in front of us.

At the conclusion of this discussion on Myth, it should be noted how, in the light of the abovementioned definitions, the hypothesis whereby the contrast between Myth and Democracy becomes so evident that demonstration is redundant, no longer applies. The assumption underlying the above hypothesis is the organic nexus between Myth and Totalitarianism. Democracy is by its very nature opposed to the policy of Myths, as the latter characterises totalitarian regimes; correspondingly, totalitarian regimes exploit political myths to overcome Democracy and prevent it from being rekindled.[309]

The above hypothesis could lead to the conclusion that in totalitarian systems, archetypes that pre-exist unconsciously in the collective memory may condition the unaware masses, but as bearers of the original models, force them to embrace the directives issued instrumentally by the elite. The symbols and models proposed as examples by the latter to the masses draw their capacity of persuasion from ancestral memory and from the liberating power of Myths and what they represent. Thus, abidance with regulations is mandatory to the spirit, a prospect of liberation. Compliance with the law, the expression of power, is comprehensive and assures a guarantee of power and self-accomplishment.

If, however, as we have already ascertained, Myth adopted by totalitarianism is nothing but a pseudo-Myth and if the emancipation of man, through the inclination for an authentically mythical view of life, is doomed to clash with the policies of the masses and the standardisation of conscience, then the axiom whereby Myth is equivalent to Totalitarianism is inevitably overturned by the principle that perceives any form of Totalitarianism as a negation of Myth itself. Myth, therefore, in its most "genuine" form cannot but be self-revealing for man on his pathway towards the progressive conquest of authenticity and the most sacred dimension of mankind, the very bastion of freedom.

308 W.F. Otto, *Essais sur le Mythe*, page 34.
309 R. Esposito, *Micromega*, 1/92, page 203.

Chapter Eight

The Tradition

'Maybe you're a Mason yourself!' suddenly escaped from Aloysha. 'You don't believe in God' he added, this time with great sorrow. Besides, it seemed to him that his brother was looking at him mockingly.

Fyodor Dostoevsky
The Great Inquisitor
The Brothers Karamazov

1. Freemasonry as a "Form" of Tradition

In the course of this book I have constantly and systematically referred to Freemasonry as the ultimate manifestation, in a temporal order, of a form of *Tradition*.

In my humble opinion, this should represent its true collocation and identification, both esoteric and philosophical, deduced from its principal aim, which is that of transmitting a Knowledge of metaphysical origin.

In the same way as all traditional doctrines worthy of this name, Freemasonry is by its very constitution immutable in its deepest essence (the *Landmarks*), even though the historic representations of them may at times present the movement with a wide series of heterogeneous versions.

When speaking of *Tradition* we are referring to a metaphysical and atemporal Truth which has crossed the history of mankind, a Truth that is transmitted with the aim of being preserved intact, as it was in the beginning. *Tradition,* as underlined by Elémire Zolla, is:

"...what is transmitted, particularly from progeny to progeny, the root of all human states or actions, the living rather than the dead or those in whom their blood flows, easily persuaded that they can invent things which are actually a sheer revival, create dialogues that move with the semblance of novelty to the degree that the ancient voice already bestowed on it achieved in antiquity. But every sort of Tradition exists. The overriding Tradition however, deserving of a capital letter for exactness rather than a rhetoric expedient, is the transmission of the highest and most perfect of things, the knowledge of perfection. This is the Tradition

that outshines all others as logically anterior, indeed implicit in the instrument used for all transmissions, language."[310] Zolla, therefore, and I fully agree with his view, considers that *Tradition* pre-eminently consists in the transmission of the ways of achieving knowledge of the Divine representing the ultimate good and, consequently, *Tradition* represents a set of *actions* suited to *"propitiating the intuition of a perfect being"* underlining in this way the intuitive and intellectual characteristic of this operation, identifying the same with beatitude and paving the way for the ultimate aim of man.[311]

As mentioned, it is the characteristic of *immutability*, despite its apparent historical modifications, that unfailingly allows *Tradition* to transmit its principles and its essence, contrary to the profane world in which all is continually subject to change and alteration. However, this immutability is only assured by the inseparable practice of *initiation* by means of which the essence of the original *Tradition* may be preserved, thus enhancing its survival and enabling its transmission even throughout the more obscure periods in the history of mankind.

To be faithful to *Tradition* however does not imply the slavish reproduction of ideas and thoughts, the re-evocation of symbols or carrying out of ritual ceremonies through which the spiritual currents were manifested in past incarnations. On the contrary, the task of the "keeper" of *Tradition* is to succeed in *incarnating* the last of the new forms in which it is manifested today, in other words to "actualise" *Tradition* in the new context in which it will reawaken.

I would moreover like to point out that Freemasonry, in addition to representing a "form" of *Tradition*, the last in a temporal order, likewise constitutes a living *Tradition* that is still in its prime. By this I mean that Freemasonry, which in my opinion has still not completed its full *esoteric-initiatic* development, interrupted frequently by adverse historical events, is still capable of terminating the project, and rediscovering its esoterism to propose it again with renewed vigour. This may indeed lead to unexpected results.

The current social unrest, the identity crisis that continually challenges the individual in a society lacking its *Centre*, provide a glimpse into the enormous potential available to Freemasonry, but on condition that its true initiatic component is *returned to the light* and its possibilities exploited in full.

To return to the concept of *Tradition,* important scholars have often provided a wide variety of definitions, all however linked to a common denominator, the *metaphysical*, *extra-spatial* and *extra-temporal* essence of Freemasonry with its ultimate aim of drawing closer to God: "deification".

310 Elémire Zolla, *La Tradizione*, Bompiani, Milan, 1971, page 97.
311 Ibid. page 387.

For Julius Evola, *Tradition* represents a *"force from on high"* that acts by conferring spiritual and super-individual ideals to the human order and, generally, is manifested to the few at the apex of the human hierarchy. It exerts an action of education and animation as it confers a higher significance and legitimacy to the latter orders. Evola opines how in the more original forms of *Tradition* there is no division between temporal power and spiritual authority, and how the latter mainly establishes and legitimises the former. He mentions that historically *Tradition* was presented as the *transmission* of an invisible and educational energy, and not as a form of abstract contemplation.

Tradition however also yielded a second esoteric and doctrinal aspect for Evola, an aspect that related to the *"transcendent unity placed in the various Traditions"*, *Traditions* which, with a view to the *sophia perennis,* could be of a religious, knowledgeable or mystic nature. Furthermore, he held the view that *Tradition* was historically manifested in two distinct forms, a primeval "hyperboreal" or "Nordic-western" *Tradition* for the entire group of traditional Indo-European civilisations, and another *Tradition* based on the culture of the Far East.[312]

I maintain, therefore, on referring once more to Freemasonry that in so far as a "form" of *Tradition*, we may observe an intention to preserve, hand down and even restore the thought and actions of the latter by creating the assumptions on which to base the establishment of a new, original anthropology and gnoseology.

Accordingly, quoting the journalist Hans Bluger, Freemasonry could be identified as a sort of *Männerbünde*, a society of men, an exclusively male Order and venue for meetings between an elite of initiates. As the German thinker Ernst Jünger accurately foresaw, the decadence of the masses marches parallel to that of individuals and will, over time, lead to the establishment of *specialist, differentiated groups* who will ultimately bear Medieval characteristics of the Religious Orders and Orders of Knighthood. In my opinion this is what Freemasonry is today.

In this perspective Freemasonry, in a certain sense and to paraphrase Evola and Guénon, is seen as a *"revolt and criticism of the modern world"*, a criticism of the contemporary world which is also a condemnation of the blind trust placed in scientific materialism, the ideology of progress, individualism, social anomia, of reason reduced to a mere instrumental rationalisation that governs over a *"reign of quantity"*: a civilisation that has lost its spiritual and metaphysical values. Freemasonry was born and developed as a "revolt" against this modern world.

To resume the discussion of *Tradition*, it is only in this that man will succeed in escaping from the vicious circle and *retracing* his steps towards his origins; a pathway of this nature however cannot be *either contingent or transient*, contrary to ideologies,

312 Julius Evola, *Imperialismo Pagano*, Mediterranee, Rome, 2004, page 47.

philosophies, religions and political regimes. Indeed, if the thought of modernity is based on an idea of "linear time", *Tradition* is largely opposed to the idea of "cyclical time" or "duration", as traditional societies are situated *beyond the confines of time* in an atemporal, metaphysical dimension.

Consequently, the opposition between the modern world and the traditional world, between modern man and traditional man, is not merely a historical issue, but is also, as Evola states, *"ideal, morphological"* and, particularly, *"metaphysical"*. The opposition between the "historical world" and the "world of *Tradition*" is similar to the antithesis between historical action and metaphysical action. The former is the distinctive sign of the modern world based on a concept of time, i.e. on a succession that divides and distinguishes events. The idea of development, of theological redemption, emancipation and progress is represented in this concept. The second is the distinctive sign of *Tradition* based on the concept of the eternal: action is; it is continually ongoing although is not expressed in a temporal, but rather a spatial context. It is the typical action of the myth, of a super-temporal and non-human nature.

I have previously referred to the Masonic "Method", and I should like to add that this necessarily resembles the traditional "Method" defined by Julius Evola:

"Thus, what is called a 'traditional method' is usually characterised by a double principle: ontologically and objectively by the principle of correspondence, which ensures an essential and functional correlation between analogous elements, presenting them as simple homologous forms of the appearance of a unitary and central meaning; and epistemologically and subjectively by the generalised use of the principle of induction, which is here understood as an excursive approximation of a spiritual intuition, in which what is realised is the integration and the unification of the diverse elements encountered in the same one meaning and in the same one principle." [313]

In the Masonic "Method" inspired by the traditional "Method" we can first and foremost observe a clear neglect of what may be termed "external" aims, and an increased focus on "personal" aims, not in an "ascetic" vision of life, a neglect of society and its dynamics, but a *facing* of the world from another point of view, a new approach that in the context of social dynamics allows us to maintain our peculiarities and individual traits, a non-defeatist participation.

In the final era defined by the Indian philosophy of *Kali-Yuga,* the "figure" of the Freemason may represent that which for Evola was the "differentiated man" and for Jünger an "anarchical", an individual intimately connected to a transcendent dimension and thus to *Tradition,* who has understood that he cannot be under any illusion, but

313 Julius Evola, *Rivolta contro il mondo moderno*, Mediterranee, Rome, 1998, page 32.

who at the same time is not overwhelmed by anxiety or frustration, *who takes care of his duties until they are completed*, who does what he has to do in full autonomy and dignity, going *beyond* nihilism. Freemasonry therefore would become a sort of *manual of inner salvation*, spiritual, that would permit us to escape unscathed from the discord of the modern world.

To the Freemason, the man of *Tradition*, an *awareness* of the crisis underlines how the modern world is lacking particularly a *Centre*, a significance, a symbol; for this reason he fights against modern nihilism that denies the transcendence and thus disintegrates the symbolic value of life.

It would then be feasible to ask oneself whether Freemasonry as a "form" of *Tradition* could ever produce an "incisive" action directly on society, transforming it, improving it? Will it ever be capable of intervening in social dynamics? A response to this query is provided by Julius Evola:

"Tradition, in its essence, is something simultaneously meta-historical and dynamic: it is an overall ordering force, in the service of principles that have the chrism of a superior legitimacy (we may even call them 'principles from above'). This force acts through the generations, in continuity of spirit and inspiration, through institutions, laws, and social orders that may even display a remarkable variety and diversity... Even where these principles (relating to Tradition) are objectified in a historical reality, they are not at all conditioned by it; they always point to a higher, meta-historical plane, which is their natural domain and where there is no change. The ideas that I call 'traditional' must be thought of along the same lines." [314] Quindi, agire sì, ma da un piano superiore, o meglio, secondo la filosofia del Wu wei, agire non agendo — *then act, but from a higher level, or better still according to the philosophy of Wu wei, act by doing nothing.*

To conclude, I would like to emphasise that what markedly divides the "traditional" world from the "modern" world is that, whilst the latter is founded on the profane criteria of the useful and time, economy and politics, the former relates unerringly to the values of the "sacred" and to "eternity", as noted by Elémire Zolla:

"The first step towards Tradition is a criticism of ideologies, of tricks, of appealing seductions which permeate the sensitive world, the world of individuals and of society. Non modo personis sed rebus ipsis persona demenda. *Tradition represents the sole warranty of a constant dissolution of all that in man is hypocrisy, and in society ideology because, removed from the game of the worldly forces, it knows no limits, it is tireless as the worldly revolutionary faced with its playthings, it never fails to display the ridicule of utopias."* [315]

314 Julius Evola, *Gli uomini e le rovine*, Mediterranee, Rome, 2001, page 64.
315 E. Zolla, op. cit., page 105.

2. The Concept of Hierarchy

For all advocates of an "egalitarian" society, every time the term "hierarchy" is uttered or perceived, there is a serious risk of endangering the indissoluble principles that safeguard equality against all forms of power that descend from the heavens to the earth.

This is not quite how things are. The social contexts in which *Homo Hierarchicus*, among which I would like to Freemasonry, is collocated, do not in any way endanger the ideals of freedom and equality. Indeed, as highlighted by the famous French Indologist and anthropologist Louis Dumont, we are not dealing with a representation, as we have been led to believe, of a *rigid system of power* but, on the contrary, the hierarchical dynamics are portrayed in the light of the principles of *Tradition*, in the form of *differences in grade rather than in power*, in a setting that has as its ultimate aim the creation of a respected principle of authority rather than authoritarianism.[316]

If *Tradition*, as observed in the definitions presented in previous paragraphs, is represented as *"the transmission of the idea of being at the height of perfection, therefore of a hierarchy among relative and historical beings founded on their distance from a specific point or unit,"* [317] it would be, in the light of these concepts, totally mistaken to take the hierarchical principle as being based on the predominance of one over the other; conversely, the term "hierarchy" should be identified with the concept of *supremacy of the all on its parts*, in the mark of an organicistic and impersonal logic.

As often happens, the interpretation of the hierarchical system in the authoritarian sense was caused by the individualistic perception of modern Western society, which is completely unrelated to the hierarchical, traditional societies in which we detect a collective idea of man.

It is here that the opposition between *individualism* and *holism*, a phenomenon that Louis Dumont frequently underlines in his works (in a holistic view, society is an individual group featuring wishes and relations, which is subjected to social regulations) was manifested, particularly in *Homo Hierarchicus*. In this work, in which the author uses the central theme of the "Caste" concept as applied in India, he emphasises the contrast between traditional, holistic, hierarchical societies and modern, individualistic, equalitarian societies.

According to Dumont, society from an ontological perspective no longer exists, with only a few remaining individuals against the background of a universal scenario, monads in a global village. Consequently, to overcome this problem, Dumont is of the

316 Louis Dumont, *Homo Hierarchicus*, Adelphi, Milan, 1991.

317 Elémire Zolla, op. cit., page 98.

opinion that we need a new synthesis between *holism* and *individualism*, in the belief that individualism alone will never be enough.[318]

However, it is particularly the interpretation of the concept of hierarchy in use in Indian societies that Dumont focuses on and that is of concern for the purpose of this study. In an Indian context the term assumes a different meaning from that generally used in the West, writes Dumont:

"For modern common sense, hierarchy is a ladder of command in which the lower rungs are encompassed in the higher ones in regular succession. 'Military hierarchy', the artificial construction of progressive subordination from commander-in-chief to private soldier, would serve as an example. Hence it is a question of systematically graduated authority. Now, hierarchy in India certainly involves gradation, but is neither power nor authority," [319] consequently, according to Dumont, *"So we shall define hierarchy as the principle by which the elements of a whole are ranked in relation to the whole, it being understood that in the majority of societies it is religion which provides the view of the whole, and that the ranking will thus be religious in nature. We are concerned in this case with concepts which have become totally foreign to us, as Tocqueville has shown us. In the modern age, hierarchy has become 'social stratification' that is, hierarchy which is shamefaced or non-conscious, or, as it were, repressed."* [320] If we wished to apply this view to the Initiatic Societies and to *Traditional* thought, it would suffice to replace the term "religious" with "sacred" and thus achieve a perfect correspondence in the application of the concept of hierarchy according to the representation indicated by Dumont.

It is however above all the *holistic* nature embedded in the hierarchical relationship that makes the hypothesis put forward by Dumont so interesting, and is represented as follows: *"Two features stand out: first in India, any totality is expressed in the form of a hierarchical enumeration of its components (thus of the state or kingdom, for example), hierarchy marks the conceptual integration of a whole; it is, so to say, the intellectual cement. Secondly, if we are to generalise, it can be supposed that hierarchy, in the sense that we are using the word here, and in accord with its etymology, never attaches itself to power as such, but always to religious functions, because religion is the form assumed by the universal in these societies."* [321]

To conclude, Dumont attempts to push a difficult and thorny concept closer to the Western world which is, however, in his opinion still present today in our culture:

"It is appropriate to keep in mind our aversion to hierarchy. Not only does this aversion explain our difficulty in deepening our understanding of hierarchy, but we are facing a kind of

318 Louis Dumont, op. cit., page 81.

319 Louis Dumont, op. cit., page 161.

320 Louis Dumont, op. cit., page 162.

321 Louis Dumont, op. cit., page 419.

taboo, an unmistakable censure, and caution requires the adoption of a circumspect approach, the avoidance of any provocative statements or premature judgements ... I believe that hierarchy is not, essentially, a chain of super-imposed commands, nor even a chain of beings of decreasing dignity, nor yet a taxonomic tree, but a relation that can succinctly be called 'the encompassing of the contrary'. The best example I have found is biblical. It is the story of the creation of Eve from Adam's rib, in the first book of Genesis, chapter 2. God creates Adam first, the undifferentiated man, the prototype of mankind. In a second stage, he extracts a different being from this first Adam. Adam and Eve stand face to face, prototypes of the two sexes. In this strange operation, on the one hand, Adam has changed identity; from being undifferentiated he has become a male. On the other hand a being has appeared who is both a member of the human species and different from the main representative of his species. In his entirety, Adam, or 'man' in our language – is two things in one: the representative of the human species and the prototype of the male individuals of this species. On a first level man and woman are identical, on a second level woman is the opposite or the contrary of man. These two relations characterise the hierarchical relation, which cannot be better symbolised than by the material encompassing of the future Eve in the body of the first Adam. This hierarchical relation is, very generally, the relation between the whole (or a set) and an element of this whole or set; the element is part of the whole, and is in this sense consubstantial or identical with it; at the same time the element is distinct from the set or stands in opposition to it. This is what I mean by the expression 'the encompassing of the contrary'."[322]

According to Dumont, therefore, hierarchy represents an unavoidable *need* of human society, in my opinion the dynamics of which can be observed to the full particularly in Initiatic Societies, for example Freemasonry. It is thanks to this "hierarchical" view of human dynamics that Freemasonry should be considered a *Society of Initiates*, with a singular "view of the world", a *weltanschauung*, and more besides; to simplify, it is an organisational system of association in which the concept of hierarchy assumes a markedly profane significance.

A hierarchical interpretation of life is not aimed at abolishing reality but at representing the same by means of a *scale of priorities*, identifying for each the human peculiarities and characteristics and an appropriate collocation in a suitable environment, in an attempt to arrange reality in a more "organic" and harmonious manner. Hierarchy should be interpreted as a natural need of society and a civil dimension suited to man.[323]

To return to the discussion of Evola, we are fully aware of how the thoughts of the Roman traditionalists were unavoidably directed *on high*, in a rigorously elitist and hierarchical manner. Evola recalls how etymologically the term "hierarchy" indicates

322 Louis Dumont, Ibid. pages 528-529.

323 Marcello Veneziani, *L'Antinovecento*, Mondadori, Milan, 1996, page 180.

"sovereignty of the sacred", and consequently the hierarchical perspective should likewise be conveyed in a synchronic sense ("the wider the base, the higher the summit") as well as in a diachronic sense as the past is by definition invariably better than the present – and gets better the further one is from it. The key notion is that the inferior may never succeed in preceding the superior, as more cannot be born from less, being indeed the main reason for which Evola has always rejected Darwin's theory of evolution.

Our ritual demonstrates that these concepts are present throughout the pathway to perfection, and this we know as at a certain point of the initiatic process we are told that *"the mysteries are not communicated indiscriminately, but are conferred on the Candidate according to his merits and skills."*[324]

Evola's criticism of individuals and values is all embracing and spares not even the Church:

"We have seen that inequality and a distance between beings is not so much a fact as an ideal, something that must be, something that is necessary, an assumption for all rational organisations of beings. But Christian morality commences from an idea of equality, on a belief that all men are equal in front of God and in relation to their common nature deriving from sin. The saying to do as you would be done by – giving rise to the saying by Kant 'Act in such a way that your best conduct may serve as a universal ideal of action' is merely one of the many that irrefutably imply the assumption of equality, the criterion of sociability and uniformity of the values, for the transcendence of a collective association, something that is maintained by means of a system of impersonal reciprocal relations so that each, although dependent on the other, seeing no-one above him, achieves the sensation of freedom."[325]

Evola undoubtedly expresses extreme concepts which are hard to comprehend beyond a "traditionalist" view; however, in the context of Traditional thought we can observe a logic and precise collocation. Evola writes:

"The lord was he who imposed himself as a power, an initiative, a capacity for resistance, heroism and generosity – featuring both an aptitude in appreciating superior forms of life (knowledge, intellect, art) – and, even more directly, a higher potential of psychic forces and suggestion (mana), with a virtue of animator and summoner. Faced with the manifestation of these qualities characteristic of a privileged being, in the souls of those who could not and did not know how to elevate themselves to gain participation, the modern population displayed *long forgotten sentiments; devotion, respect, worship, fear. Accordingly, a hierarchy was justified in an organic and direct manner... Let us thus provide support to he who in the name of this Knowledge and can attest to this knowledge are deauthored and denuded, he who in the field of religious*

324 Emulation Ritual, page 83.

325 Julius Evola, *Imperialismo Pagano*, Mediterranee, Rome, 2004, page 106.

superstitions for mere 'aspirations' of the 'soul', for dogmas, traditions, hallucinations and acts of blind faith are the keepers of the sacred and the divine. In the place of those who 'believe', the blind who lead the blind, should stand those who 'know', in the same way as the men-gods encountered in the Chinese Imperial, Persian, Egyptian and Greek-Roman traditions."[326]

To conclude, the hostility that related to the hierarchical forms, hierarchy as a view, confirms and attests overwhelmingly to a fact, decadence and the inevitable extinction, in Western society and culture, of the value of individuality and, consequently, ratifies the new dictatorship of the "masses", as stated by Elémire Zolla:

"Equality places a king of immense and disembodied tyranny on the throne: a statistical formula is used to re-establish the average. The statistically average man becomes a saviour, the imitation of whom is sought after and should enable individuals to be cleansed of the sin of possessing features; he who dares to question, or feel emotions, undertake a study, be enthusiastic about an idea not deemed by the saviour to be accessible and consumable will be sorry. By definition, an average man is not able to grasp what is rare, superior, and therefore precious; all values therefore shall have to be sacrificed, being justified solely when based on their summit... The few are aware of the disasters elicited by the cult of equality, and all seek to represent an average between incompatible fates."[327]

3. The Inclusion Theory

The "form" or the "figure" conveys the place, expressed in a symbolic form, in which following an encounter between interiority and exteriority, reality is collocated in its depth, in its own space and its own time. Ernst Jünger highlights how the latter represents a Neoplatonist return to the promethean substance, a representation of the "elementary" among the "figures", which should be included rightfully among the symbols of Freemasonry.

Jünger specified that the "figures", their singular and pregnant substance of an exhaustive nature, derive directly from the elementary forces that are released as uncontainable energies of telluric origin, with the major characteristic consequently of being manifested under a *metahistorical* aspect. The "figure" of the Freemason in this case, albeit in its relative atemporality, is invariably and necessarily incorporated in time according to its own specific meter and distance or self identification.

From this point of view it is clear how Freemasonry could not belong to one ideology rather than another. Freemasonry is.

326 Julius Evola, op. cit., page 107.
327 E. Zolla, op. cit., page 75.

The "figure" or "form" of the Freemason therefore, with his ritual, his *Landmarks*, his "Method" shaped by *ethics* leads the world that surrounds him to an "order", although it remains *independent* of all evolutionary instances as its origin and status are independent of time and of the affairs this would appear to generate. Those who maintain that to study the social, economic-political or religious situation would help to understand the reason underlying the birth of the *form* in Freemasonry or the *figure* of the Freemason would be far from the truth; the birth of Freemasonry as an Initiatic Order indeed conveys the need to regress to the "elementary", to annul the history and start again afresh.

A Freemason consequently is presented as the *enemy* of he who tends to destroy "figures" and "forms", a tendency born within a modern order as a result of technology and progress, the two great "molochs", the outcome of modern rationality.

How should we collocate Freemasonry therefore from a *Traditional* point of view? In an *atemporal* or *meta-historic* manner?

In an attempt to solve this difficult and nigh on impossible question addressed by generations of scholars, I will refer to the concept of "inclusion" used by Ernst Jünger in his wonderful novel *Eumeswil*.

In a chapter relating to the Mystery Societies I have already mentioned how the *initiatic current*, the *Tradition*, has "survived" for two thousand years until it was re-presented in the "form" of Freemasonry. In the theory of "inclusions" put forward by Junger likewise, the *initiatic currents* were once again manifested after having been occulted for centuries, although never completely extinct.

The "inclusions", in the opinion of Jünger, are a sort of "condensation" and "laceration" of the historical theme, of survivals. He defines them as petrifications, sclerosis, crystallisations of the historic structure. In the modern day the "inclusions" would thus represent a permanence or *incursions into the sacred*, the elementary, mythical or fantastical in the orderly company of the rationalisation of the world, essentially phenomena classified in the realms of irrationality. They originate from Chthonius and represent vestiges of mystic-imaginary forces and dimensions rendered possible at times by the intense Plutonic activity of technology.[328]

As stated above, Jünger refers to the "inclusions" in one of his novels, *Eumeswil*, a text that has linked his fame to the presence within the plot of the "figure" of an "anarchist" who is mentioned repeatedly by Jünger. In his novel, the author refers to the *inclusum*, explaining how the latter is, for historians, a somewhat singular problem: *"History does not merely signify a collection of occurrences, but rather their collocation in a*

328 Luisa Bonesio, *Fisiognomica del Nichilismo*, in *Ernst Jünger e il pensiero del nichilismo*, Herrenhaus, Seregno, 2002, pages 207-208.

precise order. This is undertaken first by the chroniclers and subsequently by the historian. It is implicit that in doing so not only is a choice made, but a role is also played by the style of the times. Some happenings are highlighted to excess whilst others are not even mentioned. They disappear forever or are exhumed one fortunate day by an ingenious mind… By the term inclusum I intended to allude to something quite different – to the 'everything different'. There are periods comprised within the events that the historian scarcely understands, or indeed may never succeed in comprehending." [329]

This has occurred frequently with several traditional "forms", often interpreted in a superficial or incorrect manner, largely misunderstood and, in particular, this is exactly what has happened to Freemasonry since the time of its origin.

In the "inclusions" the concept of "time" and "history" assume a different, metaphysical meaning, as underlined by Eliade:

"At times some events, although classifiable as 'historic' occurrences, may not reveal behaviours that reach beyond the historic compartments of the human being… If it is indeed true that man frequently finds himself 'in situations', this does not imply that the situation is of an historic concern, that is conditioned exclusively by an historic movement of contemporary times… Man knows, on the other hand, a series of temporal rhythms of a not unfailingly historic domain, of his own time, a historic contemporaneity… Too soon the conclusion was reached that the authenticity of an existence depends solely on an awareness of one's historic dimension. This historic awareness plays an extremely modest role in the human conscience, not to mention the areas of the unconscious that likewise belong to an integral human being." [330]

In conclusion, I have attempted to put forward in this book a representation of Freemasonry as the *ultimate* manifestation in order of time of all "traditional" forms, whilst at the same time portraying it as the final "synthesis", bearer of an enunciation of the beauty of life and a system of ethics, a *means of facing one's existence.*

329 Ernst Jünger, *Eumeswil*, Guanda, Parma, 1981, page 223.

330 Mircea Eliade, op. cit., page 34.

Appendix I

Freemasonry and the Catholic Church

On behalf of the Regular Grand Lodge of Italy I would first like to thank Prof. Giuseppe Ferrari, Italian Secretary of the GRIS (Group for Research and Information on Sects - social and religious group for research and information) for his kind invitation, a rare opportunity to freely express our views on an issue of fundamental importance in such a highly qualified context.

I have listened with interest to the previous speeches and I must confess that, further to the individual conclusions drawn, being called upon to focus on the association between the Church and Freemasonry indeed provides an ideal opportunity to clarify the complex "world" of Freemasons.

Before starting out on this dissertation of documents that in the course of history have affected the relationship between the Catholic Church and Freemasons, I wish to point out that to mention Freemasonry in a merely generic manner is somewhat vague, if not downright misleading. Indeed, one of the most frequent mistakes when dealing with issues pertaining to Freemasonry is to overlook the fact that although Freemasons throughout the world are characterised by a spiritual and formal link (Mutual Recognition) between the individual Grand Lodges, they are often divided by a substantial discrepancy in doctrines and esoteric aspects.

The involvement of Lodges on the social and at times political scene varies from country to country in line with the history of the moment, frequently forgoing the esoteric-initiatic component on which its origins are based and evolving into a mere associative phenomenon strongly resembling political parties or similar.

Therefore, when expressing one's opinion on the principles, the philosophy or the ideas of Freemasonry, I would suggest the advisability of specifying which documents and rituals, and particularly which Masonic Obedience is being referred to. Indeed, the differences and peculiarities on the vast Masonic panorama are so marked that in my opinion it would be better to refer no longer to "Freemasonry" but rather to the plural "Masonic Obediences".

As a mere example, the Scandinavian Masonic Obediences are organised on a prevailingly Christian basis, and access consequently denied to all individuals not professing this faith. Accordingly, it would be hard to justify to Scandinavian Freemasons the reasons underlying the accusation of "religious indifferentism" included in the Encyclical *Humanum Genus* written by Leo XIII in 1884.

In view of the lack of a single reference body representing the vast multifaceted international movement of Freemasons, it is of fundamental importance to be aware of the sources adopted by the Catholic Church in publishing documents to be taken into consideration here.

The documents and sources traditionally consulted by Catholic scholars in investigating the relationship between the Catholic Church and Freemasonry have, regrettably, failed to include documents originating from traditional Freemasonry, in particular British and Scandinavian Freemasonry. On the contrary, reports published by the Catholic Church with regard to Freemasonry have invariably been based on documents referring almost exclusively to two Masonic Obediences: the *Grand Orient of Italy* and the *Grand Orient of France*, accounting for a very small percentage of the international Masonic movement.

In the light of the above premises therefore, it is crucial that scholars of the Catholic Church make a committed effort in an attempt to better comprehend the multiple aspects, peculiarities and profound differences encountered in the vast multifaceted context of Freemasonry.

On undertaking a rapid digression amongst documents on Freemasonry belonging to the Catholic Church the presence of several contradictions soon becomes evident. The first document issued by the Catholic Church against Freemasonry, the Excommunication Bull *In eminenti apostulatus specula* issued by Pope Clement XII in 1738 accused Freemasons of "heresy". The Bull reads: *"Moreover, We desire and command that both Bishops and prelates, and other local ordinaries, as well as inquisitors for heresy, shall investigate and proceed against transgressors of whatever state, grade, condition, order dignity or pre-eminence they may be; and they are to pursue and punish them with condign penalties as being most suspect of heresy."*

In the Declaration on Freemasonry *Quaesitum est*, a document published on November 26th 1983 by the Congregation for the Doctrine of Faith (the prefect of which at the time was Cardinal Joseph Ratzinger) completely overturned the previous sentence and accused Freemasons of "relativism".

In addition to the above documents several others of apparently lesser importance, although crucial in illustrating the evolution of opinions and positions held by the Catholic Church with regard to Freemasonry, have been published.

Subsequent to the issuing of the document by Clement XII, an Apostolic

Letter *Providas Romanorum* was published by Pope Benedict XIV who reiterated the injunctions issued against Freemasonry by his predecessor, invoking *"the amount of harm that can be caused to the purity of the Catholic Religion by those secret Societies and Assemblies such as Freemasonry."*

However, the most injurious misunderstanding of the nature of Freemasonry occurred in 1821 when Pope Pius VII in his letter *Ecclesiam a Jesu* indicated the Carbonari as an affiliation of Freemasonry by means of falsified historical documentation that could easily be disproved but which harmed Freemasonry considerably, providing it with political connotations.

The letter initially referred to the previous documents and then expressed the following opinion:

"A long time ago this Holy See, once these sects had been discovered, cried with a great and unbridled Voice against them, and exposed their plans, which had been devised secretly by them against Religion, indeed against civil society... Indeed, men whose arrogance has always mounted, have dared to begin new secret societies... and is generally accustomed to go under the name of the Carbonari... We are also moved by the example of Clement XII and Benedict XIV, our Predecessors of happy memory, of whom the one on the 28th day of April of the year 1738 by the Constitution 'In Eminenti', the other on the 18th day of March 1751 by the Constitution 'Providas', have condemned and proscribed the societies de' Liberi Muratori, or Francs-Maçons, or called by whatever other name according to the variety of regions and idioms, of which societies the society of the Carbonari, must be considered perhaps the offspring or certainly the imitation."

Paradoxically the Carbonari themselves attempted to explain how they had nothing to do with the Freemasons, but to no avail:

"The Carbonari indiscriminately maintain that they are not included in those two Constitutions of Clement XII and Benedict XIV, and that they are not subject to the judgments and penalties provided for therein".

A similar approach was maintained by Pope Leo XII in his Letter *Quo Graviora* published in 1825 recalling how:

"... from those old Masonic sects which have never languished, many others have arisen much more dangerous and more audacious than the former. The sect of the Carbonari, which was considered the leader of all the others in Italy and in some other regions, was considered to embrace as if in its bosom all these".

The document moreover provides reference to continental Masonic documents not hailing from the British tradition. Indeed, on reading: *"Truly that abominable oath, which has already been mentioned, and which must be sworn even in that lower echelon, is sufficient for you to understand that it is contrary to Divine Law to be enlisted in those lower degrees, and to remain in them. In the next place, although they are not accustomed to commit those things which are more serious and more criminal to those who have not attained to the higher degrees...",* most certainly reference is made to the "Higher degrees" of the Ancient and Accepted Scottish Rite that, in spite of its name, was of Continental, prevalently French, origin, subsequently spreading throughout Europe.

A further change in direction was manifested in the document *Traditi Humilitati* published by Pope Pius VIII in 1829, supporting not only the previous condemnation of the political and theological positions assumed by Freemasonry but also those of a more philosophical nature. Hence, Freemasons were accused of supporting and diffusing Enlightenment philosophy condoning the idea of an enlightened, rational world opposed to religions and related secular institutions:

"You know how evil men have raised the standard of revolt against religion through philosophy (of which they proclaim themselves doctors) and through empty fallacies devised according to natural reason... The holy precepts are despised, the celebration of divine offices is ridiculed, and the worship of God is cursed by the sinner; all things which concern religion are relegated to the fables of old women and the superstitions of priests... it is then your duty, Venerable Brothers, to eradicate those secret societies of factious men who, completely opposed to God and to princes, are wholly dedicated to bringing about the fall of the Church, the destruction of kingdoms, and disorder in the whole world... Hence the supreme pontiffs, our predecessors, Clement XII, Benedict XIV, Pius VII, Leo XII, repeatedly condemned that kind of secret society."

The Encyclical *Mirari Vos* written by Pope Gregory XVI in 1832 first put forward the accusation of "indifferentism": *"Now We consider another abundant source of the evils with which the Church is afflicted at present: indifferentism. This perverse opinion is spread on all sides by the fraud of the wicked who claim that it is possible to obtain the eternal salvation of the soul by the profession of any kind of religion, as long as rectitude and morality are maintained. This shameful font of indifferentism gives rise to that absurd and erroneous proposition which claims that liberty of conscience must be conceded for all."*

Following the Encyclical *Qui Pluribus* written by Pius IX in 1846, substantially reaffirming the accusations made by his predecessors, in 1884 the renowned Encyclical *Humanum Genus* was published by Leo XIII in 1884.

This renowned document emphasises the convergence between naturalism and Masonic principles, accusing Freemasonry of attempting to abolish all forms of religion, particularly the Catholic doctrine. The document obviously evokes the climate of that period and is thus of greater political significance than documents published previously.

The documents acknowledged so far have included mention of every manner of accusation against Freemasons, although the charge of "relativism" was only proffered in a document edited in 1985 entitled *"Irreconcilability between the Christian Faith and Freemasonry. Reflections One Year After the Declaration of the Congregation for the Doctrine of the Faith. The document reads: "Even if it is stated that relativism is not assumed as dogma, nevertheless there is really proposed a relativistic symbolic concept and therefore the relativising value of such a moral-ritual community, far from being eliminated, proves on the contrary to be decisive."*

The latter accusation of relativism is something quite new. Indeed, the previous accusation of indifferentism maintaining that all religious beliefs are equally valid paths to salvation is far removed from the idea of relativism, implicating the inexistence or rather the unawareness of a universal truth.

At this point one wonders which Masonic ritual, Constitution or official document provides proof that Freemasonry refutes the achieving of, or at least a desire to ascertain the existence of a universal Truth.

Moreover, and here we have the true paradox, the idea of branding Masonic ideas and rituals as relativistic was first imparted to the Catholic Church by Freemasons themselves. Indeed, from 1974 to 1980 when the *German Episcopal Conference* set up an official Commission to evaluate the compatibility of being a member of both the Catholic Church and Freemasonry at the same time, the documents given to the Committee by Freemasons of the *United Grand Lodge of Germany* included the *International Masonic Dictionary* by E. Lennhoff and O. Posner.

The above-mentioned book states: *"Freemasonry may thus be conceived as a movement aimed at uniting men of relativistic orientation to promote the humanitarian ideal... The point of view of Freemasons on world and humanitarian issues can be deduced from relativism. Its relativistic position is clearly evidenced through its symbolism and rituals"*. One of the eminent members of the Commission, Mons. Josef Stimple, declared that the text had been provided by German Freemasons to illustrate authentic Masonic views.

On the contrary, it can be affirmed with absolute certainty that none of the texts habitually taken as reference documents by scholars of Freemasonry worldwide contain similar declarations to that reported by Lennhoff and Posner, asserting the unfailing "relativistic" conviction of Freemasons. Therefore, the accusation of relativism has arisen from a recent error originating through the incompetence and superficiality of German Freemasonry. Indeed, although in an article published in the journal *Avvenire* on December 12th 1993, Giovanni Cantoni commented that the Encyclical *Humanum Genus* issued by Pope Leo XIII in 1884 reported how *"Freemasonry is condemned as it heralds the triumph of relativism"*, the term relativism was never overtly applied throughout the entire document written by Pope Leo XIII and certainly cannot be inferred by a similarity with subjectivism, naturalism, scepticism or religious indifferentism referred to in the Encyclical.

To conclude, I would like to quote two issues of the journal *Civiltà Cattolica* published on November 2nd 1991 and April 2nd 1994. In the first the editorial entitled *The Church and Freemasonry today* recalls how according to the neo-enlightenment assumptions conveyed to Freemasonry the Church reiterated the irreconcilability *"between the doctrines of the Church and those of Freemasonry, as the latter are refractory to both the idea of a personal, charitable God and to the salvation of man"*. It would be of interest to learn which documents have provided evidence for the drawing of similar conclusions that under no circumstances could be upheld on referring to any form of Masonic ritual of British origin. Moreover, the current belief whereby Freemasonry is deemed equal to enlightenment and represents an incontrovertible truth, is finally being questioned by several scholars. In the second issue of *Civiltà Cattolica* we read: *"The Masonic view of religion is of a deistic nature... the life and practices carried out in modern-day Freemasonry, at least in Italy, are still of a deistic, positivistic temperament, remaining largely anti-clerical and opposed to Christianity."* Once again, as pointed out previously, it would be opportune to specify which Italian Masonic Obedience is referred to in this instance.

Numerous errors of judgement with regard to Freemasonry could have been avoided if in carrying out their research, historians had referred to documents that are, in my opinion, fundamental to the comprehension of the authentic principles and bases underlying the Masonic ideals: the previously quoted ritual of Emulation and the Constitutions of the *United Grand Lodge of England*, the *Grand Lodge of Scotland* and the *Grand Lodge of Ireland.*

The Emulation ritual is the ritual practised by the *United Grand Lodge of England*, founder of modern-day Freemasonry, the most widely used ritual approved in 1816, hailing from the efforts of English ritualists belonging to the *Lodge of Reconciliation* prior to the unification of the two Grand Lodges of the *Ancients* and the *Moderns.* For more than half a century this ritual did not appear in printed form and was passed down by word of mouth.

Printed copies of the Emulation ritual first started to circulate in 1870. In 1969, the *Emulation Lodge of Perfection* officially authorised printing of the ritual.

Knowledge of this ritual, also adhered to by the Obedience of which I am Grand Master, would contribute not only towards clarifying numerous misunderstandings and banalities involving Freemasonry but also in demonstrating the lack of verity in the accusations of relativism or even deism that I would be delighted to discuss elsewhere.

I am fully persuaded of the importance of promoting meetings and discussions such as the present with the aim of furthering knowledge into the mutual reasoning and contributing towards overcoming the incomprehension that has long characterised the relationship between the Catholic Church and Freemasonry.

Appendix II

The Five Signs of Decay of an Angel

We find ourselves in the midst of a world of ruins. And the question we should ask ourselves is: are there still men standing in the midst of these ruins? What should they, what can they still do?

Julius Evola
Orientamenti

The five signs of decay of the angel are an allegory provided by Buddhist thought, as listed in the text *Abhidharma Mahavibhasasastra.*[331]

We took inspiration from this allegory to analyse the severe conditions of ill health of modern-day Freemasonry, in an attempt to comprehend the causes underlying this decay and to establish which possible forms of correction may be applied to ensure its survival. We shall examine the issue by listing five stages of degeneration of Freemasonry, all of which registered internally.

Naturally, when referring to the decay of Freemasonry, we refer to the disappearance of the "traditional", "original" form of Freemasonry, conceived and empowered with the function of "Initiatory Society". At first sight, my opinion of the current state of

331 *Abhidharma Mahavibhasasastra* describes in detail the five major and five lesser signs. The lesser signs are as follows: 1) when an angel flutters and pirouettes, it creates a breathtaking music such that no musician, orchestra or choir could ever hope to perform; but as death approaches the music wanes and its voice fades to become strained and faint. 2) Under normal conditions, an angel shines with a light that gives rise to no shadows; but as the angel dies the light fades suddenly and its body is enveloped in imperceptible shadows. 3) An sngel's skin is smooth and covered in ointment which, even if immersed in a lake of ambrosia, repels the liquid as a Lotus flower leaf; but as death approaches the water adheres with tenacious persistence. 4) Habitually, an angel can be likened to an ever-revolving wheel of fire, it never stops, can never be identified in any specific place; when we think it is here, it is really somewhere else, it moves from one place to another and effortlessly fluctuates; as death nears however, it stays put in one place and can no longer stray from that spot. 5) The body of an angel abounds with overflowing energy and its eyes are firm and steady; but as death approaches its body weakens and its eyelids flutter incessantly. The five major signs are as follows: its once immaculate gowns become worn and dirty, the flowers making up the garland on its head wither and fall, sweat pours from under its arms, an overpowering smell surrounds its body, it loses its joy in being. As can be observed, other sources only list the major signs. As long as only the lesser signs are present, death can still be avoided, but once the major signs are manifested, death becomes inevitable (Yukio Mishima, *The Decay of the Angel*, page. 1546-1547).

Freemasonry may appear to be exceedingly critical, particularly in view of the fact that numerous European Masonic Obediences have reported a marked increase in the number of members. I should like to use this fact as a starting point.

The first of the five signs that herald the imminent end of Freemasonry is emphasised by the inappropriate choices made or the total lack of discernment applied in selecting new candidates for initiation as Freemasons.

Prior to deeming an initiation possible, persons capable of providing this initiation should be available. Of course, the candidate for initiation must also be suited to the purpose. Indeed, it should be ascertained whether the candidate possesses the raw material required for the task. By the latter, we imply a specific internal constitution, an inborn predisposition, in an initiatic vision that renders the Masonic experience a maieutic rather than a thaumaturgic event. This is the Socratic technique applied to uncover the light dwelling within each of us; in the same way that the perfection process is brought to the light by means of rites and symbology, knowledge hidden in the depths of the soul of a Freemason is awakened unto itself.

To use the concept of equality in the context of Freemasonry is misleading and contradictory. If the meaning of life is constituted by a continual evolution, of which the accomplishment of Freemasonry is the representation, the distinguishing of stages of development leads to an inevitable differentiation of individuals.

In the world of *Tradition*, the highest forms of initiation were conceived as an intensely real process, capable of altering the ontological status of an individual and empowering him with forces deriving from the surrounding world or superstructure[332]. Modern lay reasoning sees all rites, indeed when not viewed as ridiculous superstition or things of the past, as a mere ceremony arousing curiosity in view of its symbolic, aesthetic or emotional value. The etymological significance of the ceremony has indeed been lost; it should be taken into account how the latter derives from the root "to create", identical to the Sanskrit "kr" meaning "to do", thus the ritual ceremony should be viewed as a truly creative event.

The most evident manifestation of this phenomenon can be observed in several Obediences throughout the United States in which "mass inititiations" are frequently performed. Further to constituting a clear contradiction, I leave it up to you to imagine what manner of profound esoteric connotations a ceremony undertaken in the presence of thousands of people can have.

332 Julius Evola, *Rivolta contro il mondo moderno*, first edition Hoepli, Milan, 1934, subsequently, Mediterranee, Rome, 1998, page 108.

An initiatic society should not rely merely on an increase in the number of members, due to the clear absurdity of a concern which for its very nature and constitution is an elite society, having a high number of adepts. The race to gain the highest number of members has become a means of comparison on an international level, as proven by the question unfailingly put on all encounters with representatives of other Masonic Obediences: "How many members do you have?" If we were only capable of directing our interest towards the true essence, the authentic nature of the Obediences we represent, in the future we could compare our Research Lodges as a common project of cultural interest. We could abandon all connotations of Masonic "politics" that in recent years have badly affected the idea of Freemasonry in Europe. By the latter, I refer to laughable initiatives undertaken for the apparent purpose of spreading the "light" of Freemasonry in nations such as those of Eastern Europe.

On the contrary, considerably important initiatives have been undertaken thanks to the involvement of Lord Northampton, Pro. Grand Master of the *United Grand Lodge of England*: the establishing of the *Canonbury Centre*, the *Cornerstone Society*, the *Centre for Masonic Studies* of *Sheffield University*, have all provided an opportunity for the hundreds of scholars of history, symbology and Masonic ideals to diffuse their articles and thus spread the knowledge of Freemasonry throughout the world. The International Conference on the History of Freemasonry held at the end of May 2009 in Edinburgh, in which I had the honour of taking part as a speaker, represents one of the major outcomes of these initiatives.

Unfortunately, the ability to decipher the true message handed down to us as a heritage by the great men of culture who established the rituals has been lost over the centuries. Reciting by heart should invariably be associated with a keen awareness of the profound significance conveyed by these rituals. The behaviour displayed should not be passive, emotional, and merely open to learning a truth revealed by others. Indeed, the Masonic process assumes the existence of a dynamic relationship with the "Sacred", being a process of progressive realisation, a "Path open only to those who are willing to walk".

A detachment from the true comprehension of the rituals has led to a neglect of esoteric components and to a concurrent indiscriminate initiation of frequently inappropriate candidates, resulting in a lowering of spiritual and cultural tension within the Obediences and an increasing demand for more traditional forms. A return to a true selection of candidates for initiation is to be sought, forsaking the idea that in order to become Freemasons it is sufficient to take out membership in an Obedience and pay formal homage to the Grand Master.

The second sign is displayed by the inability of Freemasonry to provide appropriate historic, philosophical and esoteric information and, particularly, to explain the historic differences underlying its composite, non-univocal nature.

In a recent conference organised in London by the *Canonbury Masonic Research Centre* in which I took part as a speaker, one of the participants, a member of the *Grand Orient of France*, an irregular Obedience due to its atheist status, delivered a speech focusing on the Lodge of the *Nine Sisters* in Paris, asserting that Freemasonry is not an Initiatic Society, but a mere association. All right. But the problem was that minutes before I had concluded my speech on the effect produced by alchemic ideals on the symbology and principles of Freemasonry, viewed as an Initiatic Society. Undoubtedly amongst those present there was bound to be someone aware of the intricate historic problems of the regularity, or lack of the latter, although the vast majority were somewhat taken aback by the confusion in terminology emphasised following the conclusion of the two presentations.

Although it is quite unremarkable that no common opinion or views may be reached in the context of such a widely diverse audience, however, in choosing topics to be dealt with in public, great care should be taken to provide information which is as correct as possible, and to avoid speaking in the name of a Universal Freemasonry.

This project of diffusion should be promoted by Masonic institutions, in order to prevent the numerous critics of Freemasonry, invariably ready to accuse it of all manners of vile deeds, from giving a distorted, unrealistic vision of the former.

The first mistake made by anti-Masons is to attempt to define the Masonic spirit on the basis of statements made by individual Freemasons, frequently chosen for quite the wrong reasons. Their second mistake is to not take into account the fact that an ideally united Freemasonry is in truth actually divided. Its connotations and social incidence vary from one country to the next, as well as at times within the given country, particularly when more than Obedience is present and according to the environmental and historic context. Consequently, no political undertakings moved by any given Obedience can be ascribed to Freemasonry in general, frequently being the result of the political circumstances or ideas of a sole Grand Master, thus not affecting or involving Freemasonry as a whole.

The third sign is portrayed in the vulgate of historians of Masonic ideals who have attributed eighteenth-century origins and synergies based on the Enlightenment or Rationalism to the movement.

The attributing of rationalist origins, typical of a positivist movement, to a traditionally Initiatic Society, was a serious mistake that led to a series of problems and misunderstandings that Freemasons today are still called upon to face. To depict Freemasonry as a mere associative phenomenon from which modern political parties have stemmed undoubtedly gave free rein to critics of the movement who had long accused it of an involvement with the profane. These individuals never entertained the thought that traditional knowledge and political undertakings belong to two completely different contexts, as clearly emphasised in Anderson's *Constitutions* issued in 1723. For an Initiatic Society based on "traditional" ideals, such as Freemasonry, modern progress, an offshoot of eighteenth-century Rationalism, may constitute a spiritual involution, although viewed as an improvement from a material point of view.

Those pointing to rationalist and positivist origins for Freemasonry should bear in mind that the means of communication within an Initiatic Society differ substantially from other forms of profane associations. This "means" of communication could be defined, as termed by Guénon, *"intuition intellectuelle"*. As noted by Frithjof Schuon, one of the leading traditionalists of the twentieth century: *"Intellectual knowledge also transcends the specifically theological point of view, which is itself incomparably superior to the philosophical, or more specifically rationalist, point of view, since, like metaphysical knowledge, it emanates from God and not from man; but whereas metaphysic proceeds wholly from intellectual intuition, religion proceeds from Revelation. The latter is the Word of God spoken to his creatures, whereas intellectual intuition is a direct and active participation in divine Knowledge and not an indirect and passive participation, as is faith … as for intellectual knowledge, this proceeds neither from belief nor from a process of reasoning, it goes beyond dogma in the sense that, without ever contradicting the latter, it penetrates its internal dimension, that is, the infinite Truth that dominates all forms."* [333]

Accordingly, intellectual knowledge by intuition is the sole means capable of penetrating the Truth beyond all dogma, exceeding and settling all counter-positions between the Church and Creeds. It is for this reason that Freemasonry is not a religion and the reason for which individual believers will not be subject to conflict with their religious beliefs, if the case. Moreover, to further clarify the concept, I would like to refer to the words not of a philosopher or traditionalist, but of a scientist, the anti-evolutionary palaeontologist Roberto Fondi: *"This – intellectual intuition – is a form of gnoseologic experience that, although as immediate as the act of intuition, is not even remotely vague and confused in the same way as the latter and, on the contrary, is unequivocal in the way of the most impeccable of logical-mathematic developments and as crystal clear as the purest mountain springs. It is a form of knowledge based on a supersensitive and super-rational perception of Being in its 'purest' form, or of the specific context, before individual*

333 Frithjof Schuon, *Unità trascendente delle religioni*, Mediterranee, Rome, 1980, pages 10-11.

senses and reason concur to make it seem as though divided into a multitude of 'things' or manifestations which convey (for men alone) a particular significance… From this form of absolute, disinterested knowledge founded essentially on intellectual intuition, a unified, coherent vision of the world was derived – cosmology in the ancient sense of the term – indivisible, even when assuming numerous diverse forms, from the traditional knowledge and sacred aspects of pre-modern and non-modern civilisations, having taken on all aspects of community life: from politics to art, from war to the war between the sexes, from work to culture. Indeed, it is this very cosmology that constitutes the nucleus of the thing that Guénon and Evola termed 'Tradition'." [334]

The error committed by the supportersof an enlightened and progressive origin of Freemasonry was based substantially on their unawareness of the "transcendent dimension" of the movement due to its initiatic nature.

To better clarify the different contexts that differentiate a *Traditional* Initiatic Society from a profane association we should apply the Spenglerian dichotomy of *Kultur* and *Zivilisation*, whereby the former implies a qualitative, organic, differentiated society, whilst the latter refers to a rationalist, mechanistic movement lacking structure. Clearly, as an Initiatic Society with a specific spiritual identity, Freemasonry operates in the world of culture rather than in a civilisation based prevalently on material progress and technical dominion.

The modern world, a consequence of the "necessary progress" for the proponents of a deterministic theory, oriented towards material possibilities, a concept of quantity, the multitudes in which the individual disappears under the weight of the mass and its induced needs, cannot have given origin to an initiatic society, the very nature of which is atemporal and metahistorical, and has nothing in common with the ideals of *Tradition* and the original Masonic movement. It has however become a commonly held position to associate Freemasonry with the eighteenth-century Revolutions.

I am however convinced that the traditional Masonic ideals are mainly of an "anti-Enlightenment" nature, in view particularly of its abhorrence of the myth of progress and of its acknowledgement of the impossibility that mere reason may represent the spirit. Indeed, according to the Masonic "Method" it is the use of a symbolic language that expresses the integration between materials and the spirit, an esoteric language therefore that differs radically from rational, scientific language, being as it is conveyed through use of images aimed at increasing knowledge via intuition rather than reason. Intellect is seen as a tool of lesser importance than the creative process leading up to

334 Roberto Fondi, *La critica all scienza e il rifiuto dell'evoluzionismo*, in *Testimonianze su Evola*, Mediterranee, 1973, pages 262-263.

intuition-enlightenment. Masonic ritual teaches us how the purpose of the natural cycle of life and death is to rejoin us to the Divine in a special-temporal dimension in which time features a cyclic rather than a linear progression in line with the theory of an eternal return, compared to the idea of indefinite progress as upheld by an Enlightened vision. An initiatic society does not seek social progress, being as it is beyond the realms of time, beyond history; it does not strive to create a better society, or rather only as the secondary consequence of its only true aim: to provide a setting and enhance discovery in initiates of their Divine Self. This path must necessarily begin, develop and terminate inside each individual, with society and related dynamics staying in the background and the degree of evolution will represent a mere reflection, a projection of the awareness of individual Self. As Evola observes: *"Tradition, in its essence, is something simultaneously meta-historical and dynamic: it is an overall ordering force, in the service of principles that have the chrism of a superior legitimacy (we may even call them 'principles from above'). This force acts through the generations, in continuity of spirit and inspiration, through institutions, laws, and social orders that may even display a remarkable variety and diversity… Even where these principles (linked to tradition) are objectified in a historical reality, they are not at all conditioned by it; they always point to a higher, meta-historical plane, which is their natural domain and where there is no change. The ideas that I call 'traditional' must be thought of along the same lines."* [335]

The fourth sign, a direct consequence of the previous one, is the phenomenon of the "disenchantment" of Freemasonry.

Shortly after its establishment, Freemasonry was called upon to face a difficult trial. The Cartesian vision whereby nature is an inert machine devoid of vitality and at the mercy of men, embarked on the process of de-divinisation of the world, having as its culminating point the modern cult of science, its omnipotence, in the persuasion that technical progress occurs at the same rate as the inner spiritual evolution of man. However, this vision of necessary progress resulted in what was termed by Max Weber as "disenchantment", or rather the secularisation produced by scientific rationalisation, of the old vision of the mythological-religious world representing *Tradition*, and replaced by an objective image of reality. Regrettably, the removal of "Tradition" from Freemasonry is slowly leading to "disenchantment" and to its transformation into a mere associative movement.

I am well aware that an initiatic society is by its very nature reserved to an elite component. However, as mentioned previously, an increasing tendency to achieve

335 Julius Evola, *Gli uomini e le rovine*, Mediterranee, Rome, 2001, page 64.

higher numbers of members is being manifested in Freemasonry. It is clear that Initiatic Societies operate throughout the world and it is thus unavoidable that some members may be affected by *esoteric* dynamics. Within the context of Freemasonry the feature that in Muslim Fellowships is represented by the difference between the *mutabarik* who rarely deviate from their exoteric perspectives and the *salik* (those who walk) who adhere to the path of initiatic tradition, is manifested. The necessary changes having been made, in Freemasonry the superior presence of the *mutabarik* is dragging an Initiatic Society towards "disenchantment" and the mortification of esotericism.

The task of the elite component, the task of Freemasonry, is to invert this process and re-establish in man the awareness of the spiritual nature of our existence, leading, by means of this return to transcendence, to a "re-enchantment".

The fifth and last sign is represented by the transformation of Freemasonry from an Initiatic Society to a contemporary representation of Kitsch.

The consequence of the previously mentioned processes is plainly visible in the contradiction within the context of Freemasonry, between a plethoric symbolic, ritual structure and a radical void of significance. Accordingly, in its modern version Freemasonry becomes a representative of Kitsch, to use a term with which Hermann Broch describes the end of the Austro-Hungarian empire, where: *"A minimum of ethical values was to be masked by a maximum of aesthetic values, which themselves no longer existed. They could no longer exist because an aesthetic value that does not spring from an ethical foundation is its own opposite – Kitsch."* [336]

Unfortunately, modern-day Freemasonry is gradually becoming a manifestation of Kitsch, a mere aesthetic representation devoid of substance, lacking values, particularly in view of its constant, progressive involvement in profane dynamics.

Prior to asking ourselves what Freemasonry is, we should first ponder on who a Freemason is. On the basis of a predisposition, inborn attitude, talent, search for an unchanging Truth that reaches beyond history, beyond progress, beyond society with its dynamics and topics. In this regard he is detached from an external dimension, acting independently and undertaking an original, unique path. He realises that history repeats itself ceaselessly and that if he wishes to break the vicious circle he will have ideally to break out. The dimension in which he intends to operate is that of the perpetual Self rather than the changeable, unachievable, frustrating context of events. There is no Salvation or Truth beyond Self, there is no

336 Hermann Broch, *Il Kitsch*, Einaudi, Turin, 1996, pages 93-94.

reason to exist without the constant tension of what we wish to become: to be free and aware of our dignity and our power.

A Freemason belongs to nothing except unto himself, he quite simply is. The figure of a Freemason is independent of all evolutionary instances, as his origin and status detach him from time and from the events apparently underlying his generation. To some degree he recalls what Julius Evola refers to as a "differentiated man" and Ernst Jünger as an "anarchist": intimately linked to a transcendent dimension, he is not overwhelmed by an existential anguish and frustration, but carries out his duties until the end, independently and in a dignified manner.

Freemasonry is therefore situated beyond the contingent, and particularly beyond any historic confines, in an *atemporal* dimension in which the current "problem" can find no solution.

It should not however be construed that Freemasons are passive figures. On the contrary, they bravely walk alone throughout the ruins of the world to achieve their power. To use a Hindu definition, they could be seen as representing *Kshatriya*, the warrior incarnating Self-control. Power, superior order and nobility of the spirit. To be faithful to *Tradition* does not imply simply re-evoking the rites and symbols, but bringing back to life the essence, significance, incarnating the latter in the new forms in which it is manifested today. Accordingly, the Order takes on the semblance of a "militia" in which the militant-Freemason embarks on the conquest of a different, far vaster territory than that occupied by the profane world.

The existence of this Order results in what Jünger refers to as an "inclusion", a sort of condensation or laceration of a historic theme, a petrifying or crystallising of the historic structure. In this day and age, traditional Freemasonry indeed constitutes a permanence or irruption of the "Sacred", the elementary, the mythical or fantastic amongst the rational compartments of the world.

Throughout the centuries Freemasonry has formed a body which has, regrettably, lost its soul. The transformation of an association with esoteric connotations into a true initiatic society is an aim that may be achieved only by means of a radical change, a true leap forward towards our most profound, authentic ambitions.

Appendix III

Freemasonry and Mass Media

Only by overlooking the initiatic character of Freemasonry can we deny that the purpose of the latter is the perfection of self, to be achieved through perfection of the Ritual, or rather to use Masonic terms, by the skilful hewing of the raw stone and its transmutation into cubic stone according to the rules of the Craft

Arturo Reghini
Considerations on the Ritual of an Apprentice Freemason

I am often asked by Brothers how an appropriate relationship should be developed between Freemasonry and the mass media.

I would like to begin this speech therefore by focusing on the title, which could undoubtedly be defined an evident "contradiction of terms", perhaps even an oxymoron. You will be aware that an oxymoron is a rhetorical figure constituted by the concomitant use of two terms that are clearly in contrast one with the other.

This contradiction, the antithesis, should be plain for all to see, and consists in uniting two subjects that due to their very nature live in completely separate worlds, an Initiatic Order, exclusive by definition, and the so-called mass media, the means of "mass" communication.

An Initiatic Order is made up of and addressed to "initiates", therefore to an "exclusive" circle of men who have "knowingly" chosen to undertake an *esoteric-metaphysical* journey, an initiatic "method" that will allow them to establish an active process of inner transformation, to elicit a fully-fledged mutation of status.

Conversely, the mass media are directed at the "masses", towards society as a whole, devoid of all distinctions; indeed, to achieve this purpose they adopt methods and mechanisms suited to the audience they aim to reach.

An historic definition of the "masses" is provided by the Spanish thinker José Ortega y Gasset who, in his renowned essay *The Revolt of the Masses* writes: *"Society is always a dynamic unity of two component factors: minorities and masses. The minorities are individuals or groups of individuals which are specially qualified. The mass is the assemblage of persons not specially qualified... The mass is the average man,"* [337] adding *"In those groups*

337 José Ortega y Gasset, *The Revolt of the Masses*, TEA, March 1988, page 37. Original title: *La rebelión de las masas.*

which are characterised by not being multitude and mass, the effective coincidence of its members is based on some desire, idea, or ideal, which of itself excludes the great number. To form a minority, of whatever kind, it is necessary beforehand that each member separate himself from the multitude... The division of society into masses and select minorities is, then, not a division into social classes, but into classes of men, and cannot coincide with the hierarchic separation of 'upper' and 'lower" classes'." [338]

Consequently, no association should exist between Freemasonry and the mass media, as their dynamics and competences are radically divergent. Unfortunately, as I will now illustrate, things are not quite so simple.

In spite of the fact that in view of its singularities, an Initiatic Order is required to stand apart from all forms of profanity, recently Grand Masters of Masonic Obediences are becoming increasingly implicated in issues that are by no means of an initiatic nature, focusing rather on politics, social problems, and more besides.

How did all this come about?

The process in question was certainly not begun recently, and a tendency for several Masonic Obediences to become involved in matters in no way associated with the *esoteric* activity of an Initiatic Order has long been manifested. However, in an attempt to analyse this degenerative phenomenon, I would like to trace historic research back into the past with the aim of better comprehending the origins and nature of the matter.

In my opinion, this degeneration probably originated at the time when the dynamics underlying the "transmission" of the ritual, the initiatic tool of fundamental importance in the Masonic "Method", changed.

This process is marked by a specific starting date, namely the moment at which Masonic rituals were no longer guarded as they ought to be, and often through no fault of our own they started to be savagely disclosed in contexts widely diverse from the Masonic Temples, the sole context in which a ritual should be destined for use. From that time onwards, Freemasonry started to lose what the famed philosopher Walter Benjamin, in a magnificent study on the uniqueness of a work of art, subsequently termed its "aura".[339]

It should however be clarified that the loss of the "aura" by Freemasonry does not imply a loss of its "secrets". Indeed, the secret of initiatic organisations is merely symbolic compared to the unique, hidden, exclusively inner initiatic secret that can only be achieved by means of a spiritual awareness and that, in view of its inexpressibility, is necessarily incommunicable. The inexpressible may be effectively conveyed and

338 Ibid. page 38.

339 Walter Benjamin, *L'opera d'arte nell'epoca della sua riproducibilità tecnica*, Einaudi, Turin, 1966.

apprehended by means of intellectual intuition and in line with individual intellectual skills. This inner secret constitutes the true essence of the initiatic secret that a Freemason strives to achieve.

The "aura" therefore is construed as the "mystery", "fascination", "charm" that inevitably accompanies Freemasonry as a "form" of *Tradition*.

Historically, the first person to inappropriately publish Masonic rituals in October 1730 was Samuel Prichard in his *Masonry Dissected*. A full-blown scandal ensued, with mention being made in the minutes of the Grand Lodge in December of the same year: *"The Grand Master Adjunct has acknowledged a Pamphlet published recently by a certain Prichard who stated he had been made a regular Mason: By violating the commitment made for the purpose of harming Freemasonry and expressing himself with a high degree of indignation both against the man (defining him an Impostor) and against his book, stupid stuff that should not even be taken into account. However, in order to avoid the Lodge from being deceived by False Brethren or Impostors: He has Proposed that until new Disposition of the Grand Lodge no person whatsoever may enter the Lodge as a Visiting Brother unless one of those present should vouch for him and confirm his condition of regular Mason, and the name of the guarantor should likewise be noted in the appropriate Register of the Lodge. The proposal has been accepted unanimously."* This was the start of a perverse process that has now reached its apex with the publication of rituals on the most unlikely websites. An Initiatic Order has become a consumer commodity, and in the consumer universe the essence of human values shall never be contemplated.

In referring to works of art, Walter Benjamin writes that following the advent of technical reproducibility represented by photography, and particularly the cinema, this subject started to lose its "aura", its authenticity. In Benjamin's words: *"The authenticity of a thing is the essence of all that is transmissible from its beginning, ranging from its substantive duration to its testimony to the history which it has experienced. Since the historical testimony rests on the authenticity, the former, too, is jeopardised by reproduction when substantive duration ceases to matter. And what is really jeopardised when the historical testimony is affected is the authority of the object... One might generalise by saying: the technique of reproduction detaches the reproduced object from the domain of tradition... the processes lead to a tremendous shattering of tradition which is the obverse of the contemporary crisis and renewal of mankind. Both processes are intimately connected with the contemporary mass movements."* [340] The final outcome of these dynamics will lead, in his opinion, to the "*liquidation of the traditional value of the cultural heritage*".

340 Ibid. page 23.

The "exploitation" of rituals, and their "mass" printing and disclosure made possible through their publication in books and on the web, has thus resulted in the termination of their "secrecy", thereby depriving the latter of their "aura" and giving rise to a never-ending degenerative process.

The other *Traditional* "forms" which acted as forerunners to Freemasonry, numerous references to which are contained therein — the Mysterious Societies, and Hermetic, Gnostic and Rosicrucian groups — were fortunate enough not to experience the same problem, with their rituals remaining unknown to the present time. However, on referring to *Tradition*, we should not make the mistake of thinking of something relegated to the past, as underlined by Alain De Benoist: *"Tradition is linked to the past in exactly the same way that it is associated with the present or the future. It is situated beyond the confines of time. It in no way refers to ancient things, to those we have 'left behind us', but rather to the permanent state, to whatever is contained 'within'."* [341]

Communication today focuses increasingly on bringing things "closer", making them "easier to use" and "more intelligible" for the masses; indeed, the tendency is to apply the same logic to Freemasonry, obliging it to comparison with topics on which everyone has something to say.

It is therefore customary to see Grand Masters acting as opinion leaders, in no fear of being contradicted by others. To use the words written in this regard by Ortega Y Gasset: *"To-day, on the other hand, the average man has the most mathematical 'ideas' on all that happens or ought to happen in the universe. Hence he has lost the use of his hearing. Why should he listen if he has within him all that is necessary? There is no reason now for listening, but rather for judging, pronouncing, deciding. There is no question concerning public life in which he does not intervene, blind and deaf as he is, imposing his 'opinion'."* [342] The risk run by Freemasonry is that, on becoming closer to the profane and overlooking "initiatic" significance, it may be open to attack by what Max Weber termed the "disenchantment".

It could be objected that accordingly, by shutting itself away, Freemasonry is at risk of failing to diffuse knowledge of its singularities, thus preventing many potential "initiates" from becoming part of the movement. It should be underlined how the latter fear is totally groundless as, particularly in recent years in English speaking countries, Freemasonry has been able to rely on establishments of excellence which concentrate "solely" on carrying out studies in this regard.

341 Alain De Benoist, *Le idee a posto*, Akropolis, Naples, 1983, page 123. Original title: *Les idées a l'endroit*, Albin Michel, Paris, 1980.

342 José Ortega y Gasset, op. cit., page 79.

First and foremost the historic *Quatuor Coronati* Lodge in London, a point of reference for all those who undertake genuine studies into the history of our institution, to the *Cornerstone Society*, the *Canonbury Centre* (for all studies of an esoteric nature), *the University of Sheffield* and the important International Conference on Freemasonry studies held in Edinburgh, to name the better known. All the above establishments have published proceedings of their conferences which are available to all, initiates or profane, who wish to further their knowledge. I have had the pleasure of being invited to speak and to represent, I trust worthily, the Obedience of which I am Grand Master, at all the above events: in the *Quatuor Coronati* Lodge in London (*Freemasonry and Fascism*), the *Cornerstone Society* (*The Influence of Neoplatonic Thought on Freemasonry*), the *Canonbury Centre* (*Freemasonry and Alchemy*) and the International Conference in Edinburgh (*Julius Evola and Freemasonry*).

Another inexplicable phenomenon observed in some Masonic Obediences is the ongoing race to increase the number of registered members; by means of a savage proselytism accompanied by loud proclamations and trumpet fanfares, thousands upon thousands of new "initiations" are announced. In a previous chapter, I mentioned the need for an appropriate "qualification" in order to be deemed eligible for initiation, underlining the fact that the characteristics sought are, necessarily, hard to find. It is indeed this characteristic that makes Freemasonry an elite circle of "initiates". Quite remarkably, however, several Obediences manage to find "thousands" of candidates for initiation each year, in this way increasing, in their opinion, their numbers exponentially.

At this point, however, the spontaneous question that arises is: For what purpose? What is the true purpose of an Initiatic Order? To evolve into an enormous Service Club that bestows business, favours and political appointments?

As we well know, the truth is that a Freemasonry for the "masses" would clearly constitute a further contradiction of terms.

To once again quote the words of Walter Benjamin: *"The earliest art works originated in the service of a ritual – first the magical, then the religious kind. It is significant that the existence of the work of art with reference to its aura is never entirely separated from its ritual function. In other words, the unique value of the 'authentic' work of art has its basis in ritual, the location of its original use value... But the instant the criterion of authenticity ceases to be applicable to artistic production, the total function of art is reversed. Instead of being based on ritual, it begins to be based on another practice – politics."* [343] Benjamin presents art as a form of tradition, providing the impetus for a comparison with Freemasonry,

343 Walter Benjamin, op. cit., pages 26-27.

which I hope is not too daring, whereby as things change, the perverse dynamic leads to the same conclusion: the degeneration into politics.

The Masonic "Method" is based substantially on metaphysical elements, on the pure intellectual knowledge of universal principles, a super-rational transcendent knowledge. As mentioned previously, the latter poses on a basis of intellectual intuition, which the great philosopher Massimo Scaligero brilliantly defined as follows:

"Intellectual Intuition is a form of gnoseologic experience which, although equally immediate as the act of intuition, is lacking the vague, confused elements that characterise the latter, being, on the contrary, unequivocal as the most impeccable of processes of logic and mathematics, and as clear as the clearest of mountain springs. This type of knowledge is based on a super-sensitive and super-rational perception of Being in its 'unadulterated' state, or rather of reality as it actually occurs, before the senses and individual reasoning make it appear to be divided into a myriad of 'things' and manifestations which hold (for human beings alone) a particular significance." [344]

The aim of Freemasonry is Knowledge, implying a "metaphysical awareness", the supreme aim of man to be reunited with his Supreme Principle and free himself of material bonds (leaving the "metals" outside). For the purpose of achieving this spiritual objective, Freemasonry provides a means through its rituals and symbols.

To conclude, therefore, the "social function" of Freemasonry may be only of an "indirect" nature. An Initiatic Order should not be mixed with battles beyond its control, it should not be dragged into the profane, and above all it should not make use of "mass" communication methods. To do so would inevitably result in a loss of authenticity and a failure to comply with its innermost beliefs. To quote Nicolás Gómez Dávila: *"Trivialisation is the price you pay for communication…"* [345]

344 Massimo Scaligero, *Dioniso*, in *Testimonianze su Evola*, Mediterranee, Rome, 1973.
345 Nicolás Gómez Dávila, *In margine a un testo implicito*, Adelphi, Milano, 2011 page 64.